TWAYNE'S WORLD LEADERS SERIES

Felix Adler

FELIX ADLER

Robert S. Guttchen
Late Professor of Philosophy
Hofstra University

SERIES EDITORS

Arthur W. Brown, Ph. D.
Professor of English and
Dean of the School of Liberal
Arts and Sciences, Baruch College; and
Thomas S. Knight, Ph. D.
Professor and Chairman of the
Department of Philosophy, Adelphi University

Twayne Publishers, Inc.   ::   New York

163611

Library of Congress Cataloging in Publication Data

Guttchen, Robert S.   1926-1971.
   Felix Adler.

   (Twayne's World leaders series)
   Bibliography: p. 283.
   1. Adler, Felix, 1851-1933.
BJ354.A343G87   1974   370.1'092'4 [B]   73-15952
ISBN 0-8057-3650-6

Contents

Note

Dual tragedy brings this book into my hands. Robert Guttchen had written and revised the manuscript and was in the process of preparing it for publication when an accident claimed his life at his summer home in Vermont in 1971 at the age of 45. I had read the work in manuscript before his death and had helped with some of his revisions.

At this point the book came into the hands of Richard Cecil, who had been his friend and colleague at Hofstra University. Dick Cecil apparently was unable to bring the matter to a fruition before death claimed him as well.

Robert Guttchen's literary effects were then put into my hands by William Cecil, son of Richard, who was aware of my involvement in this project. I confined my efforts to tending to the physical well-being of the manuscript, reorganizing the front material, and obtaining the aid of Howard Radest of Ramapo College and Joseph Blau of Columbia University to write the biographical sketch and the epilogue respectively.

Evelyn Shirk

Hofstra University
1973

Acknowledgments

The debts accumulated in the course of preparing this study are numerous. I can acknowledge them, but I cannot repay them.

I wish first to thank Professor Louise Antz for her kindness and continuing support and encouragement throughout my doctoral studies. Both Professor Antz and Professor Maxine M. Greene have given unstintingly of their time to help shape and to comment on and criticize this study, for which I am deeply appreciative. I also wish to thank Professors John C. Payne of New York University and Joe R. Burnett (now of the University of Illinois) for their assistance.

I am particularly indebted to Professor Horace L. Friess of Columbia University and The New York Society for Ethical Culture for invaluable help. As Literary Executor of Felix Adler's unpublished manuscripts, Professor Friess made these manuscripts accessible to me for study. As a student of long standing of Adler's work, Professor Friess's comments on Part I of this study were of particular value. The several long conversations we had are, for me, memorable occasions. I am also grateful to him for permission to quote from his published and unpublished works on Felix Adler.

I would also like to thank The American Ethical Union for its kindness and support, which allowed me to participate in a two-week Leader Training Institute held in the summer of 1960. This is particularly to be noted since my purposes were not those of the Institute but were in connection with the present study.

Thanks are finally due for the cooperation of the following

publishers in giving permission to quote passages from works to which they hold copyrights: Merideth Press, for passages from *An Ethical Philosophy of Life, Marriage and Divorce, The Reconstruction of the Spiritual Ideal,* and *The World Crisis and Its Meaning,* all by Felix Adler; The Macmillan Company, for passages from *Democracy and Education* by John Dewey; Yale University Press, for a passage from *The Logic of the Humanities* by Ernst Cassirer; Harvard University Press, for a passage from *The Great Chain of Being* by Arthur O. Lovejoy; and The University of Chicago Press, for a passage from *The Human Condition* (copyright, 1958) by Hannah Arendt.

Robert Guttchen

Hofstra University

Preface

Felix Adler's writing on ethical and educational theory has received remarkably little attention from other ethical or educational theorists. With the exception of a few brief papers and some summary statements in several doctoral theses, Adler's work has been virtually ignored by scholars. No prior attempt has been made to display and analyze, much less evaluate, the central core of Adler's thought. Thus, the present essay claims to be no more than a first attempt to lay out the main lines of Adler's general position. The success of this enterprise can be measured by the extent to which Adler's thought is made more accessible for further study.

If one embarks on a study of Plato or Aristotle, or of Dewey or Whitehead, one has the benefit and burden of many commentaries—against which one can measure one's own interpretation and evaluation. With Felix Adler, we have neither this benefit nor this burden. For the most part, our appeal can be only to Adler's writings themselves. The considerable extent to which new interpretive ground is here being broken required that some rather stringent delimitations be placed on the scope and purposes of the present work.

The study deals primarily with Adler's own thought. No attempt is made to compare or contrast either Adler's ethical or educational philosophies with the ethical or educational views of other writers, except insofar as such comparison and contrast may serve to clarify Adler's position.

This restriction is most important with regard to Adler's early religious and philosophic background and particularly his relation to the Kantian philosophy. No independent analysis of Kant is offered, nor is an attempt made to evaluate Adler's understanding of Kant's views. The concern is only with what Adler understood to be Kant's views, and his own understanding of how he differed from Kant. This restriction applies also to Adler's discussion of Matthew Arnold and Goethe and to his analysis of the Hebraic and Christian traditions as well.

The study restricts itself to the most general and pervasive aspects of Adler's ethical and educational *philosophies.* Adler wrote and spoke on an extremely wide range of issues. Much of this work was in connection with his leadership of the Society for Ethical Culture, which he founded in New York City in 1876, at the age of twenty-five. A full treatment of Adler's work, in the manner of Ernest Jones's *The Life and Work of Sigmund Freud,* although in the opinion of this writer well worth the effort, is far beyond the scope and intent of the present study. What is herein offered of Adler's thought provides an introduction to the fundamental matrix of Adler's life work.

Finally, no attempt is made to evaluate Adler's position from the standpoint of any other philosophy of education, ethics, or metaphysics. The internal evaluation concerns itself with the general coherence of Adler's position and the clarity and consistency and/or compatibility of Adler's main ideas and the relations among them. The external evaluation deals with the scope of Adler's view and the significance of the problems with which he chose to deal. Although such criticism inevitably arises from a point of view, it is not offered as an articulation of, and so does not gain support from, a fully developed "position." Its only claim can be that of general cogency and inherent reasonableness.

This entire study might be titled *Adler's Conception of Human Worth.* In what follows, the concept of worth is offered as more than just a heuristic. Adler is, as Isaiah Berlin uses the term, a *hedgehog:* "The fox knows many things, but the hedgehog knows one big thing."[1] The "one big thing" which

---

[1]*The Hedgehog and the Fox* (New York: The New American Library of World Literature, Inc., 1957), p. 7.

Adler knows is that each and every human being has worth. What this means to him, in terms of ethical theory and in terms of a general conception of education, is what this study attempts to explore.

In Chapter Two, an attempt is made to make clear what Adler means by *worth*. Chapter Three deals with Adler's epistemological and ontological views as they bear on the problem of claiming anything to be real. Chapter Four develops Adler's argument that worth has objective reality.

Chapters Five, Six, and Seven form a second unit. In Chapter Four the concept of ethicizing is introduced. Chapter Five starts by showing how Adler conceived of education as a process of ethicizing. Thus the main link between Adler's ethical and educational theories is presented. The balance of Chapter Five and the whole of Chapter Six develop Adler's general educational position. In Chapter Seven the focus is on Adler's conceptions of culture, cultivating, and formal education, that is, schooling.

It will be seen that both Adler's general conception of education and his conception of schooling are attempts to articulate a means by which the objective reality of worth is recognized and striven for. This objective reality is an ideal reality, never to be fully realized. It should be, however, according to Adler, the final end toward which all human thought and activity are directed.

There is wide agreement that education is much concerned with the question of how one ought to act, and particularly with the direction of the conduct of children and youth. Adler has put this question, the ethical problem generally, at the very center of his philosophy of education. I believe that educators, both here and abroad, might benefit greatly through a study of this distinctively ethical perspective toward the educational enterprise. This perspective should be valuable, particularly to philosophers of education, but also to philosophers who have an active interest in ethics. And not least, such an ethical perspective should be of interest to teachers and the public at large.

From a technical point of view, Adler's work is worth studying because it supplies us with a metaphysical theory that is explicitly developed to deal with what Adler takes to be fundamental ethical problems. These problems are first expressed in nonphilosophic terms, then in terms of a metaphysical construction, and finally, lines are drawn from the metaphysics to the ethics and then to an expression of what constitutes an ethical way of life. The metaphysical construction is offered as a rational ground for the ethics and for dealing with the problems of life. It is also offered as a possible object of relief, or in religious terms, as an article of faith. This is philosophy in the grand tradition. There is, today, considerable discussion as to the nature of metaphysics, the proper function of metaphysical theory, and the relation between such theory and both the rest of philosophy and educational theory. We also find much dispute regarding the proper scope and function of philosophic ethics. It is reasonable to assume that there are important connections between the discussions in these two central areas of philosophic inquiry. Adler's metaphysical ethics might well serve as a basis upon which such discussion could proceed. This study might be of value insofar as it presents and analyzes Adler's position and so supplies grist for the philosophic mill.

Robert Guttchen

Chronology

1851   Born August 13 in Alzei, Germany, the son of Samuel and Henrietta Adler.

1857   Emigrated with parents and older brother, Isaac, to the United States.

1870   Graduated from Columbia College as a member of Phi Beta Kappa.

1873   Received his doctorate in philosophy *summa cum laude* at Heidelberg.

1873-   Held the chair of Hebrew and Oriental literature at
1875   Cornell University.

1875   Came in contact with Ralph W. Emerson and Free Religion.

1876   Founded May 15, 1876, the Society for Ethical Culture.

1877   Senior leader of the New York Ethical Culture School which founded first free kindergarten in the United States.

1878-   President of Free Religious Association. Resigned in
1882   protest because of organization's failure to take action.

1880   Established Workingman's school in which manual training was first used as a regular branch of instruction.
       Married Helen Goldmark, daughter of a Brooklyn chemist on May 24, 1880. Five children from this marriage: Waldo, Eleanor, Lawrence, Mary, and Ruth.

1882   Established Tenement House Building Company to erect model tenements.

1889	Developed the American Ethical Union, a federation of American ethical culture societies.
1890	Founded *International Journal of Ethics*.
1891	Spent a sabbatical year in Europe.
1894	Gave a series of lectures on the subject of the reconstruction of industrial politics.
1896	Established the International Union of Ethical Culture Societies.
1902	Appointed Professor of Social and Political Ethics at Columbia.
1904-1921	Chairman of the National Child Labor Committee.
1908-1909	Appointed Theodore Roosevelt Exchange Professor at the University of Berlin.
1911	Joined with Gustave Spiller in establishing the first International Races Congress.
1918	Published *An Ethical Philosophy of Life*.
1923	Delivered the Hibbert Lectures at Oxford.
1924	Published *The Reconstruction of the Spiritual Ideal*, a book based on the Hibbert Lectures.
1926	Formulated the "Fieldston Plan," the basis for the Fieldston School.
1929	Received an Honorary Doctorate of Literature.
1933	Died April 24 after a long struggle with cancer.

Felix Adler: A Biographical Sketch

Once upon a time, but no longer, images of America were presented in two ways. One was the frontier, the land spread endlessly before the eyes of the pioneer family as it moved westward. The second was the sea, the harbor, and the newcomers arriving to partake of the American dream. Behind them were the struggles and habits of an old world. Behind them, too, the warmth and security of rooted traditional life patterns. Before them was raw bustling America, still very much the new nation on a new continent. If there was illusion in this imagery—and there was—it was the illusion of hope, the fiction that the people could be as new as the land, and that America secure in its oceanic separation could be a place for utterly new beginnings. The reality was different, an amalgam of novelty and habit, of innovation and history, of ideals and memories. And yet, paradoxically, the illusion worked.

Arriving in New York Harbor in the year 1857, after a stormy seventeen-day crossing from Le Havre, Rabbi Samuel Adler, his wife Henrietta, and their two sons, Isaac, age 8, and Felix, age 6, took up residence in a pleasant neighborhood near Stuyvesant Square in New York City. Samuel, then nearly fifty years old, had been called to the rabbinate of Temple Emanu-el, then as now one of the leading Jewish Reform Congregations in the country. The environment was a good one, and the city, though large for its time, was not the massive incomprehensibility it is today. Nearby was the

Academy of Music. A few blocks south was the Cooper Union Institute with its library, its lectures, and its concerts. Trees and shrubs still survived. A comfortable walk led to nearby shopping or eastward to the river, as yet unpolluted.

The city with its culture, its noises, its confusions, and its promise was to be the setting for the life of Felix Adler. New York was both American and cosmopolitan. And it was this complex background that served to accent Adler's work and thought. The ambivalent quality of the American dream was never more clearly visible than in the growth of its cities and the immigrant waves that swelled their population. If the "land of opportunity" was the land of the frontier, it was also the land of an evolving business life and industrial society. The latter found its home in modern metropolis. To America came the seekers from 1850 onward—Irish and Italian, German and Pole and Russian. For the next half century or more they came by the tens of thousands to be exploited, to be "voted" by the bosses, to be crowded into the emerging slums. Here they came to watch their children grow up and grow away, to found new fortunes, build new families, create new histories.

The second half of the nineteenth century in America, as in the world, was a time of ever more rapid changes. The rural idyll was passing from view. True, America was still an agricultural nation, but the seeds for a concentration of economic and political power were being planted beneath the cobblestones of the nascent modern city. The nation-state, too, with its loyalties and its wars, was moving to the front of history's stage. In Europe, new nations appeared in the ruins of old empires. Here, young Adler's boyhood was punctuated by the sound of the Civil War, the calls to preserve the Union and to broaden the message of freedom. In the Adler household, the prose of Lincoln and the cause of antislavery accented a newly found Americanism. The historic experience of a people in search of itself was felt by young Adler in personal terms. Thus, he recalled the morning after Lincoln's assassination: "I was then fourteen years of age. I came down to the breakfast table and found my father weeping. I had never seen tears in his eyes before."[1]

Felix's adolescence paralleled the post-Civil War era. The crusade for racial justice—if that is what it was—soon gave way to business as usual. With the end of Reconstruction, the chance for equity in human relations yielded to Jim Crow and the night riders, to the KKK and new forms of peonage. Nationally, a postwar period much like other more recent ones developed, a period of rising demoralization with consequent corruption in public life and personal ambition in private life. In the cities, the political machines turned democratic politics into a moral farce:

The corruption of municipal and state politics was still more flagrant (than in national politics). Boss William Tweed's rule of New York was untypical only in the scope and daring of his grabs. . . . When Vanderbilt and another freebooter tangled for control of the Erie Railroad, hundreds of thousands of greenbacks arrived in Albany. One of Tweed's State Senators, catching the full spirit of the occasion, took $75,000 from the Vanderbilt representative and $100,000 from the other side. He preserved the morals of the new politics by voting for the higher donor.[2]

A successful, if often vicious, commercialism justified itself as the progress of civilization and the realization of an American destiny. The pirates of the new economics of industrial greed soon became the nation's heroes and replaced the unfortunate Ulysses S. Grant. The myth of America was Horatio Alger with success as its theme and hard work for private gain as its story line.

But the culture of cities and the ugliness of nationalism and laissez faire economics do not tell the story alone. A third strand woven into the complex tapestry of change which is biography's surroundings was the developing sciences of man with their corrosion of old values and their promise of new and better ones. If Darwin's evolution gave rise to the amoral-

---

[1]Cited in an unpublished manuscript by Horace L. Friess, Felix Adler's literary executor.

[2]Eric Goldman, *Rendezvous with Destiny* (New York: Knopf, 1952), p. 11.

ity of social Darwinism and the rationalization of the most vicious forms of competition, it marked, too, a part of the continuing pattern of "enlightenment." Reason and knowledge were boundlessly applicable not merely to the farthest stars and the smallest atoms but to this "middle state" called human life. Politics, economics, education, and religion were all likely candidates for the inquiring mind. A liberating force against the authority and power of the past was still the message of the life of the intellect. And this too played its role in Adler's world.

Thus, Adler grew up in a time when more and more of the elements of human experience were in flux. And nowhere was this more evident and more dramatic than in America. It was a nation given to exaggerations, unchecked by traditional memories and patterns, revealing in their crudest forms both the good and the evil of what we have come to call modern society. Through the remainder of his life and well into the twentieth century Adler was to remain both witness to, and participant in, a drama whose early acts marked his childhood, the drama of a species moving into a new, scarcely discernible stage of its collective biography.

A man's life cannot, however, really be understood merely as a function of large-scale social events important as they are for shaping the lines of intimacy out of which a particular life actually emerges. What made this man different from others of his time—and how much of this can we ever know? A background is only that and so one must turn to those relationships which in fact molded the personality and the character of Felix Adler. He was born in Alzei, Germany, in 1851 and came, as we have seen, to New York when he was six. His father was a man of the enlightenment, active while in Europe both in secular struggles for freedom and in religious reform. The marriage of a passion for social justice and immersion in scholarship characterized not only the father but the family and was crucial in shaping young Adler.

The Adler home was filled with books. Indeed, one of the best collections of Judaica in the city was to be found there.

The family's friends and visitors, fellow congregants at Temple Emanu-el, were men and women of achievement in the life of the city and the nation. This German Jewish group represented the successful immigrants in the country, those who had made their place in business, finance, and the professions. They were visible symbols of the truth of the American dream, moved by loyalty to it as by a conscientious desire to broadcast it as widely as possible. Thus, the names that appear in Felix Adler's later life as religious and social reformers include the Seligmans, the Sutros, the Prices, the Morgenthaus, the Bambergers. But it was not all sober, serious practicality. Music, art, and poetry, the features of secular culture, played as much of a role in his life as Judaism and religious reform.

Felix's father was determined to secure a good education for his children, one that combined religious and secular scholarship. For the former, the household could be the setting. For the latter, Felix and his brother, Isaac, were enrolled in the Columbia Grammar School, an elite preparatory institution. He received a strong, highly demanding education with heavy emphasis in the classics and languages—a foundation that was to serve him well all of his life.

Although intellectually stimulating, one may guess that young Felix's life was not the happiest. As he himself recalled, "A Jewish boy from a family largely German among typically American boys of the wealthy class, I found I was forced back upon myself by lack of companionship."[3] He was, we are also told, a "dreamy boy" without the "tough" mindedness of his father or older brother.

Nor was Adler's education limited to the book and the classroom. In particular, Felix shared his mother's charitable rounds, characteristic of the life of the Jewish community. With her, he visited the poor and the sick, learning at first hand the nature and smell of poverty. Even in these early

[3]Friess ms.

years, young Adler began to show some of the features of
personality which were to reveal themselves more fully as he
matured. He developed a love of language and great skill in
its use. His scholarship was to become formidable and he
found himself at home in classical and in modern literatures.
At age eighteen, he was encouraged by his father to deliver
some sermons at the Hebrew Orphan Asylum. Even then he
demonstrated his power with the spoken word and the pulpit
style, an ability to combine passionate argument with intellectual vigor.

These formative features of young Adler's life stress the
mixture of reform in religion, a breadth of scholarly influence, and above all the organizing meaning of the "good
deed," a passionate commitment to the act. Already, an ethical
centrality makes its appearance in Adler's life. Conduct prom-
ises to become the crucible for both religion and scholarship.

On completion of his work at the Grammar School, Felix
entered Columbia College, then not the great cosmopolitan
university which it later became. Of those years of undergraduate study we know little except that Felix was disap-
pointed. The college lacked that broad philosophic interest
and intellectual magnanimity which he was accustomed to look
for. It still reflected a Christian parochialism which, clearly,
suited neither his temperament nor his concerns. Following
graduation in 1870, Adler went abroad for graduate study,
enrolling at the University of Berlin for his work toward a
doctorate while simultaneously seeking to complete studies for
the rabbinate in Abraham Geiger's seminary. When this arrangement did not work out, he transferred to Heidelberg.
There, in 1873, he completed his degree in Semitics.

Again, Adler's intellectual life was well served but one has
some hint that his personal life was less than happy. A letter
from a fellow student at Heidelberg said:

a young man with a diaphanous wisp on his chin called on
Steinschneider....He was prim and neatly dressed....Twenty min-
utes later the young man went away and I returned to the office.
The homely face of Steinschneider was wreathed in smiles. "Du

Adolphe," he said, laughter choking him, "du musst recht nett sein, denn wir haben einen Amerikanischen Adler hier; er ist der Sohn eines amerikanischen Rabbiners und wird Rabbiner Werden." The old wolf knew that I had an inferior respect for foreign scholars and wanted me to be very nice to the American.

It soon turned out that the young man was Felix Adler....I....know that [he] was unmercifully twitted by the students who called him, "der Amerikanishe Adler."[4]

Adler himself recalled, in his autobiographical notes, his dismay at his fellow students' personal moral behavior.[5] Later this was to lead to a strong emphasis on "sexual purity" and the devotion of one's wealth and energies to good works.

At Berlin and Heidelberg, Adler began to discover that broader philosophic climate which his undergraduate education had lacked. He spoke warmly, yet critically, of his studies with Hermann Cohen and his first exposure to socialism. More significantly, it was Frederich Albert Lange's *Die Arbeiterfrage* which "opened for me a wide and tragic prospect." A lifelong interest in the labor movement and in the problems of industrial society began to take shape even then.

In Germany, Adler came under the influence of neo-Kantian idealism and, in particular, the consequences of Kant's thought for religion and ethics. Two Kantian concepts played a major role in Adler's development: (1) that the existence or nonexistence of deity could not be demonstrated by "pure reason" since contradictory conclusions could be drawn from the same data; and (2) that morality, "practical reason," could be established without reliance on theology. The autonomy and centrality of ethics became guiding philosophic themes for Adler. His development of these in their application to the philosophic and practical problems of industrial society was to become his life's work.

[4]Letter by Dr. Adolphe De Castro to Gideon Chagy, Dec. 17, 1948. Ethical Culture Archive.

[5]*An Ethical Philosophy of Life* (New York, 1918), pp. 11-13.

Finally, if we are to understand the shaping of the man, we must return once more to the American continent. Nineteenth-century America, or at least its intellectual life, cannot be understood apart from a grasp of the role of Ralph Waldo Emerson. Having left the Unitarian pulpit as too restrictive, Emerson through his lectures and essays set the tone and content of intellectual discussion for several generations of Americans. It is revealing that each of Adler's early colleagues in the Ethical Movement—Coit, Salter, Weston, and Sheldon—referred to Emerson in describing their spiritual biographies. And these were typical rather than unique experiences for young men of a certain bent at the time. And Adler himself, in reflecting on his own growth, singled out "Emerson" along with "Jesus" and "The Hebrew Religion" as formative influences. While he was later to deny the importance of Emerson in his own philosophy, Adler was and remained far more Emersonian than he knew or admitted. The claims of "free religion," the call for a purely ethical religion, and the insistence on "self reliance" were all to play major roles in Adler's thought though he gave them his own characteristic formulation. Adler's emerging emphasis on the uniqueness of personality in the context of an organic social relationship is reminiscent of Emerson's *American Scholar* address.

As Adler grew to manhood, one can thus identify his philosophic roots and his social sources. The labor question, Kant, and Emerson mingle with currents of the Jewish prophetic tradition and reform to set the scene for Adler's own appearance as reformer, critic, and philosopher. But these disparate lines of development are as yet unfocussed. Adler, now done with formal schooling at childhood's end, must first search out his own vocation.

At first, the question of Felix Adler's vocation did not seem particularly problematic. Trained for the rabbinate, he was expected to carry on a family tradition stretching back through the generations in Europe and now being fulfilled by his father in the new world. When his brother, Isaac, decided for a medical career, Felix's future work seemed to have become even more unambiguously defined.

Thus, on Adler's return to America from the philosophic and religious heartland of Europe, the assumption of family and friends, as of Felix himself, was that he would succeed his father in the pulpit at Emanu-el. As it turned out, the matter was not quite that simple. It was the Sabbath, October 11, 1873. As a sign of welcome, Felix was to deliver the sermon. The congregation gathered, eager no doubt to hear the intellectual news from abroad and to witness the coming of age of their Rabbi's son and probable successor. It was an occasion of justifiable pride for the family and the community. The announced theme seemed promising, "The Judaism of the Future." One can, however, imagine a growing dismay as Adler spoke:

but what now? The field is cleared. The ruins are removed but what remains? Vacancy unmeasured. . .the best spirits of the age are turning their backs upon religion; the workers who should rear the buildings are mistrusted, the ministers of religion have lost the confidence of the people. It is useless to indulge in self-delusion, to bury our heads in sand in order to avoid the peril that threatens us. . . .The crisis through which we are passing is of the utmost danger. On all sides we hear the end of religion predicted. . . .The question for us to answer now is not this form or that form, this reform or that reform, the question is life or death, is religion about to perish. . .?

Thus far, troubling though the message may have seemed, it was still within the great prophetic style of discomforting the comfortable. But then Felix turned to his proposal for meeting the "question":

religion not confined to church and synagogue alone shall go forth into the market place, shall sit by the judge in the tribunal, by the counselor in the hall of legislation, shall stand by the merchant in his warehouse, by the workman at his work. . . .Then shall religion in truth become not a cause of strife but of harmony, laying its greatest stress not on the believing but in the acting out. A religion such as Judaism ever claimed to be—*not of the creed but of the deed* . . .

. . .we discard the narrow spirit of exclusion and loudly proclaim that *Judaism was not given to the Jews alone,* but that its destiny to embrace in *one great moral state the whole family of men.*[6]

Adler's words must have come as a shock mingled with anger at the ill manners and poor grace of their Rabbi's son. The secularity of Adler's proposal is inescapable; its activism unavoidable; and its universalism a direct challenge to the "identity" of the Jew as a Jew. It was Felix Adler's first and last sermon at the Temple, though he probably did not intend it that way. Much later, Adler recalled the occasion:

In an interview. . .Dr. Adler told what happened on his return to America. "The congregation," he said, "asked me to deliver a sermon from my father's pulpit. I did so and it created quite a lot of talk. Then some members brought up the fact that I had not mentioned God in what I had to say. The committee came to me and asked whether I believed in God. I said, 'yes, but not in your God.' And such being the case, I could not conscientiously accept the ministry."[7]

The family's vocation was now closed to him. Trained as a scholar, he was also unprepared to enter the business and professional life of the time. Indeed, "There was a story in the family that they thought he wouldn't amount to much in a professional way and that maybe they had better look around for some place for him in the jewelry business."[8] Fortunately, through the good offices and financial support of some members of the congregation, Felix was appointed as nonresident Professor of Hebrew and Oriental Literature at the newly founded Cornell University.

For three years, from 1873 through 1875, Adler taught at the university. Evidently he was a brilliant and successful teacher. Philosophically, he sought to trace a direct line between Pharisaic Judaism and the American ideal. Adler interpreted the Pharisaic insistence on personal religious responsi-

[6]"The Temple Emanu-el Sermon," 1873, Ethical Culture Archive.

[7]Cited in the *New York Times* obituary of Adler, April, 1933. [IX]

[8]Conversation with Horace L. Friess.

bility, on the interpenetration of religion with all of a man's life, and on its rejection of a special priesthood as forerunners of a spiritual democracy. Clearly, Adler did not remain confined to the past but used it instead to shed light on contemporary problems like the labor struggle, power politics, and changes in education. Adler's success in attracting students and his "relevance" led to a public attack on him in the denominational press. He was, we gather, accused of atheism and of being a threat to the Christian nurture of the students. In a letter to alumni, the President of Cornell, Andrew D. White, defended the college, Adler, and more importantly, academic freedom.[9]

But, by 1875 the funds which had supported Adler's teaching had run out and the college did not wish to renew the appointment. The question of vocation was still unresolved. However, some of those who had heard the Temple Sermon in 1873 had not forgotten its promise. Led by Julius Rosenbaum, a letter with 100 signatures was presented to Felix Adler inviting him to speak on the "plan of a new organization," which would meet the situation Adler had described. Standard Hall in New York City was rented and invitations issued. Many who had heard the earlier address attended as did the family and friends. Parenthetically, though Felix had broken with the Temple, his father was to come regularly to hear his son, thus accepting the integrity of young Adler's position.

On May 15, 1876, Adler spoke:

We propose entirely to exclude prayer and every form of ritual. . . .freely do I own to this purpose of reconciliation and candidly do I confess that it is my dearest object to exalt the present movement above the strife of contending sects and parties and at once to occupy that common ground where we may all meet, believers and unbelievers, for purposes in themselves lofty and unquestioned by any. . . .For more than 3000 years, men have quarreled concerning the formulas of their faiths. . . .

. . .We shall at all times respect every honest conviction—but be

[9]Adler to Cornell Alumni, May, 1877, Ethical Culture Archive.

one with us where there is nothing to divide—inaction. Diversity in
the creed, unanimity in the deed. This is that practical religion from
which none dissents. This is that platform broad enough to receive
the worshipper and the infidel. This is that common ground where
we may all grasp hands as brothers united in mankind's common
cause.[10]

Some two months later, a group of 128 people joined in ar-
ranging for Adler to deliver a regular series of Sunday morning lectures the following fall. On October 15, 1876, again at
Standard Hall, these lectures were inaugurated and the first
step in what was to become the Society for Ethical Culture was
taken. That winter, in February, 1877, the Society was incorporated and Felix Adler was employed as its "lecturer."

But the discovery of vocation was not completed. In a sense,
it was to continue to evolve all of Adler's life. Important as the
weekly lectures were to him and to his followers, they were
not, obviously, going to be adequate for a movement that had
called for the "deed." Led by Adler, the group now turned to
give content to that promise. During the next decade, from
1876 to 1886, they began a series of innovative actions. In
1877, the first free kindergarten east of the Mississippi was
founded in New York City. A district nursing program was established, forerunner of today's Visiting Nurse Service. A
tenement house building company was organized completing
its first building to accommodate 100 families. In 1880, the
Workingman's School—today the Ethical Culture Schools—
was organized. In 1882, Adler became a member of the
New York State Tenement Housing Commission. With Ed-
mond Kelly in 1883, he founded the Good Government Club
(now the City Club) to oppose political corruption in the city.
In progressive education—before it got its name—civic reform, and social welfare Adler took the lead. The centrality of
the organized act was much in evidence.

Adler was sophisticated enough to know that important as
such activity was, it required both philosophic grounding and

---

[10]Adler, "Address," May 15, 1876, *ibid.*

a well-constructed institution to provide support and coherence. Thus, he tried not to neglect the development of Ethical Culture as idea and as institution even while he busily moved into the community at large. Classes in ethical education were developed for the children of Society members; new Societies were founded in Philadelphia, Chicago, and St. Louis; young men were recruited and trained to serve the professional needs of Ethical Culture; books and pamphlets were published.

Adler's formidable energy was matched by growing personal powers, though for a time at least philosophic analysis took second place to more urgent practical demands. Describing his public appearance, a witness reported:

He speaks entirely without notes and from the first sentences it is apparent that his intellect is of a keen, relentless, and incisive order....Absolute fearlessness seems to be one of his leading characteristics....He stood easily at the side of his desk with the air of...weighing his thoughts....His sentences seem to drop out of a great profound and his whole manner so singularly unstudied instead of suggesting glibness shows hardly a sign of preparation.[11]

Adler's efforts were matched, more often than not, by successful response. To him and his society he drew a competent and effective membership prepared to join with him in the construction of a new religious movement and its works. The members of his Board of Trustees were men of prestige and achievement. Not untypical was its first chairman, Joseph Seligman, a founder of the banking house of Seligman and Brothers and one of the wealthiest men in the country. Samuel Gompers, founder of the American Federation of Labor was an early adherent. Henry Morgenthau, Sr., was active in Adler's work, assisting in establishing the Ethical Culture School, and helping to secure the site for the Meeting House of the Society on Central Park West in New York City after the turn of the century.

[11]"The Index," *Journal of the Free Press Association,* 1877.

But Adler was not only attracting an elite. Again, a contemporary observer reports:

Two hundred new members have joined the New York Society for Ethical Culture the past year [1878-1879] nearly doubling its membership. Standard Hall no longer accommodates the audiences and next season the Society will occupy Chickering Hall. During the summer, the Sunday meetings will be discontinued but the philanthropic work in which the Society is engaged will go on. The secret of Dr. Adler's remarkable success is not fully explained by. . .devotion to truth and righteousness; it lies even more. . .in his faith in organization, his executive ability. . .his controlling purpose to found institutions that shall outlast his own individual exertions. . . .Workers are no less needed than thinkers, and it is the phenomenal combination of both qualities in Dr. Adler that is giving him great success where so many others have failed, a success not likely to be ephemeral.[12]

While never large in numbers, the Society, and the activities of moral religion, included workers and wives, businessmen and teachers, professionals and tradesmen.

Adler managed, despite the growing public character of his life, to begin a family. In 1880 he married Helen Goldmark, daughter of a Brooklyn chemist. During the summers the family developed the practice of going to Keene Valley in the Adirondacks. There Felix would give time to his scholarly work regularly each morning. The family would go for long walks. When the children came—there were five, eventually: Waldo, Eleanor, Lawrence, Margaret, and Ruth—there were games too. As paterfamilias, Adler developed the habit of formally sharing with his family some of the things he was thinking or reading about.

Adler's life was not, initially, caught up only in the work of Ethical Culture. In 1866, following a struggle between conservatives and liberals in Unitarianism, the Free Religious Association had been founded by Francis Ellingwood Abbott and O. B. Frothingham. With headquarters in Boston, it became a

[12]*Ibid.*, 1878, p. 241.

center of religious liberalism, counting among its members Emerson, Lucretia Mott, Wendell Phillips, and Julia Ward Howe. Its goal was to "liberate religion from bondage to every kind of ecclesiastical authority" and to express the religious conscience in "moral and humane deeds." Adler came in contact with Free Religion, and with Emerson, in 1875. Its platform sounded very much like that of Ethical Culture. When Frothingham gave up the Presidency of the Association, Adler was elected in 1878 and served in that office until his resignation in 1882.

Repeatedly, as President, he tried to move the Association in more practical and more unified directions. But the group of individualists who formed its membership resisted all organizing efforts as dangerous—for these might issue in a new clericalism. Finally, Adler resigned in protest. According to Persons:

Felix Adler had proposed his plan of action in 1879 and had waited for three years while the Association debated [it]. . . .Adler's patience was exhausted by 1882 and at the Annual Meeting of that year he resigned. . . .Although he remained heartily in favor of the principles of the Free Religious Platform, he was disgusted with the scrupulousness of the Association's policy. . . .Adler's personal creed of agnosticism placed supreme emphasis on benevolent action, and he measured all religious professions against that standard. It was time for the free religionists to stop talking and act. "What has Boston done for the honor of our principles," demanded Adler; "What great charitable Movement has found its source here among those who maintain the principle of freedom in religion? What living thing for the good of mankind, for the perfecting of morality among yourselves and others emanated within the last twenty years from the Free Religious circles of this city? I say to you, friends. . .these annual meetings will not answer."[13]

The center of Adler's vocation, therefore, became finally the Ethical Culture Societies. Its threefold thrust emerged as: the reform of faith through active participation in the complex life of modern communities; the reconstruction of society

[13]Stow Persons, *Free Religion,* p. 96.

through the spirit of ethical religion; and the moral growth of the person by reciprocal interaction with other persons in the process of "ethicizing" society.

During the decade following the May 15 address, Adler was working out the lines of his vocation. The rabbinate and the academy did not suit him either ideologically or temperamentally. He had begun to probe ranges of experience which were to play major roles in his intellectual evolution. Experimenting with social causes, building educational institutions, learning the skills of organization, and sensing growing powers, he came to his fortieth year a highly successful man. The lines of early development still showed—the interest in scholarship, in social and religious reform, the prophetic style and leadership skill. Still to be discovered, however, was the "idea" of his vocation, the effort to interpret its meaning and to see it philosophically. Amid the endlessly demanding round of activities, the question of coherence began to grow larger and larger. While this, clearly, had personal import, it was also the more general question of building meaningful vocations while taking seriously the conflicting pressures and opportunities of modern life.

It would be artificial to speak of the next "stage" in Adler's life as if some explicit break with the past could be discovered or to identify some dramatic shift in his biography. We find, instead, continuity and differing points of emphasis. In his earlier years, though the pressures of career and the growing Ethical Society had kept him occupied, he had tried to clarify, to criticize, to analyze experience. And in his later years, attention to the institution, to social criticism, and to religious reform were not neglected. Nevertheless, it seems to us that as Adler moved into the 1890's, he began more and more to focus on the life of the mind as the key to his practical efforts.

In 1891, Adler spent a sabbatical year in Europe. Perhaps this permitted enough distance from the endless round of activity in which he had been enmeshed to face more directly the issues which that activity entailed. Adler's formative years

had resulted in manifest successes and increasing public recognition. They also exposed him to the need to move beyond
reform. Adler had been concerned from the outset with the
danger of losing himself in merely disparate experiences, in
"this reform, or that reform." While no system builder—he
was to be criticized by his philosophic colleagues for being too
unsystematic—he nevertheless tried more and more in these
years to discover theoretical intelligibility lest the endless demands of activity result in a type of mindless activism. The
"deed" to be sure remained at the center, but the "creed"
could not be forgotten. In Kantian and in pragmatic fashion,
the deed was to become the source and the validation of
philosophy, experience giving rise to meanings which were
then to be acted upon.

As a symbol of Adler's growing interests, he founded the
International Journal of Ethics in 1890 (still published today as
'Ethics' by the University of Chicago). In its pages were to be
found work by American thinkers like William James, John
Dewey, G. H. Mead; the British idealists and utilitarians; and
indeed many of the leading philosophic figures of the western
world. It was the world scene that became, for a time, far
more central than America to Adler's thought. His travels
abroad and the growing Ethical Culture Movement resulted in
the founding of Societies in most of the countries of Western
Europe as well as in Japan. In 1896, an International Ethical
Union was established. Adler, ever an acute observer, found
his international colleagues stimulating but "too academic"
and later expressed dismay at the failure of the European
movement, by and large, to apply the idea to the act.

In 1902, Adler was appointed Professor of Political and Social Ethics at Columbia, now becoming the university it had
not been in the 1860's. He continued to teach there while still
serving as Leader of the Ethical Society until the end of his
life. In 1908, he was appointed Theodore Roosevelt Professor
at the University of Berlin. Through the International Ethical
Union, Adler helped to develop the international Moral Education Congresses begun in 1908, and in 1911 he joined with

Gustave Spiller of the International Movement in establishing the first International Races Congress. Later, in 1923, he was to give the Hibbert Lectures at Oxford together with another series of talks on the reconstruction of education. Throughout his life, and particularly in these latter years, Adler visited Europe frequently. The period from 1890 through the early 1920's saw his exposure, therefore, to a far more complex cosmopolitan and academic setting as he moved outward from his base in the Ethical Culture Society. His reputation as a national and international figure grew.

But Adler was not content to move smoothly from city to nation to world. At Cornell, while a young man, he had traced a line between Hebrew prophecy and American democracy. Now, his European experiences confirmed him—over and over again—in the thought that he could not make sense of the modern industrial world except by turning once again to America as a model for the reconstruction of the ethical life.

Even as the European setting was providing another element in Adler's thought, events in American history were raising new questions. Adler moved into the forefront of those who, in the name of an American ideal, were increasingly critical of American imperialism. From 1898 onward, in publication, on the Ethical Platform, and as a public figure, he began to raise the issue of what he came to call the "national crisis." Central and Latin American adventurism were the beginnings. World War I, and in particular Wilson's "naivete" about the League of Nations, saw the climax of the crisis from his point of view. The war was not a democratic crusade at all but evidence of conflicting imperialism. A tension between manifest destiny and spiritual democracy was growing. And if the American model was to become an ethical model, then this tension had to be made explicit and the illusions of American self-righteousness exposed. The nation itself had to be "ethicized."

Finally, in establishing the matrix of Adler's philosophic maturity, one must identify the issues which seemed to him to have become more and more serious as America and the world moved into the Twentieth century. A deep and pervasive attention to what we would call minority rights began to punctuate Adler's thought. Labor had interested him from the outset and child labor in particular was ethically troubling. The Civil War and the Lincoln influence reappeared in his concern with the question of racial justice, a concern which characteristically Adler saw not merely as a domestic but as a worldwide problem. While he opposed the popular movement of "equal rights" for women, he did so on the grounds that the problem could not be dealt with merely by a superficial adjustment of social forms like voting and the like. This would merely compound the errors of "quantitative" democracy already afflicting America and would, moreover, endanger society's basic building block, the family. He did support the rights of women to careers but more significantly and problematically saw in motherhood a vocation equal in its claims to other more traditional vocations. Adler was temperamentally very much the Victorian. Yet his opposition to divorce, to Freudianism, to anarchic individualism was a not unrealistic response to the needs for social stability as prerequisite to ethical reconstruction. It was, however, clearly an unpopular response and masked Adler's radicalism behind a seeming conservative cloak.

The European experience, the rise of American and global imperialism, and the issues of human rights might each, in turn, have led Adler to expand his role as social critic and social reformer. Certainly, there would have been more than enough to do in any of these areas, let alone all three. And certainly, the continuing claims of Ethical Culture would have been enough to exhaust the energies of any man let alone someone moving into his twilight years. But Adler saw in these issues and experiences—or thought he saw—a common thread. They represented outcomes of a society, a civilization, in deep trouble at its roots. Thus, even as he paid attention to issues of criticism and reform, he began more and more to develop his thinking on the problems of industrial society.

The time from about 1890 through the end of his life in

1933 saw Adler develop a philosophy of industrial culture. The struggle for the rights of labor was meeting violent and bloody repression. Private armies, strikes, and economic depression were joined with political unwillingness to deal with these problems equitably. In this setting Adler, together with Crawford Howell Toy of Harvard and Henry Carter Adams of Michigan, founded the Summer School of Applied Ethics at Plymouth in 1891. Among others, William James, Josiah Royce, and Jane Addams taught courses there. In 1894, Adler gave a series of twelve carefully worked out lectures on the labor question, the problems of commercial society and its ethical possibilities. He developed three coordinate themes: a concept of labor as a social and political but, significantly, also an ethical movement; a concept of vocation; and a concept of industrial politics. Adler's proposal, in brief, was that the reconstruction of industrial society was both possible and necessary. The clue to reconstruction was the development of vocational opportunity for every member of society based upon the "talents" that were to be attributed to each person. Vocation, the commitment of the person to meaningful work, was the core. Properly understood, a vocation was not merely a job or even a career. Rather, because it had historic components, involved the vocationalist in interdependent relationships with all other vocationalists, and served as a lever for social reform, vocation was the practical moral center for a truly radical attack on industrial society. In such a society at least it became the way in which the attribute of inalienable human worth became active and gained a realistic content.

Adler saw in his concept of vocationalism the possibility of a reconstruction of the democratic ideal as well. Through vocation, the participation of everyone in society would be insured. Each person, through the development of his talents and through his interaction with others, would find a place, a meaningful place, in society. Thus the pressures of alienation would be met and the deadly superficiality of the commercial spirit could be successfully challenged. The suicidal pathways of war, revolution, and anarchy could be avoided. Adler's critical neo-Kantianism had led him to reformulate the categorical imperative as follows: So act as to elicit the best in others and thereby in oneself. The realistic content of the formal imperative became the move toward vocation. Action in industrial society was work and productivity. Adler wanted these to be transformed by moving from mechanistic to organic categories, by treating man as an organism and as a whole. Kant's "kingdom of ends" became Adler's spiritual democracy. Vocation in industrial society was its empirical expression. The emphasis was not on goods and services, the cry for more, more, but on personal growth through interpersonal development. And America as the model—in its best and worst senses—of industrialism was the place where this essay at reconstruction and transformation could occur.

Philosophically, this thesis on the transformation of industrial society was to reappear in Adler's *An Ethical Philosophy of Life* (1918), where he put it in the context of a criticism of Kantianism as overly individualistic. In *The Reconstruction of the Spiritual Ideal* (1924) he saw vocational or industrial democracy as a response to the "false" civilization whose critical weakness had been revealed by the debacle of World War I. Typically, he had tried out these ideas from time to time on the Ethical Culture Platform. A fascinating example of how Adler developed an idea is to be found in *The World Crisis and Its Meaning* (1916), where the interaction of philosophic insight, systematic efforts to organize them, and *ad hoc* social criticism is quite revealing of Adler's style.

As Adler molded his philosophy of industrial democracy, he was led inevitably to reconsiderations of schooling. His interest in education dated back to the founding of the Workingman's School. Though, in part, it had been an activity of "good works" and social welfare, it was even then almost intuitively a response to Adler's recognition that somehow the reconstruction of society rested on the reconstruction of education. As Adler neared the end of his life, he began to be more and more explicit about the connection between social and pedagogical radicalism. In the 1890's, a concept of "organic"

education was germinating for him which led to a curriculum
that integrated classical studies, modern science, industrial
arts, and ethics. In 1913, an experimental Arts High School
had been established as part of the Ethical Culture Schools
seeking yet another mode of integrated education (or what we
today might call interdisciplinary study). In the 1920's, Adler
began to dream more dramatically about a major new step in
education; and in 1926, he formulated the "ideals for the new
school":

the principle of the pre-eminence of values must be adhered
to. . . .we go through the whole history of commerce and the commercial class—the kind of government it has promoted; and how it
has influenced science and the arts. . .how far commerce was the ac-
complice of tyranny; how far commerce today is a menace in the Far
East. . . .We give the young business men. . .an idea of the man of
business considered as a member of the commercial group, of the
policies to be favored in national and international life, of the attitude to be taken toward fellow workers. . .we endeavor to implant
in them the principle of watching their lives and estimating their own
value by the way in which they affect other people, to bring that
principle into the very market place.[14]

A year earlier, and less formally, Adler spoke in almost grand-
iose fashion to his Board of Trustees:

we should. . .give rein to our vastest hopes. . .think of the future
graduates of the business school as playing a great role in the
world. . . .The white races are one third of the population of the
world; the colored races. . .are showing their restiveness under the
domination of the white. . .the commercial spirit is everywhere break-
ing the hearts of the races. . . .The greatest change that the world
needs today is the creation of real men. . . .We must dedicate our
pre-vocational school. . .to the future civilization of this planet.[15]

The "Fieldston Plan" as it came to be called (and the Fieldston School) reflected once again Adler's unwillingness to rest

---

[14] *Ideals for our New Schoool,* February, 1926.
[15] Minutes, Board of Trustees, N.Y. Society for Ethical Culture, November,
1925.

content with philosophic formulation alone. He was now in his seventies. The last act, so to speak, of Adler's life was reminiscent of the first. Philosophy, unconnected with organic activity, was empty; activity untouched by philosophy was mindless. Thus, the mature Adler still reflected the young man—critic, philosopher, and educator seen as integral to each other. But now, as Adler neared the end of his life, there was a growing unity in these three elements of biography, and explicit interconnections replaced intuitive responses. Reform, which may well be identified as the initial theme of Adler's development, was transformed by philosophy into reconstruction. *Ad hoc* radicalism in the pulpit became a nearly systematic radicalism. The theme of religious reform took new shape as Adler saw in "reconstruction" not only a change in society but a change in persons, a "spiritual" reconstitution of man.

Felix Adler had a long, productive, and complex life. A child of the nineteenth century, he exhibited the traits of the Victorian gentleman: a certain rigidity of personality and a sense of unquestionable authority. Tutored in a personal community that was economically and socially quite comfortable, he began as a radical critic within it and ended, philosophically at least, as a radical democrat. The move from reform to reconstruction, from noblesse oblige to universal fellowship, is the dynamic line of Adler's biography, though it was a move never quite completed.

Unlike his philosophic mentor, Kant, Adler was a man of the academy and the market place. The continuing achievement of his life was the effort to bring these disparate environments together in idea and in action. His friendships included teachers, professionals, politicians, businessmen, and lawyers. But as important as this variety of personal relationships which provided him with a continuing source of information, the time in which he lived was one of repeated crisis and growing complexity. Adler, though he never formulated a philosophy of history, was deeply sensitive to man as an historical being. Indeed, in describing the ideal of education, he maintained that history had to be its basic discipline. Though he himself never went to war, he had from childhood onward, a certain responsiveness to the hero and the heroic. Paradoxically, his evolving philosophy had to come to terms repeatedly with the moral horrors of warfare and its aftermath: a young man witnessing the demoralization of America after the Civil War; a mature man watching imperialist wars break out in Latin America, in the Philippines, in China, in Siberia; an older man tortured by the indecency of the so-called "war to make the world safe for democracy." And while he did develop a theory of a just war,[16] he recognized, long before others did, that modern warfare was a function of industrialism gone awry.

Adler's life span was marked by a continuing round of transitional struggles. War was, perhaps, its most dramatic and visible expression. But the growing pressure of once-silent peoples for a voice in their destiny, the emerging labor movements around the world, the rise and derailment of a democratic politics all contributed to his sense of a time when events were latent with promise and awesome with deadly threat. Adler's style reflects, therefore, a need to respond to what was to him inescapable experience. This gave his work a decidedly contemporary quality since it also made it impossible for him to separate himself from history long enough to work out his ideas without the intrusion of occurrence. The acceleration of experience which is so much of the modern complaint was already underway for Adler. To keep both balance and relevance under these conditions was difficult and, at times, simply impossible. For all his lifelong efforts, his work had to remain unfinished.

Adler's style is not only responsive—and hence, occasionally at least, seemingly sporadic—but also reflexive. There was a decided realism in the man which would not let him avoid the present conflict for the sake of utopian abstraction or even pure thought. Though he insisted on the urgency of the

[16]See Appendix 11, "The Exercise of Force in the Interest of Freedom," *An Ethical Philosophy of Life.*

moral ideal, he simultaneously insisted that the ideal would only be valid in so far as it cast light on the present and offered conceivable directions to the future. Thus, he did not become a revolutionary and was clearly not a conservative. History was not historicism. And revolution was an illusion, for one could not really believe it possible to wipe the slate clear and start over again. For an historical being, there can be only one beginning—all the rest is *re*-construction. His philosophy of industrial society illustrates Adler's respect for the facts of the present. His central theme of reconstruction was premised on the persistence of a certain historic situation, industrialism. The key terms of his thinking, therefore, had to be drawn from industrial experience—work, productivity, competence, achievement. But by a type of spiritual judo, he sought to convert these from what they were into what they ought to become. This is what Adler meant by "ethicizing," the conversion of reality by the active intervention of man who lived, in part at least, as an idealist. But, and this was crucial, the starting point—the reality—could neither be dismissed nor evaded.

The market place and the academy were two points of reference for Adler. The third was his sense of the religiousness or potential religiousness of all experience. This implied that Adler could not simply be a reformer or simply be a thinker but had to entwine both in a highly personal commitment of his very being. Early in life, Adler's personalism had revealed itself. Henry Morgenthau, Sr., recalled:

Above all, however, I treasure the fond remembrance of having been a member of the "Union for the Higher Life"—an organization of a few of Adler's devotees. He always maintained that, as every man expected purity from his wife, it was his duty to enter the marriage state in the same condition, and the members of this "Union" pledged themselves to celibacy during bachelorhood. We met every week. . . .We read Lange's *Arbeiterfrage* and studied the labor question. We discussed the problems of business and professional men. I notice in my diary of April 24, 1882, we debated the simplicity of dress and the follies of extravagance. Then, as Dr. Adler wanted us to feel that we were doing something definitely altruistic, the members of the Union jointly adopted eight children; some of them were half-orphans, and some had parents who could not support them properly; we employed a matron and hired a flat for her.[17]

If the young Adler sought to show by his own conduct the connection of thought and act within personality—Adler's view of "character"—this effort continued throughout his life. He was, in short, serious about his philosophy, seeking to avoid a fatal "specialism" which put reform in one compartment, thought in another, and private life in still a third. But, as with all great seriousness, there was a sense of humor too. He was, we are told, an incorrigible punster and

was fuller of real fun, prankish, impish fun than any man I ever met. That is the way he acted when he visited us. But one day, just as we were about to finish our dinner, the front doorbell rang, the dining room had been full of joyous laughter. . . .My wife and I never saw such a change in a man as happened at that moment. As soon as our friends entered he became again the great moral leader, taking on at once all the dignity becoming the head of the Society for Ethical Culture.[18]

The "coldness" which so many report of Adler corroborates this deeply held sense of his role. He revealed himself fully only to very few intimates. His effort at personal integration suffered the weakness of a sharp division between public and private presence. Rarely do we get a glimpse of the intimate Adler, but a letter to his wife from Europe suggests it:

It is all so tantalizingly beautiful and so tantalizingly unsatisfactory. We must hope and plan and arrange somehow that we shall take this lovely trip together some day before too long. But in the meantime, my own particular lady love, there cannot possibly be a closer response than that of my thoughts to yours as they travel over the leagues of sea, annihilating space and defying separation. This makes

---

[17]*All in a Lifetime,* pp. 95-97 *passim.*
[18]Julius Henry Cohen, *They Builded Better Than They Knew,* p. 36.

me happy despite all grumbling and so I will sign for tonight your discontented, yet deeply contented,

Felix.[19]

As with any man whose career was so much in the public eye, there is a fatal temptation to take the public figure for the man. But this would not only be humanly false, it would be a misreading of Adler philosophically as well. And if he did not easily reveal himself, there were clues enough in his utterances to suggest to the sensitive listener that more was involved in the man than impressive speaker, thinker, or even social reformer. It was not merely as a philosophic notion that he referred so frequently to "spiritual pain" and made much of the experience of frustration. Behind the ideas was the struggle of the man to master experience which he was convinced could never finally be mastered by anyone, let alone himself. Now and then we get a more direct, but still indirect, expression of Adler's awareness of his inability fully to integrate thought, act, and person. For example, while ostensibly speaking of Kant, he made the following self revealing comment:

has not your experience told you—I think mine has—that those who put on the hardness of inflexible rigor are often persons who realize that they are subject to deep emotions and who fear to be carried by their softer feeling. . .and who thus assume a sternness which is not really natural to them?[20]

The ideal was quite real to Adler. It remained a source of tension and incompletion reflecting itself in his biography as in his philosophy. The contradictions of his personality could never quite be overcome by his overpowering drive for coherence. His style, his character, was a function of that tension.

On April 24, 1933, Felix Adler died after a long struggle with cancer. Though remembered within the Ethical Culture Societies as their founder, much of his more penetrating and

---

[19]Letter from Europe, dated August 20, 1896, Ethical Culture Archive.

[20]"In Commemoration of the Centennial Anniversary of the Death of Immanuel Kant, Jan. 24, 1904."

original philosophic contributions is, unfortunately, all but ignored. The literature of American philosophy treats him as an interesting but minor example of neo-Kantian religious idealism. The schools which he started and nurtured, though highly successful as educational institutions, scarcely reflect the "vocationalism" that Adler took to be his most crucial pedagogical insight. The reforms in social welfare, in politics, in labor relations in which he played so important a role continue their evolution unaware of Adler's part in their development. Except for a pious reference now and then—usually on the occasion of an anniversary—Adler is an all but forgotten figure.

It is true that those who knew him personally still speak of his influence on them. Business men, social workers, educators, housewives tell of his impact on their careers. Quite literally he helped people change their very lives. He was not only a magnificent lecturer but a great teacher too. By now, however, fewer and fewer survive and the "living presence" so many spoke of grows dim. The complexity of Adler's career hinders rather than helps his reputation. The record is perhaps overly rich and diffuse for the modern specialist perception. Philosophers tend to categorize him as a reformer and a religionist. For the activists he was too philosophic, too abstract. For the pedagogues, though he is probably better known in education than anywhere else, he is still too Victorian, too unattuned to a modern psychologized pedagogy to be quite acceptable. And for the religionists he is neither absolute enough for a new orthodoxy nor current enough for situation ethics.

Near the end of his life, Adler had some awareness of the fate which came to surround his work and his ideas. Certainly the high hopes of the younger man had given way to a quieter and more realistic acceptance of the vicissitudes of historic fashion. To his Board of Trustees in 1929, he spoke of this:

I wish to come into contact with the Trustees after the absence of last year. I have wanted to be with you as I have for fifty-four years. . .the times. . .and surrounding change, and new tendencies come up of which we did not dream in 1876. . . .There is utter chaos in. . .moral relations. . .I do not need to tell you that I stand against the skeptics, the behaviorists and the pragmatists. There is such a thing as truth, although our expressions of it need constant correction. . . .There is such a thing as right although our moral codes are being shattered because they are more or less corrupt. . . .

Some people had an idea that the Ethical Movement was going to sweep over the world like a prairie fire. That is foolish. . . .Ideas grow slowly in the lives of men. I have started my seventy-ninth year. I think of my successors. . . .I think that the lamp which we lit in the darkness of the storm may in future centuries be obscured and plunged into darkness and be again rekindled.[21]

Looking back, even over the last decade of his life, Adler could still find achievement. The mark of the man as a doer was still visible. Efforts were being made to revive some of the international work of the Ethical Movement; young men were carrying on the work in America; the Schools were flourishing and Fieldston, the new venture, had opened its doors. Many of the reforms which had seemed so tenuous in the 1880's were now part of the American scene. The books were written—though Adler never did write his book on "friendship," something he repeatedly had said he wanted to do.

Though failing physically, Adler's mind remained clear and incisive almost to the day of his death. He spoke occasionally on the Ethical Platform until early in 1930. He met with his students and his co-workers. He still sought to raise funds for his school and to keep an eye on the institutions that were his life work. For example, on April 13, only ten days before his death, he met with V.T. Thayer, Director of the Schools, to discuss a foundation grant received for the development of "pre-vocational" courses at Fieldston.

Unlike fiction, human existence does not meet the dramatic unities of beginning, middle, and end. Yet Adler's life came closer than most. It is illustrative of his own philosophy of continuing effort, continuing integration, continuing recon-

[21]Minutes, Board of Trustees, New York Society for Ethical Culture, October, 1929.

struction. A colleague recalled the Ethical Leaders' Seminar in the fall of 1932, the last which Adler was able to attend:

He had on his frock coat. . . .It was a late afternoon in the autumn. . .the golden sunlight from the west came into the room and shone on the beautiful rug and on him. He started to read. . . .He got about 2 sentences into his paper and he got lost. . . .He started over again and got about 3 or 4 sentences and got lost again. Very slowly and deliberately, he took out his watch. . .a gold watch, and he pressed a little button and opened it. Then he said, "I guess my time is up." Slowly, he closed it and walked out. . . .[22]

Howard Radest

Associate Professor of Philosophy
Ramapo College

---

[22]Interview with Algernon D. Black, 1963.

Part I. Ethics

CHAPTER 1

Felix Adler's Concept of Worth[1]

Felix Adler is today better known as a teacher and as the founder of the Society of Ethical Culture than as a philosopher specializing in ethics. He taught a course in ethics at Columbia University for many years and there are generations of colleagues and students who revere his memory. He was one of the founders of the *International Journal of Ethics* in 1890. He wrote two major works, *An Ethical Philosophy of Life* (1918) and the *Reconstruction of the Spiritual Ideal,* which is the publication of the Hibbert Lectures delivered in Oxford in 1923.[2]

The above paragraph reads as if it were an obituary notice paying proper respects to the dead. But it is my contention that Adler is deserving of critical attention and not merely devotion. A few words about his background, however, are quite pertinent. Adler's family life and education were focused on the religious. He received much of his religious education from his father, Rabbi Samuel Adler, a leader of Reform Judaism in Germany, who had already emigrated to the United States when Felix was nearly six years old. He had taken over the leadership of Temple Emanu-el in New York City. Felix started in his father's footsteps, and his graduate work in

[1]This chapter originally appeared as an article by the same title in the *Journal of the History of Philosophy.* Copyright 1973 by the JOURNAL OF THE HISTORY OF PHILOSOPHY, Inc. Reprinted from the *Journal of the History of Philosophy,* XI, No. 2 (April, 1973), by permission of the Editor.

[2]*An Ethical Philosophy of Life: Presented in its Main Outlines* (New York: D. Appleton and Co., 1918), and *The Reconstruction of the Spiritual Ideal* (New York: D. Appleton and Co., 1924). These two works are cited below as *EPL* and *RSI* respectively.

Germany was to prepare him for the rabbinate. It is clear that he drank deeply of the teachings of both early Hebrews and Christians in formulating his concept of worth.

Adler's concept of worth is multidimensional, and the following major aspects can be distinguished: an historical dimension; a psycho-social dimension; a logical dimension; an ontological dimension; and an ethical dimension.

The Historical Dimension of Worth

Looking back at his own development, Adler wrote in 1918, at the age of sixty-seven:

> The predominance of the ethical principle in religion dates from the prophets of Israel. The religious development of the human race took a new turn in their sublime predictions, and I for one am certainly conscious of having drawn my first draught of moral inspiration from their writings.

However, by the age of twenty-two, he had already separated himself from Judaism, and he never accepted Christianity. He did not simply reject these religious doctrines, while retaining the ethical aspects. Instead, he worked out his own ethical philosophy, which he thought of as building upon the best in these ancient religious and ethical traditions. The development of a new position required an intellectual justification for it, and this justification involved criticism of these traditions. The result might be called a philosophy of ethical history.

In his Hibbert Lectures, Adler proclaimed: "out of the depths into which it has fallen humanity cries today for help."[3] But "in order to reconstruct society we must reconstruct the moral ideal."[4]

Adler's general argument can be outlined as follows: (1) we seek to reconstruct society; (2) this reconstruction must be responsive to the spiritual problems of the age, and so we must reformulate our conception of the spiritual or moral ideal; (3)

[3]*Rsi*, p. 1.
[4]*Ibid.*, p. 12.

however, the moral ideal is based upon a conception of the spiritual nature of man; (4) this conception of the spiritual nature will be objectively based if it is responsive to the "spiritual pain" of the age; and (5) recognition of this spiritual pain makes it possible to see the objective *worth* of man and his proper role in the processes of social and spiritual reconstruction.

In the actual analysis that Adler offers, only three phases in Western history are discussed: the Hebrew, the Christian, and Adler's own, which we can call the Modern phase.[5]

Adler locates the primary pain suffered by the early Hebrews as being associated with the tremendous oppression which they suffered as a people. The conception of the spiritual nature of man, which was forged out of this pain and suffering, was that each man contained within himself a spiritual part that was "holy." In the world the early Hebrews knew, trespassing was the actuality. The holy thing, the inner reaches of man, his true reality, his spiritual nature, was defined as that where there would be "No Trespassing!" *The spiritual ideal was formulated primarily in terms of the concept of justice.* Persons have rights because of the holy presence in them. Respect for the rights of others (conceived in an almost wholly negative way) was what it meant to be just. And, of course, the Hebrew God is the God of Justice. The ideal society is that society where justice rules supreme. And mercy and humility follow from justice. Adler quotes from Micah: "For what doth the Lord require of thee, but to do justly, and to love mercy, and to walk humbly with thy God?"[6]

Mercy follows, for we must respond when we see a human being—who is holy ground—reduced in any way from his full stature as a dignified, sovereign being. Humility follows, as

[5] The discussion of the Hebrew and Christian traditions is drawn mainly from Chapter II, "The Spiritual Ideal," in *The Reconstruction of the Spiritual Ideal;* from Chapters II and IV, "The Hebrew Religion" and "The Teaching of Jesus," in *An Ethical Philosophy of Life;* from Chapter IX, "The Founder of Christianity," in *Creed and Deed* (New York: G. P. Putnam's Son's, 1877); also Appendix II, "The Evolution of Hebrew Religion," in *Creed and Deed.*

[6] *RSI*, pp. 37-38.

one recognizes how far one fails to live according to the high moral standard that is set.

Worth is attributed to that which one must not invade. The objective ground for this attribution lies in the fact that it is the spiritual part of man which responds with such great pain when any invasion takes place. The fact that the pain is intense is taken as an indication that there is something that is part of man's nature which ought not be invaded. The reasoning is circular. If the argument has force, it is because the assumption is made that what is here spoken of as spiritual pain cannot be ignored; it may not be set aside.

Adler seeks the source of the Christian ideals in the distinctive pains suffered by early Christians. The Hebrews had thought of themselves as a holy people and their ideal was framed in terms of community. But the early Christians, or more accurately, those living near the beginning of Christianity, were unable to find any state or community with which they could identify and which they could idealize. The pain experienced was the pain of an individual lost, without roots, homeless.[7]

Adler sees the Christian approach to the spiritual nature as offering worth in individualistic terms. We might say that the individual took the place of and became the community. For it is the spiritual part of each man that is here seen as complex: peopled, as it were, with both holy and profane elements. Thrown back upon himself, the individual makes the move that the Hebrews could never make. He attempts to enter and describe the spiritual nature. He still finds a holy part. But he finds much that is not holy:

The territory of the inner life was boldly entered. The awful sense of aloofness had to some extent diminished, and a bifurcation was attempted within the inner man. The holy thing in him was separated off by a sharper distinction between it and the things in him that are not holy, such as appetite, anger, passion, pride.[8]

[7]*Ibid.*, p. 40.
[8]*Ibid.*, pp. 39-40.

With the new conception of the spiritual nature of man a corresponding spiritual ideal appears. The Christian retains the ideal of holiness. But whereas the Hebrew conception was written in terms of social justice and made reference to the way in which people acted toward one another, the Christian turns his attention on himself. Adler says that the starting point was individualism. The spiritual ideal of the individual was purity of self. The social task was to help others in the difficult process of purifying themselves. Thinking in these terms, the Christian, as such, does not envisage a reconstruction of society in any direct sense. The important thing is the purification of the inner man.

Adler's own view develops from the Hebrew and the Christian concepts. First we must identify the spiritual pain because this pain is the primary element in the recognition and reconstruction of the ideal of worth, which, as we have seen, is essential for social and spiritual reconstruction. He locates three major sources of such pain.

The first of these three kinds of spiritual pain, in Adler's view, was the growing sense of the smallness and insignificance of man in the universe: "never has the Lilliputian disparity between man and the magnitude of his world, the immensities of space, come home with such crushing force as it has to our own generation."[9] This is the Copernican revolution come home to roost. And the theory of evolution also helps to make it less possible to think of man as the center, and the highest point, and the *raison d'être* of the universe. Adler quotes Hume to the effect that man is of no more account than an oyster in the sight of the universe and adds, "If Hume were living today, with what more drastic emphasis would he propound this depressing conclusion."[10] The results of science cannot be set aside, but there must be a way of mitigating the pain caused by these results:

[9]*Ibid.*, p. 13.
[10]*Ibid.*, p. 15.

Now no intelligent person will publish himself an obscurantist and a fool by disputing the teachings of science. The problem is to extricate oneself from this heavy burden that rests upon selfconsciousness, without stultifying the mind by subterfuges or evasions. The truths of science must be received as such, but a way must also be found of not only vindicating, but enhancing the spiritual prerogative of man, of establishing as a fact that there exists in him a spiritual nature which exalts him, which gives him a unique place in the scheme of things. Seen from one point of view he is like Hume's oyster, or like oxen and sheep, a mere product of physical evolution; known from another point of view, he is far more than a development of the inferior life-forms. He is a witness of the infinite striking into the finite world. A reconstructed ethical ideal must make good this proposition, must relieve mankind of the pain, the depression, due to profound self-depreciation and self-contempt.[11]

The second pain is that which is associated with having to stand witness to the millions of humans who suffer and die. Today, we could add what Adler did not know—that there were those doomed to die in gas chambers, purges, brainwashing, and radiation poisoning. "We stand, as it were, on the shore," he said, "and see multitudes of our fellow beings struggling in the water, stretching forth their arms, sinking, drowning, and we are powerless to assist them."[12] Adler goes into some detail and says finally:

We must sharpen the effort to improve these conditions which are instrumental to the development of the moral nature of man. . .and at the same time we must vindicate the present worth which is independent of conditions.[13]

Finally, the third kind of pain is tied to the "intolerable strain of the divided conscience":

Felt by men who are eagerly desirous to make their life whole, all of a piece, of achieving consistency in their conduct throughout, and who do not see how to do it because they find that the ethical standard which they acknowledge in their private relations, and which they would like to expand so as to cover their business and profes-

[11]*Ibid.,* pp. 16-17.
[12]*Ibid.,* pp. 17-18.
[13]*Ibid.,* pp. 22-23.

sional relations, their conduct as citizens, is incapable of such expansion. In other words, they have a moral standard to hold to when they deal as individuals with other individuals, but find themselves destitute of any sufficient moral standard to guide them where they are required to act as members of a group.[14]

In a footnote Adler adds:

A man engaged in large business transactions approached a Christian clergyman of my acquaintance with this request: "Can you tell me how I can lead the Christian life in business?" and the clergyman confided to me that he had found it difficult to give a satisfactory answer. Difficult—I reflected—on Christian premises, is it possible?[15]

Adler concludes that the reduction of this third kind of pain requires an ethic regulating the morality of groups.

Several propositions would seem to issue from the kind of historical analysis that Adler offers: (1) that the conceptions of the spiritual nature and the spiritual ideal do in fact change; (2) that these changes are accounted for primarily as responses to the spiritual pains, suffering, and frustrations that pervade an era; (3) that deliberate changes in these concep-

---

[14]*Ibid.,* pp. 24-25.

[15]*Ibid.,* p. 25. Adler might well agree with the following analysis by Hannah Arendt. It makes clearer than Adler's presentation how the Christian ideal of *inner* purity makes it, at least difficult, on Christian premises, to develop an ethic relevant to the relations among men. According to Arendt, "The one activity taught by Jesus in work and deed is the activity of goodness, and goodness obviously harbors a tendency to hide from being seen or heard. Christian hostility toward the public realm, the tendency at least of early Christians to lead a life as far removed from the public realm as possible, can be understood as a self-evident consequence of devotion to good works, independent of all beliefs and expectations. For it is manifest that the moment a good work becomes known and public, it loses its specific character of goodness, of being done for nothing but goodness' sake. When goodness appears openly, it is no longer goodness, though it may still be useful as organized charity or an act of solidarity. Therefore: 'Take heed that ye do not your alms before men, to be seen by them.' Goodness can exist only when it is not perceived, not even by its author; whoever sees himself performing a good work is no longer good, but at best a useful member of society or a dutiful member of a church. Therefore: 'Let not thy left hand know what thy right hand doeth." *The Human Condition* (Chicago: University of Chicago Press, 1958; Anchor Books, ed.), p. 664.

tions are possible; and (4) that such changes, that is, such conscious reformulations, should be made in response to the widely experienced spiritual pains directed toward the alleviation of those pains.

Ethical formulations should be responsive to the deep felt spiritual needs of men, claims Adler. These needs, when unfulfilled, are experienced not as physical pain (although that too is possible), but primarily as what we may call spiritual anguish. This anguish shows itself as a function of the conception of man that is held in a particular historical epoch. Adler seeks a criterion on the basis of which one can claim validity of objectivity for a spiritual conception of man and of the ideals formulated in terms of that conception. Spiritual suffering is the reality to which any spiritual conception of man and any spiritual ideal must answer.

But Adler seems to want to go much further than this as he suggests that there is a spiritual nature which somehow exists without change through history and that formulation of it may be more or less an approximation of a true formulation. For he writes:

> The historical situation, and the needs in it as felt by ethically sensitive minds, is ever the challenge that provokes the construction or reconstruction of the spiritual ideal. Not that the historical situation is the cause, it is the evocative occasion. . .the triple need of our own generation. . .more particularly the need of a group morality. . .is the challenge to those who are ethically sensitive for the formation, the reformation, the reconstruction of a spiritual ideal that shall be apt to respond to the need. How shall this be produced? . . .By definition, by a stricter nature, taking hold of it mentally with a firmer grasp.[16]

It would seem that the underlying ideal, which Adler seeks to formulate more clearly than had yet been done, the ideal of worth, must be a root or generic ideal that appears through history in different guises. Adler seems to suggest that the spiritual ideal of worth is responsive to a spiritual need which men will experience in one way or another in all historical

[16]*RSI*, pp. 46-47.

periods. The context of the pain and the specific form it assumes, as well as the corresponding formulation of the ideal, will differ in different historical periods. But Adler wants to say that the pain does not change, that it is the same pain, appearing in different forms throughout human history. The attempt to alleviate this pain takes many forms and the spiritual ideals that issue from such attempts can be judged to be more or less successful, more or less objectively grounded in reality.

As one looks back at Adler's characterization of the Hebrew, the Christian, and his own period, it is apparent that what is faced, in one form or another, is the demand made by an individual or a group that it counts, that it makes a difference.

The Hebrews spoke of themselves as a chosen people, finding holiness—that which is sacred and to be revered—in each man and in the people as a group. "Thou shalt not trespass" is primarily a negative dictum in response to oppression. It can be interpreted as one way of affirming the need to be counted, to be taken as having some significance in the world. As such, it may be considered as one way of trying to assert their worth. Inner purity gave significance to the early Christian in a social context that otherwise offered him neither position nor leverage for defining some sense in which he "made a difference." The three kinds of spiritual pain that Adler claimed for his own (modern) time all mark the individual as having a sense of insignificance, impotence, homelessness, meaninglessness.

It would seem that more recent literature and experience would support Adler's emphasis on this phenomenon. Nationalism and the ideas of independence and self-determination, which began in Europe and the United States, are now sweeping Asia and Africa with the breakdown of colonial empires. Insistence on the right to independence, the right to self-determination, the rights of minority groups, women's rights, and not least, the human rights of all—they seem to attest the fact that the need for "counting" at some level or in some way or another is widespread. We can recognize it as a persistent and insistent demand—sometimes articulate; sometimes repressed; sometimes manifesting itself in violence; sometimes showing itself in quiet resignation, even deprecation of oneself and/or others. The violent rebel represents a dramatic instance of this demand. But the monk, the recluse, the Taoist, and the Buddhist, the Stoic and Epicurean, in practicing a form of renunciation, might also be understood as seeking a place for themselves and a meaning for their lives.

We might pause here to consider more closely Adler's claim that in connection with the "pain of the divided conscience," what is most needed is a morality of groups, that is, a public ethic. The Hebrew conception of justice was the center of a public ethic. We may assume that Adler was influenced by this conception and sees it as the *kind* of ethic that is needed. But the pain of the Hebrew must be distinguished from the modern pain. The Hebrew suffered from invasion from without. The "modern man," according to Adler, suffers from internal division as the result, as it were, of not having an adequate map of the human dimension of the external world. The group ethic of the Hebrew might be seen as a protection from the outside world. It was framed in group terms because it was the group that needed protection. The Hebrew people came to view themselves quite literally as a "chosen people." Chosen, that is, for bondage. As far as we can see, the logic of the Hebrew ethic could apply as well to an individual as to a group or a "people." But either way, justice assumes a public world. This is in sharp contrast with the modern situation, if Adler is right. For the modern demand for a group ethic is made in a context in which no generally accepted definition of a "public world" is recognized. We may read the demand, in effect, as the demand to recognize, or find, or even build such a world. As we will see later, it is the latter idea of world-building that Adler thinks is necessary.

Much recent literature might be cited to support the claim that there is a problem of the nature and existence of a public realm and its relation to individual human beings. Discussions concerning "man in a mass society," "the organization man," "the other-directed man," and the considerable literature on agreement, consensus, cooperation, togetherness, human relations, inter-personal relations, inter-group relations, and also much of the recent existentialist and psychiatric writings, with their emphasis on anxiety, homelessness, and particularly the problem of human identity—all would seem to support the claim that there is a problem regarding individual men living as members of groups.[17]

Of the three "modern" pains Adler described, the first refers to the relation of man and the universe, the second concerns man in relation to the suffering of other men, and the third reports a pain connected with the individual's own internal division. Presumably these pains would disappear if men (1) had a sense and conception of a significant place in the universe; (2) could recognize themselves as in some way able to alleviate the sufferings of others; and (3) could find an adequate way of connecting the private and the public dimensions of their lives.

Adler's conception of worth is framed so as to supply what is here demanded. Without worth, man could not have a sig-

---

[17]A sampling of this still growing body of literature might include: M. R. Stein, A. J. Vidich, and D. M. Whited (eds.), *Identity and Anxiety: The Survival of the Person in Mass Society* (Glencoe, Illinois: The Free Press, 1960); William H. Whyte, *The Organization Man* (New York: Simon and Schuster, 1956); David Riesman, Nathan Glazer, and Reuel Denney, *The Lonely Crowd: A Study of the Changing American Character* (New Haven, Connecticut: Yale University Press, 1950); Dorwin, Cartwright and Alvin (eds.), *Group Dynamics: Research and Theory* (second edition; Elmsford, New York: Row Peterson and Company, 1960); A. P. Hare, E. F. Borgatta, and R. F. Bales (eds.), *Small Groups: Studies in Social Interaction* (New York: Alfred A. Knopf, 1955); Rollo May, Ernest Angel, and H. F. Ellenberger (eds.) *Existence: A New Dimension in Psychiatry and Psychology* (New York: Basic Books, Inc., 1958); Rollo May, *The Meaning of Anxiety* (New York: The Ronald Press, 1950); Erich Fromm, *Escape From Freedom* (New York: Rinehart and Company, 1941); Franz Alexander, *Our Age of Unreason: A Study of the Irrational Forces in Social Life* (Philadelphia, Pennsylvania: J. B. Lippincott Company, 1942); W. O. Stanley, *Education and Social Integration* (New York: Bureau of Publications, Teachers College, Columbia University, 1953); R. B. Raup, G. F. Axtelle, K. D. Benne, and B. O. Smith, *The Improvement of Practical Intelligence* (New York: Harper and Brothers, 1950). Also see material of the Adult Education Association and of the National Training Laboratory for Group Development.

nificant place in the universe, nor be able to alleviate the sufferings of others, nor have an adequate way of connecting the
private and public dimensions of his life. In Adler's view,
then, *worth* is essential to mankind.

The Psycho-social Dimension of Worth

Most contemporary value theory is marked by an empirical
orientation. As *value* is defined in terms of organic drives, appeal
is immediately made to the biological sciences for the most adequate formulations. When *value* is defined as feeling, or as an
object of interest, the articulations of these definitions are sought
in psychological and sociological theory. We have seen much in
Adler's historical discussion that suggests connections with material discussed particularly in psychology and the social sciences.
But whereas a definition of value as an object of interest will be
offered with a scientific or empirical theory of interest in mind, so
that the empirical material appears in the axiological theory in a
fairly unambiguous way, Adler's conception of worth does not
permit a direct empirical reading. For Adler, the distinction
between value and worth is fundamental:

Value is subjective. The worth notion is the most objective conceivable. Value depends on the wants or needs of our empirical nature.
That has value which satisfies our needs or wants. We possess value
for one another, for the reason that each of us has wants which the
others alone are capable of satisfying, as in the case of sex, of cooperation, in the vocation , etc. But value ceases when the want or need
is gratified. The value which one human being has for another is
transient. There are, in the strict sense, no permanent values. The
value which the majority have for the more advanced and developed
members of a community is small; from the standpoint of value most
persons are duplicable and dispensable. Consider only the ease with
which factory labor is replaced, in consequence of the prolific fertil-
ity of the human race. The custom of speaking of ethics as a theory
of values is regrettable. It evidences the despair into which many
writers on ethics have fallen as to the possibility of discovering an objective basis for rightness.[18]

The concept of worth refers to something that is permanent;
it is not an empirical phenomenon. It is not a value, not even

[18]*EPL,* p. 117a.

an intrinsinc value, for intrinsic values are not necessarily more enduring than any other kind of value. Does this mean that it is idle to speak of a psycho-social dimension of worth? We find no unequivocal answer to this question in Adler's writing. The issue is an important one, insofar as one would want to know how far and in what way, research into such matters as anxiety, frustration, the psycho-social genesis of self, the role that ideals have historically played in human lives, the mechanisms that men use for alleviating psychic pain, and much else, would be relevant to considerations of worth.

Adler speaks of spiritual pain. Some psychologists, psychiatrists, and social scientists speak of psychological or psychic pain. All speak of this pain as a part of human experience. Are these two different pains or only one pain? It would seem that for Adler it is one pain considered in two different ways. As experienced, the spiritual pain and the psychological pain are identical. As an empirical event, the feeling is the effect of previous events and a cause of subsequent events: it is an item in a causal nexus. It is an event in time and in other respects as well as simply a natural event.

As a spiritual event it is taken up by Adler in a nontemporal matrix. It is taken as a criterion, that is, a valid basis on which to proceed. As a natural event, the pain is one pain among many. It may be ignored, or become the focus of attention. As a spiritual event, the pain may not be ignored. It is understood as a distinctively ethical experience, requiring an ethical response. This difference between the natural and the spiritual or ethical may be likened to the difference between judging, which is an event in time which itself takes time, and a judgment, which is nontemporal. This would suggest that the difference between the natural and the ethical is analogous to the difference between the empirical and the logical.

Adler demands an objective basis for rightness and for human worth. He also requires that "worth" refer to something permanent. He knows that in the natural world everything is in a process of change. Worth, therefore, cannot be part of the natural world, and must be sharply distinguished from value. Here we are only concerned with the question as to whether it is possible, within Adler's theory, to speak of a psycho-social dimension of worth. The answer would seem to be yes, and in the following sense. If we are right in saying that spiritual pain and psychological pain are the same pain considered in different contexts or in different ways, then whatever one knows about pain as a natural event enters into a determination of *what it is* that is being considered in the spiritual context. If this analysis is correct, Adler's entire historical discussion is vulnerable to criticism, and particularly his characterization of spiritual pain and its relation to the spiritual ideal, which was formulated as a response to that pain. This is so despite Adler's view that worth is not an empirical matter.

We can conclude by saying that Adler's conception invited the fullest possible empirical findings with regard to the matters which it encompasses. Historical research and psychological and social theory can serve to inform, support, or call Adler's conception into question. What a follower of Adler must show is that these inform and support. He must also show that these natural and empirical considerations do not invalidate his conception of worth. For worth is not a natural event.

Logical, Ontological, and Ethical Dimensions

As Adler uses the term *worth,* a necessary condition for something to have worth is that this "something" must be indispensable. He argues that if something is both required and irreplaceable it must be unique or else there would be a duplicate of it. But irreplaceability is logically part of worth; therefore, that which has worth must be unique.

A further requirement is that worth is indefeasible, that is, incapable of being voided. But indefeasibility pertains to necessity, irreplaceability, uniqueness, and induplicability. More directly it is meant to apply to some X, insofar as X can be properly said to have worth. A companion requirement is that of inalienability or the impossibility of being surrendered or transferred.

Further meaning is disclosed as we find that the term *worth* is not to be used as a comparative. Adler would never say that X had more or less worth than Y. This might suggest that worth is meant as a superlative, so that one could say that X or Y had the most worth. There is this suggestion in Adler as he speaks of "worth" and "best" together. "Worth" does refer to the highest, but not as a superlative. For to suggest this meaning of best or highest is to invite comparisons. Adler's meaning is rather to be understood as we would intend as we speak of something as "in-comparable," or "in-valuable," or "price-less"; that is, neither comparisons, valuations, nor pricings are relevant.

These, then, are the most general things that can be said about Adler's conception of worth: that which has worth is indispensable, necessary, irreplaceable, unique, induplicable, incomparable, and the worth itself is both indefeasible and inalienable. Taken together, these might be seen as the logical skeleton of Adler's meaning of *worth*.

We may now add some additional meaning. As Adler thinks of worth, he is not just thinking of a logical property of a logical system. He means by worth something objective, real. Adler wants to be able to say that human beings really have worth. For this he has to establish that worth is a real property within the universe. Human beings, if they have worth at all, do not have it because someone thinks they do. The having of worth is not at all dependent upon what anyone happens to think or feel, believe or disbelieve, nor is it to be understood as a function of knowledge or lack of knowledge. Adler's concept of worth is, therefore, not subjective idealism.

This leads us to one of the most important characteristics of worth, as Adler understands it; namely, that worth is an ideal. It might appear from what has already been said that Adler could be an idealist of either the Hegelian or Platonic variety. In fact, Adler's idealism is mainly Kantian, but with differences and difficulties all its own. Adler is, by his own words, not a follower of either Hegel or Plato. In any event, Adler does claim objective reality for his conception of the ideal of worth.

Adler uses Kant's expression "man as an end *per se*." Adler's own meaning for this expression is not exactly what Kant intended. The expression, however, marks the direction of Adler's thinking. Part of his meaning, surely, is that man, having worth, is an end *per se*.

Now one of the major ways in which ethical theories differ from one another—and, therefore, one of the ways in which one can speak of *kinds* of ethical theory—is in terms of the weight assigned such basic ethical conceptions as right, good, obligation (duty), freedom, pleasure-pain, and happiness. More particularly, it is often possible to characterize an ethical theory in terms of the concept which it takes as central.[19]

Adler has chosen to make worth the central issue of ethics. The focus of such a theory is clearly on the human being as the bearer of the highest ethical attribute and the center of the ethical concern. All other concerns will be derivative and secondary. As Adler understands worth, it either applies to all human beings or to none, and so the scope of ethical theory includes reference to all men.

Ethics has often been defined as a discipline primarily concerned with the proper direction of conduct. So defined, it is usually *right* that is taken to be the basic concept. Now Adler is of course concerned with the proper direction of conduct, but *right* conduct is defined by him as conduct which pays due accord to the worth of man.

Similarly, obligations, duties, and the motives attaching to them, are defined in terms of worth and are judged as valid

[19]It cannot be part of the present work to develop this idea in any detail. But we may venture the claim that such differences among ethical positions are by no means simply verbal or even in the broadest sense, conceptual. We would suggest that the difference, for example, of taking worth as the central concept as against good, right, obligation, or happiness may mark an important difference in basic philosophical orientation that will determine the very content of the field of ethics discussed by the given position.

only insofar as they are framed with due respect to worth. The good, varied goods, and the life good to live, all receive their sense and significance in strictly human terms. No life can be judged a good life, and no pleasure or happiness as good—nor, for that matter, any pain or misery as bad—except as it is understood in terms of men who are unique and induplicable. Adler claims that all persons have worth, and as such, are unique, that is, essentially different from one another. It follows that obligations or duties are not identical for any two persons. Obligations are not transitive, and any moral law that might specify obligations, prohibitions, and the like, cannot apply in the same way to any two people. To ignore the difference is to ignore the special worth of each person. Statements may be framed of an order of generality that would apply equally to all, but they must be understood as applying differently to each.

A similar analysis is required for all of the other major ethical concepts. Every man has rights, but each man's rights are different. Adler expresses this idea by saying that rights and obligations are *equivalent* rather than equal.[20] If the complications and difficulties are kept in mind, we may summarize the above by saying that a worth-centered ethic is a human-centered ethic that has due regard for the difference among humans.

If we shift from the *unique* to the *indefeasible* and *inalienable,* we see further implications of the idea of worth. Consider again the matter of obligation. An obligation which is indefeasible is such that one cannot be relieved of it by another. No person may properly say that you may put such and such an obligation aside. The locus of obligation in such matters lies wholly with the individual. No ethical hierarchy is, in this sense, possible. There is no absolution, no possible ontological

[20]"Instead of moral equality it were better to use the term 'moral equivalence.' The differences are to be stressed; they are the coruscating point in the spiritual life of mankind. That every man is the equal of his fellows means that he has the same right as each of the others to become unlike the others, to acquire a distinct personality, to contribute his one peculiar ray to the white light of the spiritual life." *EPL,* p. 143.

forgiveness. And since an obligation of a person who has worth is also inalienable, it is neither possible for that person to turn over the obligation to someone else, nor would it be proper for anyone to seek to take over someone else's responsibilities. A similar analysis would apply to rights.

According to Adler's specifications, all that has worth is an element in a system in which all the relations are internal. Any change in one element will effect a change in all other elements. This is Adler's abstract formulation of "being efficacious." If a person had worth, he would be efficacious in his relations to other persons. Of course the fact that one had impact on others would not be morally equivalent to an ability to alleviate the sufferings of others. The impact might involve such power, but it is likely also to carry with it the power of increasing the suffering of others. One would have to have more than power, and more than a sense of power, if the problem is one of pain in the face of the suffering of others.

In considering the idea of indispensability, that is, requiredness and irreplaceability, we may say that just as each person is required, so too are his obligations. Each person's obligations are his own, not to be set aside; they are linked and dependent upon the obligations of others. A change in the obligations of one person will call for changes in the obligations of others. We see that not only worth, but obligations, rights, and the like, although distinctive for each person, are social in their implications insofar as the worth of each person is dependent on the worth of all other persons. Thus, Adler's ethic of worth is at once both an individual and a social ethic.

If man, each and every man, were indispensable, necessary, irreplaceable, unique, induplicable and incomparable and also had that about him which was indefeasible and inalienable—it would be an understatement to say that he had a significant place in the universe. And a man who conceived of himself in this way could hardly suffer from the pain of believing himself insignificant, presented above as the first type of spiritual pain. Adler here seeks to affirm, through the concept of worth, that people do count, do have a place in the world, do make a difference. From a psychological point of view, the value of this argument rests on the empirical generalization that, if people have a sense of making a difference, the pain will be reduced. The validity of this generalization is at least open to question. If Adler's claim involves more than a syntactic argument—and there is little doubt that he intends much more than an analytic truth—then we would require very careful experimental tests to determine, for example, what effects a sense and conception of "being indispensable" would have on people. And we would want to know whether it has the same kind of effect on all people. It would be necessary to know whether there might be some people for whom having such a sense would precipitate the deepest sort of melancholy. One thinks here of the radically different effects that the idea of being immortal has on people; some find meaning in their lives only if they can believe that they are immortal; others find the ideal of immortality, of a life without death, to be thoroughly revolting and to drain life of all possible significance.

We have mentioned above that for the second kind of spiritual pain—witnessing suffering—Adler's solution was to intensify the efforts to improve the conditions of others and so to help give them a justified sense of their worth. But this is not simply charity because "grounds of immediate experience of man's worth and what worth implies. . .means the consciousness that one lives in promoting the life of another, and reciprocally in being awakened to true life by the effect of oneself on another's life."[21] Thus activity to improve the lot of mankind can alleviate without removing this cause of spiritual pain. As philosophical formulations in themselves cannot prevent wars, hunger, social injustices, and such causes of human suffering, Adler's answer is not entirely satisfactory even to him, but it does point to the need of social action in order to satisfy man's ethical needs, and he calls for "a morality of

[21]*RSI,* p. 207.

groups" as essential.[22] This conclusion leads directly to the third kind of spiritual pain, "the pain of divided conscience." Adler's conception of worth provides a basis for relating the inner and the outer, the private and the public, the individual and the group. There cannot properly be separate private and public moralities. One must act so as to seek to elicit the uniqueness in others and to achieve the maximum development of each individual as a part of what is best for mankind in general.[23]

Adler is thus concerned with much more than the psychological effects of the idea of worth and its various aspects. It is of great importance to him to offer a satisfactory proof of the objective reality of worth. The psychological phenomena referred to above are subjective. Even if support is offered for the empirical assumption that we have attributed to Adler, this action would not constitute, in his own eyes, proof of the claim to the reality of worth.

It is of first importance that the problem of worth, as Adler saw it, was not primarily a philosophical problem. No nicer contrast could be offered than that between Adler and G. E. Moore. Moore has said that none of the problems with which he dealt arose for him within his own life. They were all problems that he perceived as the result of reading other philosophers. Adler, on the other hand, is responding to the problems of men. War, human slavery, suffering, and frustration are the facts that seemed to stimulate Adler in all his work. He was also much concerned with the inadequacies he found in democracy, particularly in the United States. The entire question of the way men thought about, dealt with, and treated one another affected him deeply. Adler's theoretical work is perhaps best seen as a response to such problems. He believed there was a crying need for clarification of the ethical aspect of the relations among men and of the foundations of

[22]*Ibid.*, pp. 47-60.
[23]*Ibid.*, pp. 50, 214a.

democracy. In this connection it is interesting to read Felix S. Cohen writing in 1933:

It would not be unfair to say that no avowed ethical philosopher in the last hundred years has made a single fundamental criticism of the established institutions of modern society.[24]

Even if this claim was largely true, it was not true of Felix Adler. He is surely an "avowed ethical philosopher," and just as surely did he offer not only fundamental criticism of established institutions, but also some wide-ranging proposals for reconstructing these social institutions. He even set up a school based on the application of his principles to the education of children, which he hoped would serve as a model for education that would help to build a genuinely ethical society: hence the Ethical Culture Schools.

Adler's theoretical discussion of worth may be seen, then, as a part, and the fundamental part, of his diagnosis of the basic problems of his time. What men lacked, Adler thought, was an adequate conception of themselves as human beings. Intimately related to this was the lack of an adequate conception of the way in which men should live together. If Kant's idea that men were ends in themselves, and should be treated as such, gave direction to Adler's thought, Adler early criticized Kant for not sufficiently clarifying this idea. *What does it mean to treat men as ends per se? To what extent may one treat others as means?* Adler wanted clearer and more determinate answers to these questions than he thought either Kant or anyone else had given.

The measure of the task he set for himself is evidenced by the three-stage history discussed earlier. He presented what he conceived as the three stages in the history of the spiritual ideal: The Hebrew, the Christian, and the Modern (or Ad-

---

[24]*Ethical Systems and Legal Ideals: An Essay on the Foundations of Legal Criticism* (Ithaca, New York: Cornell University Press, 1933), p. 16.

lerian). Adler offers his conception of worth, his reconstruction of the roots of religious thought in the West. It was not only a noble attempt, but one whose accomplishments, imperfect as they may be, deserve the attention of others with similar objectives.[25]

[25]In addition to Adler's writings, the history of the still very active Ethical movement that he founded is worth attention, as it is given in the thoughtful volume by Howard B. Radest, *Toward Common Ground* (New York: Frederick Ungar, 1968).

CHAPTER 2

The Rational Ground of Worth

In Chapter 1 we attempted to give a sense of what Adler meant by *worth*. We have said that Adler was convinced that we must think of humans as having worth and that he sought to prove that we are justified in claiming worth for every human being.

The argument that Adler advances in justifying this claim is primarily metaphysical in character. It depends in part on his conceptions of the synthetic activity of the mind: what he calls the mind's "reality producing functions." It also rests on a sharp distinction between empirical and nonempirical (sensible and supersensible) existence, which, like his conception of mind, is a modification of what is fundamentally Kant's position on these matters.

When Adler speaks of offering a rational ground for something, he is thinking of offering a theoretical framework within which that something is an element. As the mind can understand some X in its relation to other things—that is, as part of a system, with the relations of that system defined —the mind rests and accepts the "reality" of the X.[1]

It should not be expected that Adler is going to prove, or even attempt to prove, that human beings have worth, by referring us to some empirical or observable human trait or set of traits. Rational grounding is not verification by the methods of empirical science. It is rather an offering of a system of thought within which what is being grounded or justified is

[1]Compare Ernst Cassirer, *Substance and Function*, trans. W. C. and M. C. Swabey (Chicago, Illinois: The Open Court Publishing Company, 1923), Part II.

71

comprehended. And it is the comprehension within such a rational scheme that constitutes rational grounding for Adler.

This chapter will be concerned with the details of Adler's conception of "offering a rational ground," taken in the most general sense, that is, apart from the specific justification for human worth. In the next chapter we will consider both how this conception of a rational ground relates to the conception of human worth, and also the specific rational framework in which *worth* is comprehended and thus given "objectivity."

Adler was a neo-Kantian, critical of both extreme empiricism and any form of absolute idealism. Yet he feels compelled, within the "critical" and "transcendental" framework and method developed by Kant, to gain more than logical or ideational reality for human worth. The shadow of Hume falls on Adler as it did on Kant. The rational grounding, the conceptual framework which Adler developed, is meant to be more than just relations among ideas. The problem Adler faces is that of establishing a reality for a nonempirical something; and to do this with first principles drawn from Kant rather than Plato or Hegel. What we confront, then, in dealing with Adler's conception of rational ground is Adler's basic metaphysical and epistemological views, views forged to make sense of Adler's conviction that every human being has worth.

Adler accepts the fact that, with regard to matters of fact, complete rationality is impossible. He insists, however, that although this is no problem for science, it is a serious problem for ethics. For he holds that an adequate ethical conception must be fully rational: it must allow for no irrational surds.

Unfortunately, Adler never worked out a full and systematic metaphysical position, so that many questions we would like to ask must remain unanswered. He has, however, written enough to suggest the lines along which he thought and the problems which he saw.

Knowledge

One of the most important things Adler learned from Kant was that mind is not a passive receptacle or receiver of impressions from an external world, but an active instrument with a pattern of functioning which supplies ineradicable ingredients to our knowledge.

We find in experience a wide range of phenomena. Any attempt at understanding requires some ordering of these phenomena. But whatever ordering we do, however we draw the major categorical lines within experience, Adler claims that we will be confronted with (1) a multiplicity of items, and (2) some way of taking this multiplicity as a unity. Further, he claims that we have no choice in this matter. This is the way the human mind works. We recognize it as a brute, inexplicable fact. We are unable to explain why the mind works in the way it does. All we can do is recognize that it does function in this particular way. But we can discover *how* the mind operates by reflecting upon the past operation of the mind, by carefully surveying the activity and the product of our intuition and understanding. Adler holds, with Kant, a middle position between extreme empiricism and extreme idealism. Adler is as critical of one as he is of the other. He would fully agree with Kant's opening remarks in the *Critique of Pure Reason:*

There can be no doubt that all our knowledge begins with experience. For how should our faculty of knowledge be awakened into action did not objects affecting our senses partly of themselves produce representations, partly arouse the activity of our understanding to compare these representations, and, by combining or separating them, work up the raw material of the sensible impressions into that knowledge of objects which is entitled experience? In the order of time, therefore, we have no knowledge antecedent to experience, and with experience all our knowledge begins.

But though all our knowledge begins with experience, it does not follow that it all rises out of experience. For it may well be that even our empirical knowledge is made up of what we receive through impressions of what our own faculty of knowledge (sensible impressions serving merely as the occasion) supplies from itself. If our faculty of knowledge makes any such addition, it may be that we are not in a position to distinguish it from the raw material, until with long practice of attention we have become skilled in separating it.[2]

Following along these lines, Adler asks:

What. . .is the most general expression by which to designate the singularities of the human mind, the principles on which it acts, its immutable modes of behavior, the invariants that recur amid all the complex varieties of its processes?[3]

And he answers as follows:

The principal invariants are the positing of a manifold of some kind, and the apprehending of that manifold as coherent. The manifold is not given, but is posited by the mind. The positing is a mental function, just as much as the apprehending of the plurality as coherent is a mental function.[4]

Now although these constitutive principles of the human mind cannot be explained or understood they can be verified, Adler says, by exemplification. By exemplification Adler means the continual discovery of examples in experience.[5] Let us consider some of the examples of what Adler would take to be exemplification of the dual yet simultaneous root activity of the mind.

Space and Time. As we consider what we mean by space, we realize at once the possibility of a plurality of individual spaces and also a unity of all these local spaces. We speak of "this space" being "in space." Similarly, time is both the unity of all times and this time and that time, this interval, that moment,

[2]*Critique of Pure Reason,* trans. N. K. Smith (second edition; London: Macmillan and Company, 1933).
[3]Adler, *An Ethical Philosophy of Life,* p. 107.
[4]*Ibid.*

the past, the present, the future. From the point of view of the unity, we make cuts in space and time. From the point of view of the multiplicity, the unity is a unifying of the particular loci or moments.

Concepts. Adler would argue that this dual functioning of the mind appears whenever concepts are being used. Any concept, in its character as general, or as a universal, is an illustration of a unity. The diversity lies in the particulars which are "included in," "subsumed under," "referred to," or "denoted by," the concept.

We recognize that the precise nature of the kind of unity achieved by concepts has been a matter of dispute throughout the history of philosophy. A full history might be written from Plato's theory of participation to Wittgenstein's family resemblances. Adler does not, and we need not, deal with this issue. It is enough for our purpose that some kind of connection among the particulars is involved, some unity of a diversity.

Physics and Biology. Specific subject matters also will appear under the double aspect of unity and plurality:

> In the physical sciences we are compelled to assume on the one hand the atomic or granular constitution of matter, in other words, manifoldness. On the other hand, if "action at a distance" is to be escaped, we are bound to assume a continuum of some sort like the ether.[6]

Adler's physics may be somewhat dated, but the point is clear. As regards the life sciences, he writes: "in the organic world there is the manifold of structures and functions, and the unity of the organism."[7] The moral of the story is that.

> Wherever we turn we find the assurance of reality depends on the joint use of the two principles mentioned, the joint operation of the two kinds of mental action; that is to say. . .on the positing of a manifold and on the simultaneous apprehension of the subject matter to which it relates as coherent, as unified. . .to whatever object of in-

[5]*Ibid.,* p. 112.
[6]*Ibid.,* p. 109.
[7]*Ibid.*

quiry we give our attention, we find ourselves not only restricted fundamentally to the two functions described, but we discover that to their insunderable cooperation, we owe whatever of truth we possess.[8]

It should be clear that Adler holds that any knowledge —and this means, of course, any knowledge of reality—is had and is possible only by virtue of the joint use of these two functions. Any claim regarding the reality of something is analyzable into these two components, but neither of the two components ever appears alone. Adler speaks of our "assurance of reality" as dependent on the joint use of the two principles. This suggests that we might try to use one of the principles without the other, but that such attempts will not succeed, will not, that is, give us the required assurance of reality. The distinction to be noted is the distinction between the constitutive *principles* and the reality-producing *functions* of the mind. The principles are to be understood as symbolic formulations of the functions. Adler holds that the functions are operative whether we like it or not, or know it or not. The attempt to operate at the theoretical level with only one of these principles is bound to lead to insolvable theoretical problems for the reason that one is not taking proper account of the central fact that the primary functions of the human mind are two in number.

The truth is that unity and plurality are two blades of a pair of shears and that one can cut with neither singly, that one can derive neither from the other, the mind being constrained to use them jointly. It is this joint use that has led to every actual gain in knowledge.[9]

Speaking generally of the difficulties that have arisen from not taking into account both functions of the mind, Adler says:

The jointness or inseparableness of the two acts out of which cer-

[8]*Ibid.,* pp. 108-109.
[9]Adler, *The Reconstruction of the Spiritual Ideal,* p. 51.

tainty or reality issues has created all the difficulties. The fact that the manifold must be regarded as remaining a manifold, unaltered in its character as such, not derivative from the One (there is no such One), and that the unity does not contrariwise result from the manifold in the sense of springing from or being derived from it;—in other words, that we must see the same landscape of things and events both *sub specie pluralitatis* and *sub specie unitatis*—has been the stumbling block. The history of philosophy might be written under the two headings: (1) monistic systems that undertake, collapsing in their futile effort, to derive the world and its plurality from the One, as if there were such an One, out of whose bosom philosophy might evoke the many (creational systems, pantheistic systems, emanation systems, evolution systems); (2) pluralistic systems that essay, with equal lack of success, to explain the unity as somehow the offspring of the plurality.[10]

We are offered, here, not only a principle of criticism, but also a proposal as to how adequately and properly to construct theories in any area of inquiry. Acting in either of these capacities, the formulation is an epistemological principle. Furthermore, insofar as the claim is taken as a statement of a necessary condition for knowledge of reality, it is a metaphysical principle. It seems clear that Adler meant it in both of these ways.

But Adler, like Kant, would not hold that these constructive principles of mind were both necessary and sufficient conditions for knowledge. They are necessary, but not sufficient, conditions, for we are dependent on experience which is not, in the first instance, generated or produced by mind.

Now when Adler speaks of certain knowledge or knowledge of reality, he means a rational apprehension of an object—and the object itself is also characterized as rational. In this sense Adler would say that the real is rational. But Adler also recognizes an irrational element in all knowledge insofar as it relates to the empirical realm, the realm of sense experience, the sensible realm. It is best here to quote Adler in detail. He is speaking of Kant's *Critique of Pure Reason,* but he is also speaking for himself:

[10]Adler, *An Ethical Philosophy of Life,* pp. 109-110.

It is a mistake to speak of Kant as a rationalist pure and simple. When he expelled the older metaphysics he antagonized pure rationalism. The older metaphysics held that the mere existence of the conditioned proves the existence of the unconditioned, requires the unconditioned. In Kant's answer to this lies the gist of his enterprise in philosophy: You are quite right, he says, that the *idea* of the conditioned requires the idea of the unconditioned, logically, rationally. But observe well, nature is not just logical or rational. There is an irrational element in it, namely, extended manifold and temporal sequence. Juxtaposition and sequence are irrational, because, if I interpret him rightly, in the case of each the relation presented to the mind is that of parts outside each other—in the one case alongside, in the other before and after; while in the logical or rational relation the parts are implicit in the whole as in the case of the premises of a syllogism and the conclusion, the relation of a genus to the species, the universal to the particular.

We have in nature, according to Kant, a partnership between the irrational and the rational factors. And thereupon he proceeds to argue that we impose laws on nature, understanding thereby that we get hold of reality or objectivity in so far as we are able to imprint the rational element upon the irrational. The positing of the thing *per se,* which has proved a stumbling-block to many, is no more than a confession that we shall never succeed entirely in this business of subjecting the irrational to the rational factor. The thing *per se* is the X that remains over when the rational function has done its utmost. A thing, a real object, is that which is imprinted with, penetrated with, rationality. The manifolds of space and time, of juxtaposition and sequence are incapable of completely receiving this imprint, that is, of completely responding to our quest for reality, and thus their incompetency is expressed in the notion of the thing *per se.*[11]

Empirical science, then, is always less than wholly rational. But this is not cause to lament. It is just important to recognize the fact. If it is a limitation, it is one that, if ignored, leads to empty metaphysical speculation under the guise of knowledge. But this stricture against metaphysics is a great boon for science. For, given these views, the success of science does not require a conception of the unconditioned—the One, the Absolute, the Whole of things—and so is able to operate free from metaphysical speculation. In not requiring an idea

[11]*Ibid.,* pp. 95-96.

of the whole, it can fully direct its attention to the particular phenomena with which it is concerned.

In this connection Adler speaks of kinds of manifolds and the kinds of unities to which they are susceptible. In these terms one may distinguish one area of inquiry from another. As we speak of physical, biological, chemical, psychological, or social phenomena, we are speaking of different manifolds selected from within experience. We can speak of the physical manifold, *et cetera*. The theories that are proposed would then be seen as attempts to unite the particular manifold. Each of these manifolds is seen as part of the world, but the success of a particular science is in large measure a function of the fact that scientific explanation does not (and cannot) depend on knowledge of the whole for its knowledge of the part. As regards empirical knowledge, Adler writes:

> The certainty is in the linkage. We may add link to link of the chain of reality without troubling to consider by what piers it is supported or on what shore the piers rest—if indeed there be piers or shores at all.[12]

It is characteristic of all empirical phenomena to include an ineradicable irrational element. Adler understands himself to be following Kant. The space and time manifolds present us respectively with "bare juxtaposition," that is, parts external to one another, and "bare sequence," that is, parts before and after one another. By contrast, logical or rational relations are such that the part is conceived as implicit in the whole. Bare juxtaposition and bare sequence yield only external relations.

Hume argued that no certainty at all was possible with respect to connections between matters of fact.[13] Adler accepts Kant's view that, by virtue of the nature of the human mind, there is a "projection of the rational factor upon the irrational."[14] This projection accounts for the element of certainty in our knowledge

[12]*Ibid.*, p. 95.

[13]David Hume, *An Inquiry Concerning Human Understanding* (section VII; La Salle, Illinois: The Open Court Publishing Company, 1946).

[14]Adler, *An Ethical Philosophy of Life*, p. 103.

of matters of fact, of phenomena, of the sensible or empirical world.

Adler sees Kant's major effort as accounting for the element of certainty in experience. In countering Hume's scepticism, Kant insists that there is a radical difference, a difference in kind, between "expectation of future happenings, founded on previous association, and the prediction of future happenings, founded on scientific certainty. . . ."[15] The *a priori*, which is that part of experience that is contributed by the human mind, is what accounts for this certainty. Adler suggests that these *a priori* elements might better be called the elements or factors of certainty.[16]

It is worth quoting Adler at length on this point.

And what are these *a prioris?* They are the factors of certainty. The substitution of the term 'factor of certainty' for the term *a priori* might be a gain. The term *a priori* suggests independent existence which Kant, far from asserting, constantly and strenuously denies. It suggests a pretended insight into the aboriginal constitution of the mind, into the germinal principles out of which intelligence has developed. And this claim of pretended insight, I take it, was equally foreign to Kant's conception. At any rate, the validity of his theory of knowledge does not depend on the admittance of any such claim. The term *a priori* suggests chronological antecedence and, in this respect, it is particularly misleading. The Kantian *a priori* is discovered not in its origin, but in its operation. The *a priori* in the Kantian sense may be synchronous with its product, may be born at the very moment when it yields its first effect. If a new science were to arise, containing some new element of certainty heretofore unmanifested, we should be compelled to formulate a new variety of the so-called *a priori*, and we should be justified by the spirit, if not the letter, of Kant's teachings in so doing. The doctrine of the *a priori*, often confused as it is with the doctrine of innate ideas and of intuition, is really as unlike these doctrines as it is possible to be. The thinker of the Kantian type does not attempt to discover a mental content which is common to the Fiji Islander and to Lord Kelvin, does not attempt to acquaint us with an *a priori* which consoled the cave man in his mo-

[15]Adler, "A Critique of Kant's Ethics," *Mind,* New Series, XI (October, 1902), 162-195.
[16]*Ibid.*

ments of meditation. Nor does he speak of truths which are apprehended in a flash of intuition, apart from experience. The thinker who follows along the Kantian lines lies in wait, watching how the human mind behaves when it exercises its power. He observes how the mind reveals itself in the exercise of its power, and these moments of self-revelation he fixes on his philosophic camera. He watches to see what harvest of assured knowledge the soil of the human mind produces under the rarest and most favorable conditions, and from this crop he makes his inference as to the seed. But as to the origin of the seed itself, as to how it came to be planted in the human mind,—into such questions as these he forbears to inquire, and the whole question of genetic development he leaves to the psychologist to deal with it as he may see fit.[17]

But we have seen that scientific certainty is certainty within very carefully prescribed limits.[18] The limits are stated by Kant in terms of his distinction between phenomena and noumena. Recognizing that all our experience is a function of the nature of mind, we accept the rational certainty that the mind contributes to our experience. But the elements of certainty apply only in the phenomenal realm. With regard to the way things are, apart from human experience—the way they are *per se,* in themselves—we not only lack certainty, but we have no experience or knowledge whatsoever. Nor can empirical science ever yield a completely rational scheme.

The positing of the thing *per se.* . .is no more than a confession that we shall never succeed entirely in this business of subjecting the irrational to the rational factor. . .[for] our knowledge of nature is relative, which means incompletely rational, because of the foreign element in nature unamenable to the operation of the rational, the synthetic function. This relative knowledge is none the less certain, that is in some sense absolute, because of the partial coincidence of the phenomena of nature and the synthetic processes of the mind.

---

[17]*Ibid.,* 166-167.

[18]The question of the source of the limits might well be a matter of dispute. Adler suggests that "One might even say that, according to Kant, the mind itself produces the irrational factor, since the intuitions of space and time are, according to him, functions of the mind itself—the mind setting up a manifold so constituted as to receive sense impressions." Adler, *An Ethical Philosophy of Life,* p. 103.

With this degree of certainty we must perforce content ourselves, in dealing with outside nature. In trying to understand and interpret that which is not ourselves, we hit upon barriers which cannot be transcended, upon a foreign factor which opposes itself to our endeavors.[19]

At this point Adler introduces an idea that leads him to draw a sharp distinction between science and ethics and the methods appropriate to each. This is a crucial turn in Adler's argument and must be dealt with in detail.

Adler claims that conduct, insofar as it is to be thought of in ethical terms, requires reference to an inclusive plan. This is what Adler means by the "fully rational." Conduct is always directed action. An evaluation of the conduct involves reference to the direction of the conduct. An evaluation of the direction requires an end, a total plan, in terms of which the direction and the conduct itself has significance. According to this view, there cannot be any single, partial, ethical rule of conduct such as "Thou shalt not kill." Nor can any single and separate act be properly judged in ethical terms. An ethical judgment must take its significance from a completely rational plan.

if there is to be certainty at all, in regard to right as distinguished from wrong. . .we cannot content ourselves with the paradoxical, relative-absolute [that we find in science]. For [as regards conduct] we not merely interpret but act, and we must possess an ideal plan of the whole if we are to be certain of our rightness in any particular part of conduct. For in conduct there is no such partial coincidence *between the rational and the irrational as in the case of physical law.*[20]

Rules of conduct, acts, and evaluations of both, must take their "ethical quality from the plan of conduct as a whole, and without reference to the whole. . .[they are] devoid of rightness."[21]

To ask for an ideal plan of the whole is clearly to make a

[19]*Ibid.*, pp. 96-98.
[20]*Ibid.*, p. 98 (Italics in the original).
[21]*Ibid.*

request that cannot be satisfied by science, for science always deals with the conditioned, limiting itself to parts and avoiding any empty claims about the whole of nature. Adler is asking for something that science and scientific method cannot supply. He seeks a completely rational framework.

Partial coincidence of the rational with the irrational is expressed in physical law; absence of such concurrence destroys any attempt to build up an ethical theory on the empirical method.[22]

Adler claims that science cannot supply the kind of results demanded by an ethical theory. Thus the method of empirical science cannot be the method of ethics, and scientific knowledge must be distinguished from ethical knowledge.

We can see that Adler must find himself in a peculiar position at this point in his argument. He is demanding complete rationality in his conception of an ethical plan. This means, for him, that he cannot go the way of empirical science. But Adler is no Hegelian-type metaphysician. He takes seriously Kant's critique of metaphysical speculation. He would follow Kant's philosophic middle path between empiricism and idealism. But how can he do this and still insist on an idea of the whole which shall be more than either a formal logical system or an empty metaphysical construction? And we may most properly ask *why* Adler insists upon a completely rational ethical theory: for a "plan of the whole" as the necessary framework for any ethical rule, act, or judgment. It will be the task of the next section in this chapter to attempt to answer the first of these two questions. The second question we will deal with now. But because Adler himself gives no direct answer to this question, our response is of necessity of an interpretative nature.

Why does Adler insist upon a completely rational ethical theory? He can see that if human conduct is "explained" within the framework, and by the methods, of empirical science, it will be viewed under the categories of space, time, and

[22]*Ibid.*, pp. 99.

causality. A given instance of conduct will be reported as occurring at a given time, at a given place, and as being caused by some prior event or events and also as being the cause of a subsequent event or events. Even if the conduct has a purpose, this purpose will be seen both as effect and as cause.

Adler seems to hold that unless something more can be said about human conduct than referring it to a causal nexus, ethical theory is an impossibility. As unified by the method of science, the relations between elements in a manifold are all external relations. We must think here of Newtonian science in which all movement is "explained" in terms of forces lying outside the body that moves, or more accurately, that is moved. Adler here faces the now historic problem of finding a place for ethics in a Newtonian world. The nub of this problem, it would appear, is to make a case for human agency.

The terms of the problem are set, because the distinction is made by Adler between scientific explanation and ethical explanation. Scientific explanation is said to be in terms of causes. Ethical explanation, which is called *justification,* makes reference not to causes but to reasons. Further, if scientific explanation (the scientific way of unifying manifolds) is stated in terms of external relations between the objects (the items of the manifold), ethical explanation or justification yields a unification of its manifold in terms of internal relations.

Now, according to Adler, to offer even one adequate *reason* for something requires a complete system of reasons. Thus the justification of a single act requires a "plan of the whole." This, we think, must be a part of Adler's answer to the question of why a complete rational system is necessary for ethical theory.

We may go further and note that the relations among terms in a completely rational system are internal and logically necessary. Given an item of human conduct, the scientific question has to do with causes and consequences. The ethical question relates to the reason or the purpose of the act. A teleological orientation, which is completely missing from science, as Adler conceived it, becomes central for ethics. Ethical theory, for Adler, must yield a completely rational system of purposes or ends, that is, a system in which all ends are related internally and necessarily.

It is in these terms that Adler meets the problem of human agency. Ethically considered, the purposes of a human agent do not stand or exist in external relations. The human agent is a locus of purpose, internally related to other human agents, that is, other loci of purpose.

We have offered an explanation of why Adler calls for a system in which all irrational elements are eliminated, and we have indicated that this system is a system of ends. We must now consider the other question raised above: given his Kantian orientation, how can Adler claim that such a system is more than merely a formal system and not an empty metaphysical construction?

Let us briefly summarize what we have found so far. Knowledge of reality depends on the joint operation of the two reality-producing functions of the mind: (1) the positing of a manifold and (2) the apprehending of the plurality as coherent. We note that neither the manifold nor the unity of the manifold is given. In science we never achieve complete coherence or rationality. Ethics, however, Adler says, requires a complete rational plan. We can settle for no less if we want well-grounded judgment, justification, and guidance of human conduct. The method of ethics, therefore, cannot be the method employed by empirical science.

Adler's difficulty is clearly that of offering a rational plan that has ontological validity. What is at stake is the objectivity of ethical claims and what we might call "ethical knowledge." In particular, what is at issue for Adler is the ontological status of the products of "reason." This would be no problem if he could accept a metaphysics of objective idealism or rationalism, following Hegel or Plato. But for someone who is committed to following Kantian lines, the difficulty might appear to be insuperable.

There are two conditions for objective experience: the elements of certainty and laws. Scientific knowledge is a function of a particular range of *a priori* elements and empirical laws of nature. As far as science is concerned, Adler takes no exception to Kant's views. Ethical knowledge also requires at least one element of certainty and also a law or laws to order its own manifold. Now Adler's demand for a complete system may be read as a demand for a complete system of laws governing the ethical manifold. But the "whole" of the ethical manifold cannot mean the whole of nature, for it is not possible to frame such a whole. Adler calls the whole that he seeks an ideal whole or an ideal plan. He says he seeks a plan of the *universe* (the ideal whole), rather than a plan of the *world* (the impossible conception of the unity of nature).

The alien or irrational elements in scientific knowledge that prevent such knowledge from ever being complete are the presentations that impose themselves on the mind from without. The source of the manifolds that are unified by the sciences are external to the mind. The ethical manifold, by contrast, must both have its source and its mode of unification in reason, or more precisely, the functioning of the mind. Herein lies the basis of Adler's construction of an ethical universe, his ideal plan of the whole.

This construction of a completely rational plan is perhaps the boldest part of Adler's entire philosophic enterprise. The whole of the next chapter will be devoted to it. But we may here lay down the main outline of his argument.

For the construction of the conception of an ideal ethical plan, Adler takes his clue for a starting point from his conception of the nature of mind. We will remember that Adler says the reality-producing functions of the mind are two in number and that they always act together. We always find both a manifold and a unity of that manifold. These two primary and invariant functions are then used as the basis for characterizing the two fundamental constructive principles which serve to give us certainty, the assurance of reality. These two principles, the positing of a manifold and the offering of a mode of unification of the manifold, must both be invoked for any adequate theoretical work. The key concepts are clearly manifoldness and unity.

Now, argues Adler, an ideal whole may be conceived, and conceived as real, if we follow the lead of the reality-producing functions of the mind. Ideal manifoldness is infinite manifoldness. Ideal unity is complete unity. The ideal ethical plan, the completely rational plan, the ethical universe, is thus characterized as manifesting infinite manifoldness and complete unity, or, the complete unification of an infinite manifold.

Adler says that Kant's entire philosophy is primarily intended to account for the element of certainty in experience. We may say that Adler's primary concern is to account for the element of certainty in ethical experience. This element of certainty is, for Adler, the fact of human worth. To offer a rational ground for worth is to establish the objective certainty of this fact. We quoted Adler earlier, speaking of Kant's conception of the *a priori*, as follows:

If a new science were to arise, containing some new element of certainty heretofore unmanifested, we should be compelled to formulate a new variety of the so-called *a priori*, and we should be justified by the spirit, if not by the letter, of Kant's teachings in so doing.[23]

The idea of human worth is not new to ethical theory, but Adler does offer a new formulation of it. The complete rational system Adler calls for has, as a primary purpose, to afford an adequate vindication of this new element of ethical certainty.

An Ethical Ontology

From an empiricist point of view, such as Hume stated, any wholly rational scheme would have the merits of a logical system, but *as such* it could not claim to be saying anything about experience or the world of experience. This particular limita-

[23]Adler, "A Critique of Kant's Ethics," *Mind*, New Series, XI (October, 1902), 166.

tion of the significance of logical formulations Adler accepts entirely. He, of course, as we have already seen, agrees with Kant regarding the synthetic activity of the mind. He also agrees that one is barred from constructing a metaphysics based on noumena, that is, things as they are in themselves apart from any human experience.

His argument is that the reference of a wholly rational plan is neither to phenomena nor to the noumena. With respect to noumena, he writes:

They are limiting concepts intended to serve as incentives or lures, winning the mind to continue, without cessation its advance along certain paths within the field of experience; but they are not supposed to give any clue as to what is beyond experience. That which is beyond the field of experience is simply unknowable. Thus the noumenon called "things *per se*" is notice given to the mind not to be deterred in its proper business of unifying the space and time manifold by the difficulties which arise when the time and space manifold is taken as an ultimate account of reality. The thing *per se* is a welcome to science and not a bar set up in its path. . . .

The noumena, then, are apparitions that appear at the end of certain paths in the field of experience, far off where the sky and the ground seem to meet. These paths run off in different directions. At the end of each is one of these limiting apparitions, and the society of noumena is disconnected internally: there is no relation of unity between the unifiers.[24]

Adler is speaking here of Kant's conception of noumena, which he gives every indication of accepting. But in the same note Adler is critical of some specific points.

The noumenon of freedom is an incentive to man urging him to act as if he were capable of practicing the law of universality and necessity. In fact the phrase "as if" plays a leading role in the Kantian philosophy. The noumenon of God. . .is afflicted with this conditional "as if" character to even a higher degree. We are to assume God in order to look upon the vast field of possible experience as if it were unified, as if a being who himself stands for unity had been its creator. This assumption is supposed to be necessary in order to encourage the scientist in his search for the thread of unity, lest he

[24]Adler, *An Ethical Philosophy of Life,* pp. 127-128n.

flag by the way. As a matter of fact scientists have contented themselves with the simple assumption of the uniformity of nature as necessary to the prosecution of their investigations, and have as a rule troubled themselves little to hypostasize the notion of unity. Nor has recent progress in science been associated with and influenced by the belief in an individual Deity. The noumenon of God is unnecessary for science while in Kant's ethical application of it is positively harmful. He introduces the God notion as an artificial device for linking together happiness and virtue, a device quite inconsistent with the noble austerity of his ethical system, whatever its other defects may be.[25]

It would appear that Adler accepts the general idea of noumena, and sees them as performing an important function, if not in the actual scientific activity, at least in the understanding of the limitations of that activity and its results. But a dispute arises with respect to specific kinds of noumena and the need for assuming or presupposing them for any particular empirical discipline to function properly. This, however, is a minor issue in comparison with the question of the status, not of the noumena, but of what Kant called the Ideas of Pure Reason. The issue most directly concerns the idea of perfection. Adler sets the problem in terms of Kant's alleged disproof of the Ontological Argument:

Did Kant. . .annihilate the Ontological Argument? Yes, in the scholastic form in which it was held. No, in a form, based on the idea of the ethical manifold, in which it can be restated. In the scholastic form it runs: "There is such a thing as the idea of a perfect being. Existence is an element of perfection. If the perfect being did not exist it would be less than perfect. But the *ens realissimum*, the perfect being, is present as an idea in the mind. Therefore it exists." The disproof of this amounts to the curt statement that what exists in the mind does not necessarily exist outside of it, or, as Kant put it: "The idea of 100 thalers in the head of a man is one thing, lacking no element of conceptual integrity; while the existence of the 100 thalers in the man's purse is an entirely different matter." The evidence of existence, in other words, depends on the synthesis of the data of sense as arranged in the space and time manifold in accordance with the categories of the understanding. Existence is temporal and spa-

[25]*Ibid.*

tial. To prove that God exists we should have to prove that he exists in the world of the senses. Of any other kind of existence we are agnostic. Kant's disproof of the Ontological Argument thus depends on his agnosticism.

But suppose that on ethical grounds we find ourselves compelled to affirm that there is an object which has worth, and that to account for the inviolableness, indispensableness and preciousness of this object we are compelled to give free rein to the reality-producing functions, and to place this object having worth as a member in a manifold not spatial and temporal but infinite; and suppose we say that the existence of this worth-endowed object, of this ethical unit with its compeers, is as certain as the notion of rightness is certain, have we not then without blame widened the conception of existence, and placed the Ontological Argument where Kant's disproof does not even touch it?[26]

Adler adds to the above a broadened characterization of rationality:

One more important remark is here in place, suggested by Kant's designation of God as the ideal of reason, and by his designation of our highest nature as the rational nature.

Is "rational" equivalent to intellectual? If it be so, then feeling must be classed as irrational, and impulse likewise, since neither feeling nor impulse is subject to logical rules. And then the war will be on between the intellectualists or rationalists and the champions of irrational conceptions of life, since feeling and impulse actually make up the major part of life, and can neither be left out of account nor compressed into intellectualist formulas [In a footnote here Adler refers to "the anti-intellectualistic philosophy of Bergson, with its emphasis on planless spurts of energy," and "The irrationalist philosophy of Schopenhauer. . ."]

Plainly, there is a deep misunderstanding between the two parties. An error is involved somewhere. It appears to consist in assuming that objectivity can be supplied only by the intellect, in overlooking the fact that the feelings and still more the volition possess intrinsic controls and norms of their own, that Science, the work of the intellect, and art and ethics, spring from a common root, namely, the reality-producing functions. The manifolds with which each of the three respectively deals are different, the methods of synthesis are different, but the root principle, synthesis of the manifold, is identical in all.

[26]*Ibid.,* pp. 129-131.

To describe our highest nature, therefore, as the rational nature is perilous, since the word rational suggests intellectual. Either we must strain the signification of reason to include feeling and will, which is contrary to common usage, or we should select some other term, such as spiritual, to designate that nature within us which operates in science and art and achieves its highest manifestation in producing the ethical ideal.[27]

Kant did not raise any question about the conceptual or subjective integrity of either the idea of 100 thalers, or the idea of perfection. It is the objectivity of these ideas that is at issue, that is, whether the idea refers to something other than itself. Adler claims that Kant's position is that we decide whether an idea is objective by being able to find the referent of the idea in the world of sense experience, in the phenomenal world. If the idea does not refer to something that could possibly appear in experience, then the idea is only subjective.

Along these same lines Kant argued against all absolute metaphysics. It is an improper understanding of a transcendental ideal to assume that any referent for it could appear in experience. Adler agrees that the idea of the whole never appears to man except as an idea. But he does say that the idea refers to what he calls the supersensible realm. This realm, also called by Adler the "ultimate reality" and the "divine ideal," is the closest we come to finding an absolute metaphysic in Adler. But this supersensible reality is more like Kant's noumena than Hegel's absolute. For the supersensible is unknowable, incognizable.

Science deals with what is, with what is actually the case. Ethics deals with what ought to be, with the ideal. What is, can be experienced. What is ideal is never actual. We can, as human beings, formulate ideals, but if they are only our personal ideals they have nothing more to recommend them than our own personal preference. But Adler wants to show that not only is the ideal of worth not merely subjective, but that it is the most objective of all notions.

[27]*Ibid.*, pp. 131-132.

In demonstrating how Adler does this, we must consider his rendering of the Ontological Argument, and the meaning he gives to the term *spiritual*. Kant's disproof of the Ontological Argument rests on a sharp distinction between ideas and matters of fact, or we might say, between relations among ideas and relations among matters of fact. Adler accepts this distinction and the argument that Kant offers, pointing out that if by *existence* one means empirical, spatio-temporal being, then the older form of the Ontological Argument fails to prove the existence of a perfect being.

Now Adler also offers us the idea of a perfect being, that is, a being which has worth. How does his argument for its existence avoid what for convenience we might call the "empirical criticism"? First of all we must note that the conception of *existence* is changed—Adler says "widened." There seem to be two senses in which *existence* is widened. Adler speaks of giving "free rein to the reality-producing functions" of the mind. We have seen that "free rein" means conceiving each of the two fundamental functions in infinite terms.[28] Adler points to an infinite manifold grounded in one of the dual functions, and total unity grounded in the other function. The first and most obvious meaning of "widening" would be this extrapolation to infinity. But we notice that in the widening something is lost, namely spatio-temporal existence. Adler's widened sense of existence does not include the narrower empirical sense at all.

We could perhaps stop here and say simply that Adler has indeed placed *his* Ontological Argument out of Kant's reach, not so much by widening it as simply by changing the conception of the existence that he seeks to establish. But if this is all that Adler is doing, his "victory" is merely verbal. Nor does tying the certainty of the existence of an object with worth to the certainty of rightness help very much in establishing the objectivity of worth. For the critic may be equally skeptical about the objectivity of rightness.

A better case can be made in terms of the second sense in which

[28]*An Ethical Philosophy of Life,* p. 166.

existence may be thought of as widened, that is, in connection with Adler's proposal for an expanded meaning of *rational* to include feeling and volition.

We spoke earlier of the two conditions of objective experience: elements of certainty and laws.[29] Of course, as we speak of objective experience, we must admit some kind of experience into the picture. Both Hume and Kant think in terms of sense experience. Adler wants to include feelings and willings. Adler claims he *feels* compelled to affirm worth. This feeling is as little a matter of conscious and deliberate decision as the sights and sounds that impinge upon him when in a waking state. If such a feeling can be taken up within a framework of law, and its *a priori* elements recognized, then one has met Kant's conditions for objectivity, that is, one could claim objectivity for the given feeling.

The logic of the argument is supplied by Kant. The new element is the admittance of feelings as possible objective experiences. We may add here that Adler seems to put considerable stress on the idea that these feelings are given internally and in this sense are not alien elements, as opposed to sense experiences, whose sources are external to the person. Part of his argument for the possibility of a completely rational scheme is dependent on the fact that experiences of a distinctively ethical nature do not contain this alien, external, spatio-temporal, irrational element.[30]

Now one of the difficulties of including feelings and the like among those kinds of experience that admit of the possibility of objectivity is that it is not at all clear what the referent of a feeling might be. It is clear enough *what* one is seeing when one sees a table. And we are supplied with quite adequate means for determining when such seeing is merely subjective and when we agree that what is seen "is really a table out there." Following this model of argument, if one reports a feeling that people have worth, one is unable to supply means for deciding whether the feeling is a "mere" feeling or whether it is responsive to the fact that people have worth. Part of this problem may lie in the attempt to apply a com-

[29]*Supra.,* p. 85.
[30]For a discussion of these experiences see the next section in this work.

mon sense conception of the relation between an experience and the object of experience, that is, of an isolated experience of seeing connected with a particular spatio-temporal event. This is a conception that *is* well-grounded in ordinary sense experience. But it is not as well substantiated by modern physical science where the significance of a particular sense experience is read into and in terms of a very complex theoretical system. The kind of objective reference Adler seeks to claim for feeling and volition is more like the kind of reference or interpretation that is made of an instance of sense observation in the more advanced sciences.

We may distinguish between the experience as immediately had and the interpretation placed on that experience. This would apply as well to the observation of a needle on a Geiger counter as to a feeling that one has when waking in the middle of the night. When Adler reports that he finds himself "compelled to affirm that there is an object which has worth," we may read this as Adler's interpretation of a feeling that he had, either all the time or at least very often. If we admit this distinction between the experience and its interpretation, we can say that *worth* names a theory, an interpretation of experience. This may permit us to say with more clarity what is at stake in both of the Ontological Arguments.

It is clear that what is not at stake is either the existence of the feeling or the existence of the idea of the 100 thalers. But Kant's report about the *fact* of the 100 thalers in the man's purse short-cuts his criticism. What Kant must do is report about a sense experience which is interpreted as an experience of the 100 thalers, then admit corroboration for this interpretation. By introducing the fact of the thalers' existence he makes it clear that he will not admit the terms of Ontological Argument at all. His disproof is an *obiter dicta.* Its force will only be felt by one who is already convinced that the Ontological Argument is a piece of specious reasoning.

Adler, it seems to us, does not do any better than Kant in the way in which he presents his argument, for Adler also fails to draw the distinction between the experience and the interpretation of the experience.

If one admits that ideas, sense experiences, feelings, volitions, are all different kinds of experiences—and it would appear that this is the direction Adler takes as he expands the meaning of "rational"—then with respect to all of these we can draw the distinction between the experience and an interpretation of the experience. We might then argue that both Ontological Arguments, the older scholastic argument and Adler's, are attempts to interpret experience. In the first case the experience is the idea of perfection. We would agree that the interpretation is a failure. Adler's argument is an attempt to interpret, not an idea, but a complex of feeling and willing. Not only is the experience complex but the interpretation is also.

We have titled this chapter "The Rational Ground of Worth." We have seen Adler suggest that the use of the term "rational" is dangerous insofar as it tends to suggest the intellectual, to the exclusion of feeling and will. Thus Adler proposes *spiritual* "to designate that nature within us which operates in science and art and achieves its highest manifestation in producing the ethical ideal."[31] Following this terminological proposal our chapter could be titled "The Spiritual Ground of Worth." But this would probably be even more misleading to most readers. It would appear that we do not have a word which carries the weight of Adler's meaning without considerable danger of confusion.

This terminological situation is a reflection of the fact that Adler's conceptions of experience and of man's nature are not familiar. It is the status given to feeling and willing that is the most distinctive feature of Adler's formulation. He is arguing that these kinds of experience are a source of objectivity or objective knowledge.[32]

---

[31] Adler, *An Ethical Philosophy of Life*, p. 132. Also *Supra.*, p. 90.

[32] The traditions of rationalism and empiricism have, for the most part, dominated discussions of objectivity. Philosophies of science, in recent years, may be characterized as representing a synthesis of rationalism and empiri-

Categories for an Ethical Ontology

We are able to discern five major terms that Adler uses throughout his work: empirical, moral, ethical, spiritual, and divine. Adler is not entirely consistent in his use of these terms, but there is sufficient constancy in his usage to permit us to consider these terms as marking categories of an ontol-

cism. For an early statement of this synthesis see William Pepperell Montague, *The Ways of Knowing or The Methods of Philosophy* (New York: The Macmillan Company, 1925), particularly Chapters III and IV. Ernest Nagel's *The Structure of Science: Problems in the Logic of Scientific Explanation* (New York: Harcourt, Bruce, and World, 1961) is a recent formulation. Neither Montague nor Nagel would be particularly sympathetic to Adler's formulation.

Two major efforts may, however, be read as attempts to offer the kind of "extension of the rational" that Adler proposed. We refer to the work of Ernst Cassirer and Justus Buchler. Cassirer writes: "If. . .the time has come when philosophy itself must decide on a new interpretation of its own concept, it still finds itself confronted with the enigmatic problem of 'objectivity,' the burden of which cannot be entirely assumed by the separate sciences. For, taken in its full generality, this problem belongs to a sphere which cannot be comprehended and exhausted by science taken as a whole. Science is only one member and one factor in the system of 'symbolic forms.' In a certain sense it can be regarded as the keystone in the edifice of these forms; but it does not stand alone and it cannot perform its specific function without the coexistence of other energies, sharing with it in the task of 'synoptic vision,' of spiritual 'synthesis.' " C. S. Howe (trans.), *The Logic of the Humanities* (New Haven: Yale University Press, 1961), p. 64. Language, myth, religion, art, are all sources of objectivity for Cassirer. See in addition to the work just cited, Ralph Manheim (trans.), *The Philosophy of Symbolic Forms.* 3 Vols. (New Haven: Yale University Press, 1953-1957), and *An Essay on Man: An Introduction to a Philosophy of Human Culture* (New Haven: Yale University, 1944).

Justus Buchler in his two works, *Toward a General Theory of Human Judgment* and *Nature and Judgment* (New York: Columbia University Press, 1951 and 1955, respectively) argues for equal status for what he calls active, exhibitive, and assertive judgments. As assertive judgment is meant to comprise what generally is understood under the heading of man's rationality, Buchler is concerned with an extension of the notion of man's judgmental function to include, in addition to man's intellectual production, all that man does and makes. Buchler has the same kind of problem with the term *judgment* as Adler has with the term *rational.*

Ethics does not appear as a central concern in the works of either Cassirer or Buchler, but we think that Adler's attempt to broaden the conception of reason gains support from these two writers. Both Cassirer's idea of a range of symbolic forms and Buchler's treatment of judgment are fruitful approaches toward the kind of understanding of human experience Adler sought.

ogy. Adler does not speak, in this connection, of levels of reality or of a hierarchy of categories; but, from his ethical standpoint, such expressions would appear to be appropriate. We may even speak of the ontology as an ethical ontology, for there is no attempt on Adler's part to disguise the fact that "ultimate reality" and "highest good" are synonymous.[33]

Of the five categories, only the first can be understood as ethically neutral, answering to the range of phenomena as they are. The *empirical realm* is the realm investigated by the various sciences as they attempt to describe the account for *what is* and predict *what will be*, avoiding the question of *what ought to be*.

Moral refers to human activity and relations among humans insofar as they are good, by reference to a judgment of what is good. Moral conduct is a product of training, upbringing, and habit. The conduct conforms to what is good, but the individual need not be aware that he is acting according to any ethical principle. For example, a person who has learned not to kill other people because it "just isn't done," or because it is an "unhealthy" response, or it is always inexpedient ("there are better ways of getting what you want") or even "because it's wrong," might not kill—not because he understands why it is wrong, but simply on the basis of well-ingrained habits. A person may act *morally* without any *ethical* awareness.

The *ethical* realm is composed of the conduct of human beings, as spatio-temporal entities acting morally, but with explicit reference to the spiritual ideal. Ethical conduct is distinguished from moral conduct not by its goodness or its strict conformity to the ideal (which would be contradictory and impossible since the ideal can never be wholly actualized), but rather by the individual's conscious attempt to embody the

---

[33]C. J. Ducasse points out that "An ontological position. . .is a rule one adopts, or tacitly proceeds under, as to what things one will regard as alone of interest, or will rank as basic or primary." *Nature, Mind, and Death* (LaSalle, Illinois: The Open Court Publishing Company, 1951), p. 76. We would agree with Professor Ducasse and add that the pervasive "ontological sin" is to claim primacy without making clear in what sense one is making the claim. Adler's explicitly ethical ontology leaves little doubt as to what he takes to be primary.

ideal in his conduct. Ethical conduct is not characterized by its success in realizing the ideal, but by the attempt to act with reference to the ideal. There may, of course, be striving connected with moral conduct, but it would not be striving in terms of the ideal. The ethical level may be compared with Kant's conception of decision made in accordance with, and for the sake of, a maxim capable of being universalized and conforming to his categorical imperative, that is, willed as a universal law for all men. Adler does not draw and use Kant's distinctions between actions, decisions, maxims, and the moral law or categorical imperative, although these are implicit in his theory. The distinction between moral and ethical is simply drawn between acting with, and acting without, reference to the ideal as formulated in Adler's own categorical imperative.[34]

When Adler speaks of ethical conduct he is thinking of the actual conduct of human beings insofar as they strive to realize the ideal. Such conduct takes place, or can take place, and we can know about it.[35] So far we are dealing in terms

[34]As we have written, it might appear that a moral act was better than an ethical act. For we said that the moral act was in conformity with the ideal and the ethical act is only characterized by a striving for such conformity. It should be made clear that moral acts are only possible as training can effectively set some patterns of behavior bringing a person to a point of rough and crude approximation to the standard. The ethical response suggests reflection and care in the interpretation of each situation as it arises. The moral response is more in the nature of a conditioned response.

[35]It is at least knowable in principle. The difficulties of knowing when someone is actually acting and striving with reference to the ideal and not with some other motive in mind are legion. Adler faces the same kind of problem Kant faces in ever knowing whether an ethical act has been performed. As Kant writes: "it is absolutely impossible to make out by experience with complete certainty a single case in which the maxim of an action, however right in itself, rested simply on moral grounds and on the conception of duty. Sometimes it happens that with the sharpest self-examination we can find nothing besides the moral principle of duty which could have been powerful enough to move us to this or that action and to so great a sacrifice; yet we cannot from this infer with certainty that it was not really some secret impulse of self-love, under the false appearance of duty, that was the actual determining cause of the will." Immanuel Kant, *Fundamental Principles of the Metaphysic of Morals* in *Kant's Critique of Practical Reason and Other Works on the Theory of Ethics,* trans. T. K. Abbott (sixth edition; New York: Longmans Green and Company, 1909), pp. 23-24.

which any empiricist or naturalist would understand. However, the move to the *spiritual* level in this ethical hierarchy marks a sharp distinction in Adler's total ontology. It also introduces some serious difficulties in the interpretation of Adler's meaning.

Adler draws a primary distinction between the sensible and the supersensible realms. The three levels already discussed —the empirical, moral, and ethical—all clearly fall within the sensible realm. The highest level, the *divine,* clearly falls within the realm of the supersensible. But the status of the *spiritual* is not quite clear.

For the most part, Adler follows Kant in claiming that the sensible (or the phenomenal) is knowable and the supersensible is unknowable or incognizable. We have seen Adler characterize man's highest nature as *spiritual.*[36] It is not too much to say that Adler's entire defense of his Ontological Argument rests on the claims he makes about man's spiritual nature. This would suggest Adler believes that at least some knowledge of this spiritual nature is possible.

But Adler also speaks of the spiritual as the ideal and as supersensible. In these terms the spiritual is clearly unknowable. As unknowable, the spiritual might be understood as noumena which stand behind our distinctively ethical experience. Such spiritual noumena would stand in much the same relation to ethical experience, that is, experience which involves feeling and willing, as the "physical" noumena which Adler (following Kant) admits as lying behind our perceptual experience.

This interpretation of Adler's intention is satisfactory, but only insofar as Adler thinks of the spiritual as unknowable. Yet we must not ignore the sense in which Adler wants to claim knowledge of the spiritual.

The claim to unknowability cannot be taken literally, or as the whole of Adler's meaning. We would suggest that Adler is led to the claim as he borrows the language of Hume and Kant and accepts the view that knowledge comes from sense

[36]*Supra.,* p. 90.

experience. On empirical premises, the claim to the unknowableness of the spiritual may be taken literally. For the empiricist, knowledge not only comes from sense experience, but *all* knowledge requires the component of sense experience. As Adler speaks of nonempirical realities, he finds himself saying that they are unknowable. But, in our discussion of Adler's Ontological Argument, we have seen that Adler means to say that knowledge and the grounds of objectivity are broader than Hume or Kant would allow. He is claiming that nonempirical knowledge is possible. Adler's construction of the spiritual ideal, or as he calls it sometimes, the spiritual universe, depends for its validity on the strength of his extension of the Ontological Argument. Kant would have to reject Adler's claim to the reality of his spiritual ideal. From Kant's point of view Adler is caught by a transcendental illusion: Adler, in Kant's terms, is characterizing noumena.

We must conclude that the spiritual is partly knowable and partly unknowable. As the sensible realm is expanded to include the experiences of feeling and willing, the spiritual nature of man falls within the range of the knowable. But Adler is also led to construe a supersensible realm—an ideal realm. This supersensible realm as the level of the *divine* is unknowable. But it is the ultimate reality which the ethicist attempts to formulate. What Adler calls the spiritual realm, or the spiritual ideal, is this attempt to formulate the unknowable. He admits that such formulation is never successful, partly because of the infiniteness of the divine, but also because one has no real clues as to what ultimate reality is in itself.

Despite this guarantee of failure, an attempt must be made at a formulation. We note that *spiritual* refers both to the highest nature of man and to an ideal realm of reality. Adler uses the formulation of the spiritual nature of man to lead him to a conception of a spiritual universe. But this latter conception is clearly understood by Adler as an attempt to do the impossible.

Has Adler avoided Rationalism? The answer must be *yes* to the extent that he claims the certainty of worth issues from the deepest and most persistent impulses in man. We may intellectualize it, but impulses, deep feeling, are not themselves intellectual entities. On this broader use of *rational,* which includes the sweep of man's response to the world as it appears in science, art, and ethics, Adler would claim a rational, but not simply a logical or intellectual grounding. The other side of this issue relates directly to the ideal of worth. The impulse or certainty of worth is not a logical thing, nor is the ideal of worth, considered as a supersensible fact, to be understood as merely a logical entity. It is conceived, as we have seen, as the objective counterpart of the unity of man's spiritual nature.

The claim might still be made that Adler takes the position of an anti-Kantian Rationalism, as he insists on the validity of his version of the Ontological Argument. This may be the case, but several points would suggest that at least the major tendency of Adler's thinking is opposed to absolute metaphysics in any of its various forms.

First we may note that Adler's mode of questioning is Kantian in character. That is, Adler starts from a truth he does not doubt and then asks what must be true in order for that which he does not doubt to be true. What is presupposed by what I do not doubt? Adler's approach, even to the Ontological Argument, is precisely this presuppositional approach. His response can be stated: for worth to be objective, my form of the Ontological Argument must be valid. We notice also the qualifying statement Adler makes "that the supersensible is as certain as the notion of rightness is certain."[37]

A second point is that Adler speaks of the "divine ideal as that unknown truth of being of which the moral ideal is the best provisional symbol."[38] He goes on to state:

the universe has no ontological reality; there is no such thing as a universe. It is only an idea. Our notion of an ontological universe rests upon a generalization from experience. We can never get at a totality through experience, because experience is fragmentary, and

---

[37] Adler, *An Ethical Philosophy of Life,* p. 130.
[38] Adler, *Ethics Based on the Organic Ideal,* p. 12.

deals only with particular things, no amount of which will give us a totality. The universe is an ideal. The divine ideal is that unknown truth of being, of which the moral ideal is the best provisional symbol.[39]

Adler speaks here of the twofold functions of the mind, the positing of unity and plurality, as a flaw in the mind, "for the two factors considered by themselves are repugnant and repel each other."[40] We are unable to operate with only one of them, but we simply cannot understand how they are related to one another so "the moral ideal. . .which is the last realization of these two factors, cannot. . .be possessed of absolute certitude."[41] Adler may be understood here to hold the same view as Kant to the effect that the activity of the mind prevents us from having access to ultimate reality. And the passages just quoted add a further factor cutting man off from absolute certitude. The reality-producing functions of the mind are not only polar in character, but this polarity is given to us as an inexplicable ultimate. Whatever access we have to reality we have by use of these polar functions, but we can offer no explanation for the mind's being the way it is and functioning the way it does. We have no way of understanding the relation that binds these two mutually "repugnant" functions of the mind. This inability to comprehend the full reality of the reality-producing functions is reflected in the inability, which Adler insists upon, to have absolute certitude in any matter whatsoever, and certainly in the matter of the nature of the ultimate reality.

Our third and final point we draw from an unpublished paper on symbols. Here Adler writes regarding the characterization of the supersensible realm:

The main point. . .is, whatever signs we may choose, to keep vivid the consciousness of the distinction between them and the thing signified. There is an order of reality. There actually is. The negative-

[39]*Ibid.*
[40]*Ibid.,* p. 13.
[41]*Ibid.*

positive influence upon man's agency proves that there is, that which, however, in its nature is beyond our ability to know or to imagine. These imaginative figures by which we try to symbolize are hieroglyphs or picture-writing, necessarily cryptic.[42]

The dominant thought in Adler's mind appears to be thus: the very fact that mind makes an inexpungible contribution to our knowledge prevents us from ever making absolute claims about reality. For Adler, there is no road back from Kant's critical position. One might say that to attempt any characterization at all of an "order of reality. . .beyond our ability to know or imagine" is to do no more than extrapolate from human experience and to be faced still with a purely human production. Adler would agree. What he can claim is that the derivation of his conception is in accordance with a carefully formulated procedure. In this sense his hieroglyphs are not merely subjective or arbitrary. And Adler also seeks to submit the implications and consequences of his view to test in the active life experience of man.[43]

---

[42]Adler, *Symbols,* pp. 1-2.

[43]Horace L. Friess writes, on the matter under discussion, as follows: "Adler's two ways of expressing himself about the validity of his highest idea—the transcendent ideal—may be called respectively the spiritual or religious and the intellectualistic or rationalistic way. It seems as if in the case of the second he overlooks that neither 'pole' of the ideal—neither the infinite unity nor the infinite plurality—is given to sense, but only to idea, and this is after all the basic fact on which the Kantian criticism of the "ontological argument" turns. It would appear that Adler has, in this second way of expressing his claim, reverted, therefore, if not to a pre-Kantian at least to an unKantian rationalism. The first way of expressing his claim, the spiritual or religious way, which regards the transcendent ideal simply as the best available 'symbol' of faith would seem to accord better with his general disavowal of and strictures against intellectualism. Following this first way, the transcendent ideal will be more than an arbitrary 'symbol' insofar as (a) its derivation is by a coherent procedure, and (b) its implications or further consequences are satisfactory. The derivation has already been indicated, except that it may be added as most significant that Adler regards his reconstructed ideal as flowing not from the reason or intellect alone but from the entire unity of man's spiritual nature. And one of its most crucial tests, in terms of consequences, will be whether it can prove this derivation by aiding to effect a progressive harmony of intellect, feeling, and will." Horace L. Friess, *Ethical Theory and the Quest for Truth* (unpublished manuscript on Felix Adler, 1943), pp. 35-36. We would not argue with this statement except insofar as it might sug-

It would seem that Adler could have made his position clearer if he had not presented his conception of the nature of the spiritual within the Humean-Kantian framework. He might have presented it directly, for it is quite different from what either Hume or Kant would have entertained.

If we ask about the ontological status of the supersensible ideal, we are referred to the conviction of certainty that issues from the use of the reality-producing functions of the mind. It is not just a set of relations among ideas. It has a nonspatial, nonsensible reality—the claim for which, Adler argues, has as much warrant as the claim for the reality of the conceptions of the physicist. In both cases a manifold is unified and it is in terms of such unification of a manifold that we have whatever sense of reality we do in fact have.[44]

gest that Adler's "two ways" receive equal attention in his work. As we read Adler, his primary emphasis is on the spiritual or religious way of dealing with the ideal. This is more than a matter of being consistent with "his general disavowal of and strictures against intellectualism." As regards reading Adler's meaning, it appears to us that Adler takes the "spiritual" approach, not only most of the time, but at all the major junctures of his work.

[44]One might be tempted to say that Adler's distinction between sensible and supersensible is equivalent to Plato's distinction between the objects of sense and the objects of cognition. There is surely a similarity between the two conceptions. But two essential differences may be pointed out. Adler's conception of mind is very different from Plato's. This makes an important difference, since Adler's conception has the mind supplying an inexpungible substantive factor into what is known. The second major difference lies in Adler's use of the term *rational* to include more than the cognitive or intellectual. For Adler, the rational part of man comprehends intellect, feeling, and will. Platonic Ideas are known by the rational faculty, which means intellect alone.

CHAPTER 3

The Ideal of Worth

Adler's "ideal plan of the whole" is the rational structure within which, and in terms of which, the objective status of worth is to be understood; for

no detached thing has worth. No part of an incomplete system has worth. Worth belongs to those to whom it is attributed in so far as they are conceived of as not to be spared, as representing a distinctive indispensable preciousness, a mode of being without which perfection would be less than perfect. . .morality depends on the attribution of worth to men, and worth depends on the formation in the mind of an ideal plan of the whole—or instead of a complete plan let me say more precisely a rule of relations whereby the plan is itself progressively developed.

To rate anyone as an end *per se* means that in a world conceived as perfect his existence would be indispensable. The world we know may not be perfect, is not perfect, but we do conceive of an ideal world that is. To ascribe to anyone the quality of worth, to denominate him an end *per se,* is to place him into that world, to regard him as potentially a member of it.[1]

Adler speaks of his ideal conception variously, as the spiritual ideal, the organic ideal, and the spiritual universe. He also sometimes calls it the ethical ideal. Strictly, the term *ethical* is reserved for use concerning the relations among persons, which can never be ideal or perfect. We will, when the context is clear, speak simply of *the ideal* or of Adler's ideal. It is to the derivation, nature, and use of Adler's ideal which we now turn.

---

[1]Adler, *An Ethical Philosophy of Life,* pp. 99n and 101-102n.

Derivation of the Ideal

The abstract derivation of the ideal can be stated quite briefly. Adler combines two of his basic conceptions. (1) To be certain of our rightness in any particular part of conduct, we must possess an ideal plan of the whole, "For in conduct there is no such partial coincidence between the rational and the irrational as in the case of physical law."[2] (2) The reality-producing functions, the principal invariants in the operations of the human mind, by which Adler claims that we assure ourselves of reality, are two in number. They are "the positing of a manifold of some kind, and the apprehending of that manifold as coherent."[3]

To derive or construct the ideal of the whole one need only give these two functions of the mind free rein to expand or extrapolate to infinity. The extension of the principle of manifoldness yields the idea of infinite manifoldness. The extension of the principle of unity or coherence yields the idea of complete and flawless unity or wholeness. But as Adler points out again and again, these two functions always operate together. The principles, which are nothing more than formulations of the way in which the mind operates, must be applied together. The conception of the idea, therefore, must be formulated so as to answer to the demands of both principles. The ideal must be seen as the flawless unity of an infinite manifold. Adler writes:

The ideal of the whole, as the terms imply, must fulfill two conditions; it must be a whole, that is, include all manifoldness whatsoever; and it must be ideal, or perfectly unified. In such an ideal whole the two reality-producing functions of the human mind would find their complete fruition.

Point 1.—The totality of manifoldness must be comprised.
Point 2.—The connectedness must be without flaw.[4]

[2] *Ibid.*, p. 98.
[3] *Ibid.*, p. 107.
[4] *Ibid.*, p. 114.

Adler offers two important propositions in connection with the two functions of the mind. (1) These two functions are "reality-producing," that is, it is through their action that we gain whatever assurance of reality we have. (2) Although these two functions always act together and jointly, they always remain for us disparate and separate. We never find one without the other, but we cannot derive one from the other. Plurality or manifoldness cannot be derived from unity and unity cannot be derived from plurality. Both functions of the mind are primary or root functions. The relation between them is inexplicable.[5]

Adler offers another approach to the ideal through the concept of organism. Early in his life Adler came to the conclusion that however one made the case for worth and dignity of men, it could not be made if one insisted on viewing men as self-sufficient islands. One of the most important points on which he broke with Kant was that he understood Kant's ethics as based upon an atomistic conception of the person, in which the individual, in contrast to the group, was given priority. On the basis of his principle of polarity, Adler chooses neither the individual nor the collectivity as prior in importance. Instead, he insists that neither the whole nor the part can be considered apart from the other. It is not a question of priority at all but of mutual existence and interdependence.

Adler found that the model of a perfect organism, an ideal conceived such that the relations among the members were organic, was precisely the symbol he required for explication of the spiritual ideal.

A primary intellectual source of this idea for Adler is most probably Kant's discussion of the organic in the *Critique of Judgment*. But the idea is common enough and experience serves us with many different kinds of organisms. Of course,

---

[5] Adler's view that we are able to account for the relation between these two reality-producing functions leads him to claim that we can never fully know the nature of reality. Adler does claim, however, that we can have an "idea" of ultimate reality.

Adler's conception is not that of any particular empirical organism. His notion is of a perfect, an ideal organism in which each part (or member) is different from every other part and in which each part has its own unique function to perform within the totality of the organism.[6]

The model is clearly not mechanical in any sense. The whole is not a sum of parts but itself a function of the functions of the parts. And the parts are accountable, as parts, only as they function in relation to all the other parts. This is to say that the parts are reciprocally interdependent. If the organism is now conceived as infinite, we have an infinite number of elements. And the reciprocal interdependence is universal in the technical sense in which Adler wants to use the term *universe*—that is, a flawless totality, as contrasted with *world*, which names the fragmentary thing we know through the various sciences.

The relation of reciprocal interdependence is of considerable importance, particularly as it stands as the primary relation among the units of the manifold that ethical theory must comprehend. The relation of reciprocal interdependence among elements of the ethical manifold is contrasted with the causal relation among elements dealt with by the empirical sciences. This marks another sense in which the ideal is not mechanical.

Universal reciprocal interdependence is stated by Adler, then, both in terms of an extrapolation of the two constructive principles of the human mind and in terms of an ideal organic model.[7]

The Ideal of Worth

The principle of manifoldness (or to use the more common

[6]Adler, *Ethics Based on the Organic Ideal.*

[7]Friess, reporting conversations with Adler, indicates that Adler saw some similarity between his own view and Leibnitz's conception of monads. The change that Adler would make would be to introduce windows into the monads. This would be a third route to the idea of universal reciprocal interdependence, but Adler did not develop it.

term—plurality) requires that each and every member of the manifold be distinct and distinguishable from every other member.[8] That is, each member must "differ uniquely from all the rest, and preserve [its] irreducible singularity".[9]

[8]Adler entered the following footnote when he introduced the term *member* into his discussion: "Say not *part* or *element*, but member, to distinguish the components of the ethical manifold from such concepts as are used in mathematics and physical science." Adler, *An Ethical Philosophy of Life*, p. 115n.

[9]*Ibid.*, p. 115. The following passage by A. O. Lovejoy helps to put this demand for uniqueness into historical perspective: "Thus for two centuries the efforts made for improvement and correction in beliefs, in institutions, and in art have been, in the main, controlled by the assumption that, in each phase of his activity, man should conform as nearly as possible to a standard conceived as universal, uncomplicated, immutable, uniform for every rational being. The Enlightenment was, in short, an age devoted, at least in its dominant tendency, to the simplification and the standardization of thought and life—to their standardization by means of their simplification. Spinoza summed it up in a remark reported by one of his early biographers: 'The purpose of Nature is to make men uniform, as children of a common mother.' The struggle to realize this supposed purpose of nature, the general attack upon the *differentness* of men and their opinions and valuations and institutions —this, with the resistances to it and the eventual revulsion against it, was the central and dominating fact in the intellectual history of Europe from the late sixteenth to the late eighteenth century.

"There have, in the entire history of thought, been few changes in standards of value more profound and more momentous than that which took place when the contrary principle began widely to prevail—when it came to be believed not only that in many, or in all, phases of human life there are diverse excellences, but that diversity itself is of the essence of excellence. . . .

"It is, however of no great consequence whether or not we apply to this transformation of current assumptions about value the name of 'Romanticism'; what it is essential to remember is that the transformation has taken place and that it, perhaps more than any other *one* thing has distinguished, both for better and worse, the prevailing assumptions of the mind of the nineteenth and of our own century from those of the preceding period in the intellectual history of the West. That change, in short, has consisted in the substitution of what may be called diversitarianism for uniformitarianism as the ruling preconception in most of the normative provinces of thought." *The Great Chain of Being: A Study of the History of an Idea* (New York: Harper and Brothers, 1960), pp. 292-294. The whole of Chapter X, "Romanticism and Plentitude," from which the above passage is taken, is relevant to the matter under consideration.

Interestingly, despite the fact that Lovejoy finds diversitarianism to be a pervasive mode of thought during the time Adler was writing, Adler finds ethical theory almost wholly unresponsive to this idea. In fact, it appears he thinks himself to be alone in insisting upon uniqueness as a fundamental *ethical* concept and characteristic.

In the ethical manifold each infinitesimal member is indispensable, inasmuch as he is one of the totality of intrinsically unlike differentiae. A duplicate would be superfluous. Inclusion implies indispensableness; no member acquires a place within the ethical universe save on the score of his title, as one of the possible modes of being that are required to complete the totality of manifoldness.[10]

The manifold is composed of an infinite number of unique members.

From the requirement that "the totality of manifoldness must be comprised,"

it follows that the ethical manifold cannot be spatial or temporal, since juxtaposition and sequence lapse into indefiniteness, abounding without ceasing, but never attaining or promising the attainment of totality. . .the ethical manifold is non-temporal and non-spatial.[11]

Since neither of the two functions of the mind is derived from the other—each operating, as it were, on its own terms—the plurality must not be understood as derived from the unity nor the unity as derived from the plurality. Neither the unity nor the plurality has any priority, either temporally, causally, psychologically, logically, ontologically, ethically, or in any other way. Nor has any member of the manifold any sort of priority over any other member, despite or in face of the fact that each member is discrete and unique.

The manifold being nontemporal, neither the category of creation nor any concept of causality is relevant to the ideal. Adler speaks of the items of the manifold as "unbegotten,"[12] but it would probably be more accurate to refer to them as abegotten—suggesting that the notion of begottenness simply does not apply one way or the other.

The principle of unity requires that the manifold, that is, the infinite number of members of the manifold, be conceived of as flawlessly unified. What is required is that every member be related to every other member in such a way that a com-

[10]Adler, *An Ethical Philosophy of Life*, p. 115.
[11]*Ibid.*, p. 114.
[12]*Ibid.*, p. 115.

mon pattern of relation can be traced throughout the totality. In logical terms we would say that every member must be internally related to every other—every member must be implied by every other and by all others and by groups of other members. We must have a common rule of relation or implication.

Furthermore, if each member in the infinite manifold is unique, then it would follow that a loss of a member would be a flaw in the total infiniteness. The ideal requires that each member be indispensable and irreplaceable.

Adler recognizes unity, the One, taken by itself, as an empty concept. And this is equally true of the idea of a distinct, unique unit. Totality is never given—it leads nowhere and implies nothing—and uniqueness is "incognizable." Adler therefore turns his attention away from the individual members to the relations among them. He speaks of the relation of reciprocal universal interdependence as supplying both an ideal plan of the ethical universe and a first principle and rule of ethics:

> Consider that an infinite number of ethical entities is presented to our minds—each of them radically different from the rest. In what then possibly can the unity of this infinite assemblage consist? In this—*that the unique difference of each shall be such as to render possible the correlated unique differences of all the rest.* It is in this formula that we find the key to a new ethical system, in this conception we get our hand firmly on the notion of right, and by means of it we discover the object which Kant failed to find, the object to which worth attaches, the object which is so indispensable to the ideal of the whole as to authenticate unconditional obligation or rightness in conduct with respect to it. It is as an ethical unit, as a member of the infinite ethical manifold, that man has worth.[13]

Borrowing the format Kant used with his categorical imperative, Adler frames three formulae to express the rule stated above in italics:

> A. Act as a member of the ethical manifold (the infinite spiritual universe).

[13]*Ibid.,* pp. 116-117 (Italics in the original).

B. Act so as to achieve uniqueness (complete individuation—the most completely individualized act is the most ethical).

C. Act so as to elicit in another the distinctive, unique quality characteristic of him as a fellow-member of the infinite whole.[14]

These are not to be understood as three separate steps to be taken one at a time. Rather, to act in accord with A is to produce the uniqueness mentioned in B. And since uniqueness is itself to be understood by way of contrast with something or someone else, seeking to bring out the uniqueness of another is thought reflexively to help elicit one's own uniqueness. But Adler recognizes that the particular character of any individual's uniqueness is not knowable:

The actual unique quality in myself is incognizable, and only appears, as far as it does appear, in the effect produced by myself upon my fellows. Hence, to advance towards uniqueness I must project dynamically my most distinctive mode of energy upon my fellow-members.[15]

The rules are framed by reference to an infinite ideal pattern so that it would be impossible for anyone to succeed fully in following them. It is at this point that Adler makes a crucial move. No results actually achieved will ever satisfy the ethical demand. The *is* never coincides with the *ought.* What ought to be is that which can never become actual, empirical, phenomenal, or appear in any way to sense experience and become available to scientific scrutiny. He who seeks to fulfill his ethical obligation as a member of the ethical manifold will be sure to meet with at least partial frustration,

and yet in virtue of his ethical character he will always renew the effort. While in physical science the recurrence of phenomena supplies the occasion for exemplification or verification, in conduct, or the sphere of volition, not recurrence but the persistence of the effort

[14]*Ibid.,* p. 117.
[15]*Ibid.,* p. 118.

after defeat is at least a help to verification, arguing in one's self a consciousness, however obscured, of the relation of reciprocal interdependence and of subjection to the urge or pressure thence derived.[16]

What one does experience is the effort, and the pain associated with a striving, in which fulfillment is always only partial. The frustration can serve as a block to further effort, but it may also be seen as a sign of the partial realization of the ideal as an active force in one's life and may serve to intensify and vivify the ideal as an end to reformulate and strive for again. Adler offers a final formulation of his ethical rule, in order to connect it with actual and possible experience:

So act as to raise up in others the ideal of the relation of give and take, of universal interdependence in which they stand with an infinity of beings like themselves, members of the infinite universe, irreducible, like and unlike themselves in their respective uniqueness. . . .Whatever the symbolism may be, inadequate in any case, the idea of the enmeshing of one's life in universal life without loss of distinctness—the everlasting selfhood to be achieved on the contrary, by means of the cross-relation—is the cardinal point.[17]

It is clear that the units in the infinite manifold are human beings. Adler speaks of *members* of the ethical manifold instead of *parts* or *elements,* to distinguish the components of the ethical manifold from similar concepts in mathematics and the physical sciences. It is equally clear that the properties of the system, *qua* system, are precisely those which Adler takes to be necessary components of the idea of human worth.

The ethical ideal may be spoken of as the organic ideal if it is kept in mind that the organism is no natural phenomenon but an infinite organism. The *idea* of worth is to be understood in terms of the *idea* of the organic whole. The units of the infinite manifold, the parts of the infinite organism, *qua* units or parts, have worth. Making the application to human

16*Ibid.*
17*Ibid.*, pp. 118-119.

beings Adler says: "It is as an ethical unit, as a member of the infinite ethical manifold, that man has worth."[18]

Adler is very much aware that such a general account, taken by itself, must remain unconvincing. He is concerned primarily with the live human being. The meaning of worth must be seen to apply to the human being; it must not be lost in some abstract formulation. In the search for an adequate formulation of human worth, however, Adler is forced to a conception in which it may seem that the human person is lost. It is in this connection that he writes:

For the average man, and indeed for all men, the test of the truth of a theory is in the practice to which it leads. Abstract metaphysical arguments appeal only to a few, and even for them the formula in its abstract guise is unconvincing. Look at the mathematical figure, and see whether the axioms hold good. Look at the sequent phenomena and see whether the so-called law of nature is exemplified. And so with respect to conduct: look at the ways of human behavior traced out in accordance with the plan of the ethical manifold, and see whether such behavior wins the approval of the spiritual nature implicit within you.[19]

In a footnote to this paragraph, Adler adds: "The idea of the infinite society is a fulguration *out of* ethical experience, to be ever renewed in it. We build not only·our world, but our universe."[20]

Adler's statement of a categorical imperative serves as the base on which one can build the ethical universe, create the ethical manifold. Closer scrutiny of the various formulations of the rule is now in order.

First, for purposes of comparison we bring together Adler's three-step formulation, and then what he called his "final formulation." The three-step formulation is:

A. Act as a member of the ethical manifold (the infinite spiritual universe).

[18]*Ibid.*, p. 117.
[19]*Ibid.*, p. 134.
[20]*Ibid* (Italics in the original).

B. Act so to as to achieve uniqueness (complete individuation—the most completely individuated act is the most ethical).

C. Act so as to elicit in another the distinctive, unique quality characteristic of him as a fellow-member of the infinite whole.[21]

The final formulation is:

So act as to raise up in others the ideal of the relation of give and take, of universal interdependence in which they stand with an infinity of beings like themselves, members of the infinite universe, irreducible, like and unlike themselves in their respective uniqueness.[22]

Elsewhere Adler states this "chief ethical principle or rule" as follows:

So act as to release the best in others, and thereby you will release the best that is in yourself. Or, so act as to assist in bringing to light the unique excellence in others and thereby you will bring to light the unique excellence that is in yourself. Or, more precisely still, So act as to evoke in another the efficient idea of himself as a member of the infinite organism, and thereby corroborate in yourself the same efficient idea with respect to yourself.[23]

The main distinction to be marked between the three-step formulation and the final formulation is that the former is framed entirely in ideal terms. It could be call the supersensible imperative. The final formulation, which we will call the ethical imperative, takes account of the fact that we do not confront uniqueness. Adler says that uniqueness is incognizable. To ask that one act so as to achieve uniqueness in oneself and elicit uniqueness in others, as the supersensible imperative requires, is in effect to ask that man do the impossible. The ethical imperative recognizes this fact and requires only that

[21]*Ibid.,* p. 117.
[22]*Ibid.,* pp. 118-119.
[23]Adler, *The World Crisis and Its Meaning,* pp. 212-213 (This entire quotation is italicized in the text).

one act in terms of the idea and ideal of uniqueness, not in terms of uniqueness *per se*. The rendering of "uniqueness" as "the best in oneself" and as "unique excellence" is made to suggest the empirical aspect of the ethical rule.

Adler could not rest with only a supersensible formulation of the imperative because, stated wholly in ideal terms, the rule gives no lead at all to ethical action in the human community. Our concern at this point is to ask why the ethical formulation reads in just the way that it does.

We can divide this question into three parts. The first part concerns Adler's emphasis on "raising up in others the ideal. . . ." The question to be asked is: Why does Adler put such stress on the consciousness of the ideal?

The second part of the more general question is related to Adler's stress on uniqueness or distinctive excellence. The third part concerns the matter of the relations between persons. The second and third questions can be framed as follows: What has uniqueness to do with the ethical life? and What is the ethical significance of human interdependence?

Answers to these questions depend on an understanding of the general "connections"[24] Adler makes between his theoretical construct and the empirical world.

There are three major connections that Adler makes between the infinite ideal and the finite realm. The first connection has already been suggested. It is the idea that the elements or members of the infinite assemblage may be thought of as human beings. We may now add that in considering this manifold as infinite and nontemporal, it is possible to think of

---

[24]"Connection," as will be seen, does not refer to an ontological relation. Adler is not claiming knowledge of the relation between the sensible and supersensible realms. The idea of connection might be adequately rendered in the following phrase: treat such and such empirical phenomena as if they corresponded to such and such part of the supersensible complex. Technically what is at issue is the assignment of semantic meaning to parts of the supersensible "construct," which up to this point we have treated mainly as a syntactic system. The next step in Adler's argument is to call for an alteration of the empirical phenomena so that they will be more like their supersensible correlates than is now the case.

all human beings—the dead, the quick, and the as-yet-unborn—as having equal status in the manifold. Ethically considered, one does not cease to exist when one dies and the as-yet-unborn have as much right to consideration as those who are now alive. It should be stressed that this first connection is vital: without it the supersensible ideal would have no human significance.

The second assignment of semantic meaning is the connection Adler introduces between the concept of uniqueness and the actual, empirical differences among human beings. We must learn to prize differences above similarities:

a new habit [is] to be acquired in regard to the practical consequences of the theory. The chief of these is the prizing of distinctive difference above uniformity or sameness. The ethical quality is that quality in which a man is intrinsically unique. The ethical act is the most completely individualized act (I ought perhaps to say personalized, but the completely individualized act *is* that of a unique personality). In brief, the emphasis is here put on that in which a man differs from all others, and not on the common nature which he shares with the rest; or rather, since the common nature is not denied, the stress is put on the intrinsically different mode in which the common nature is expressed in him. . .[but]difference in the ethical meaning is not to be confounded with mere idiosyncrasy, or originality, not to say eccentricity. It is the kind of difference which elicits correlated difference in all spiritual associates.[25]

[25] Adler, *An Ethical Philosophy of Life*, p. 142. The balance of Adler's discussion at this point is not *directly* relevant to our present concerns, but it is of considerable historical interest, particularly in connection with Lovejoy's discussion of "Romanticism," which suggests that Adler might appropriately be called an "Ethical Romanticist." Adler writes: "The accentuation in current ethical discussion of the common nature of man, and the fallacious assumption that the common interests are the pre-eminently moral interests, that uniformity is the test of ethical quality, is easy to understand. It is the reaction of the modern world against feudalism, a social system not yet entirely outgrown, in which the empirical differences of rank and birth were made the basis of intolerably oppressive discriminations, and in which it was an accepted axiom that some men are baked of better clay than others. It is also a reaction against the capitalistic system that has taken the place of the feudal, in which wealth is to a considerable extent made the standard of social appraisement.

"It is against these false discriminations that the voice of humanity is now indignantly raised, affirming the moral equality of all men. But equality is

"The ethical act is the most completely individuated act." It
is also the kind of act which evokes in reaction individuated
(that is to say, ethical) acts from others. Adler does not allow
for the possibility that an act fully expressing a unique personality might fail to be answered in kind. In this context
Adler does not draw the distinction between the individuated
act and what we might call the individuating act or the act as
individuating. The difficulty is recognized, however, as Adler
speaks of acts that are merely idiosyncratic, original, or eccen-
tric. At the empirical level the problem is one of clearly identifying the act that is ethical and distinguishing it from the
merely odd or unusual act. In any event, Adler claims that
one should cultivate those differences "which elicit correlated
differences in all spiritual associates."[26]

mistakenly taken to mean likeness in the sense of sameness, not in the sense
of that fundamental likeness on the background of which the desirable unlikenesses stand forth. And this notion of equality as identical with sameness
leads to great practical aberrations. Thus, for instance, women are not only to
be recognized as the equals of men, but are to be the same as men,—their
education patterned on that of men, their specific functions, as far as possible,
ignored. For unlikeness is supposed to connote inferiority, and inferiority is
justly repelled as morally intolerable. But aside from this one example, the
stressing of the common nature, or of the basis of likeness at the expense of
the outstanding unlikenesses, leads to other leveling tendencies of which
modern democracies furnish many unpleasing illustrations. Thus uniform
popular opinion, encompassing the individual on every side, penetrates into
his inmost thinking, so that he hardly ventures to hold to his own judgment
against the judgments of the majority. And the impulses of the mass tend also
to threaten his independence in action. There is indeed a certain intoxication
in the very sense by being submerged in a large whole, a certain glad loss of
self in great impersonal movements, a certain strain of democratic pantheism,
as it were, that takes place with some of the mystic absorption in Deity. But
whatever the value that may attach to these unwellings of feelings, it is coun-
terbalanced by the circumstances that in proportion as indiscriminate devotion
to society as a whole becomes the paramount motive, the suborganisms of society, the family, the vocation and the state, in which the ethical personality is
ripened, are threatened with effacement. Instead of moral equality it were
better to use the term "moral equivalence." The differences are to be stressed;
they are the coruscating points in the spiritual life of mankind. That every
man is the equal of his fellows means that he has the same right as each of
the others to become unlike the others, to acquire a distinct personality, to
contribute his one peculiar ray to the white light of the spiritual life." Adler,
An Ethical Philosophy of Life, pp. 142-143. This aspect, at least, of Adler's position, could appropriately be termed "Ethical Romanticism."

[26]We note the similarity between Adler's formulation concerning differ-

Another citation from Adler will serve to illuminate the point just discussed and will also lead us to the third and last of the major connections we are considering. Adler writes:

For it must be remembered that the latent distinctive excellence which is here taken as the foundation of worth or personality is not a static, but a dynamic quality. It is not to be discovered by isolating man, by seeing him detached from his fellows. The idea of worth is a social idea. It deals with man in his relations. It sees in him a being essentially active, whose very life consists in affecting the life of others. *Worth, therefore, may be defined as that which provokes worth in others*, distinctive excellence as that which calls forth a reaction in others in the direction of their distinctive excellence. Ethics becomes a science of reactions.[27]

Adler's conception of uniqueness is part of the spiritual ideal. Ethical difference is its empirical counterpart. Ethical difference is the mark of the ethical person in Adler's philosophy of human worth.

Now "difference" names a relation. For X to be different, it must be "different from" something else. "Difference" names a connection. Worth, also, is attributable in terms of relations among humans. Worth is a social idea. The third assignment of semantic meaning to the spiritual ideal relates the organic character of the ideal, and the relation of reciprocal universal interdependence, with the actual social world in which man lives. Adler is not claiming that existent human society is ideal. Social and ethical relations are neither synonymous nor coincident. In fact, they are often contradictory. The interdepen-

---

ences and Dewey's statement as to the kind of growth he would foster. The following statement is characteristic of Dewey on this point: "That a man may grow in efficiency as a burglar, as a gangster, or as a corrupt politician, cannot be doubted. But from the standpoint of growth as education and education as growth the question is whether growth in this direction promotes or retards growth in general. Does this form of growth create conditions for further growth, or does it set up conditions that shut off the person who has growth in this particular direction from the occasion, stimuli, and opportunities for continuing growth in new directions." John Dewey, *Experience and Education* (New York: The Macmillan Company, 1938), pp. 28-29. Borrowing a phrase from the atomic age, we might call these the *fission* theories of ethical difference and growth respectively.

[27] Adler, *The World Crisis and Its Meaning*, p. 213 (italics not in the original).

dence of slave and master would be an example. But the social relations may be viewed as the substratum in which the
ethical relation may be worked out. The actual relations
among individuals, groups, nations, are the material to be organized, or as Adler says, ethicized.

Summarizing the three connections which for Adler connect
the infinite and the finite realms, we have (1) the members of
the infinite manifold seen as human beings, (2) supersensible
uniqueness linked with ethical differences among men, that is,
those differences that call forth correlated differences in
others, and (3) the possibility of universal reciprocal interdependence tied to the partial interdependence existing at all
levels in the human community.

We may now return to our three questions and consider
them in order. First, why does Adler put such stress on the
consciousness of the ideal? Part of the reason for his claim
that worth is an ideal is that, at the empirical level, human beings display many undesirable traits; furthermore, empirically,
it may sometimes be difficult to locate sufficient difference
among people to argue that one person could not be replaced
by any number of persons who are, for the most part, similar.
More importantly, worth is considered an ideal because, at the
sensible level, Adler attributes to all human beings the potential ability to elicit the distinctive mode of being in others and
themselves. That is to say, worth consists in large part in the
human being's potential for helping create a world in which
persons are in fact indispensable.

Now the demand that the ideal be conscious is made
primarily for two reasons. The first reason is simply that for
people to know where they are going, they must have an end
in mind. The ideal, ethically interpreted, is Adler's statement
of the highest end or goal. The second reason why Adler requires that the ideal remain conscious is somewhat more complex. If he is right in his claim that the demand for believing
oneself to have significance is in some sense or another virtually universal, then how can one account for the tremendous
amount of deprecation—of one's self and others—that we find

in human history? In this connection Adler stresses the fact that people do not seriously entertain even the possibility of their own worth. In these terms, the imperative to "raise the ideal" is to be understood as offering people a basis for conceiving of their own worth and the worth of others. If a person believed he had no potentiality for helping elicit the potential worth of either others or himself, he would seek no means for realizing this potential. To entertain an ideal seriously is to believe in the possibility of its realization. The ethical imperative may be interpreted as an attempt to bring people to an awareness of their ethical potential, their potential worth.[28]

Our two remaining questions are What has uniqueness to do with the ethical life? and What is the ethical significance of human interdependence? The primary point to be made is that the categorical imperative serves as a rule for marking out what is important in human life. It is true that the imperative also calls for action. But the action is focussed on specific aspects of man's existence. In the ideal formulation, the organic relation among unique entities is the focus of attention. At the empirical level their correlates are what should command our attention. Our first answer to both these questions is perhaps so obvious as to appear trivial: Adler is claiming that the relations between human beings are of prime importance. However, the force of this claim—and the sense in which it is not trivial, even in an ethical theory—becomes clear in contrasting Adler's claim of what is important with claims of the same order made in other ethical theories.

Without going into detail, we need only mention a few of the ethical positions against which Adler contrasts his own

[28]It is part of Adler's view that no one should think he had ever fully realized the ideal, or reached a point at which he could say about himself (or anyone else) that he actually had worth. Adler uses the term *actual* to describe the empirical realm. But it is not just as a logical contradiction that Adler means to say that empirically one cannot have a supersensible property. A full consciousness of the impassable gulf between the finite and the infinite is necessary on Adler's view. Adler does not put it this way, but it would appear that the sin of pride lies at just the point where one ceases to appreciate the existence of this gulf.

view. He sees all theologically-oriented ethics as taking the relation between men and God to be more important than the
relation between man and man. Evolutionary ethics, particularly the views we have come to know as "social Darwinism,"
put the highest value on the survival of the fittest. Plato and
Aristotle find the life of rational contemplation as most important. Capitalist ethics stresses individualism and the sacredness
of property, and socialist ethics stresses equality and improvement of material conditions. Adler would argue that, although he puts considerable stress on the spiritual ideal, this
ideal is so formulated as to place the human being at the very
center of the ethical concern.

The second part of our answer to these two questions (What
has uniqueness to do with the ethical life? and What is the
ethical significance of human interdependence?) relates to the
action required by the ethical imperative. Adler writes:

The task of mankind is to arrive through its commerce with the finite world, through its unremitting efforts to incorporate the infinite
plan within the sphere of human relations, at an increasingly explicit
conception of the ideal of the infinite universe; and through partial
success and frustration to seize the reality of that universe.[29]

In all situations Adler distinguishes between an empirical
substratum and the ethical relation potential in that substratum. The actual relations among men and groups, the actual difference among men and groups, the pain and frustration men suffer and the joys they realize and the work they
perform—all these are to be *used* to achieve and enhance a-
wareness of the ideal of the interdependence of unique persons. Adler speaks of this conception of use as "instrumentalism." It should not be confused with Dewey's use of the
term. Instrumentalism, for Adler, means simply that the empirical substratum should be used for ethical ends.[30]

[29]Adler, *An Ethical Philosophy of Life,* p. 175.

[30]"Thus the things of earth are to be used as instrumentalities by which we
are to become aware of the spiritual reality. Only that the disparateness of the
physical world and the ethical universe should ever be kept in the fore-

In its most simplified form, the process Adler envisages, and which is called for by the ethical imperative, may be stated as follows:

1. In some way, usually through some striving or effort associated with pain and/or frustration, one comes to a sense and conception of the spiritual ideal.
2. One recognizes that this ideal is a formulation of the most basic demand that he makes of life.
3. One proceeds to attempt to realize the ideal plan in his life.
4. It becomes clear that this attempt requires great and constant effort.
5. One sees some partial glimmerings of success, but mostly one meets with failure.
6. The experience of failure and frustration, despite the intense effort put forth, comes to be recognized as intrinsic to, and unavoidable in, the process of ethicizing.
7. The failure serves to clarify the meaning of a possible success. It is through failure and frustration that a more explicit conception of the ideal arises in one's mind.
8. A fuller awareness of the ideal brings a fuller sense of the unbridgeable distance between the finite life and the infinite ideal. This introduces a further frustration and hence a further possible heightening of awareness which in turn elicits renewed effort toward the realization, clarification, and reformulation of the ideal.

It should be noted that the above analysis is perfectly general in the sense that *any* empirical situation can be the theatre for the activity, the effort, the experiences of success, failure, frustration, and the possible fuller realization and appreciation of the ideal. Whatever situation man confronts may serve as a matrix for this process of ethicizing. Whatever empirical conditions exist, they are the conditions to be worked with and on. They are the substratum which is to receive the imprint of the ideal pattern. It is with the empirical conditions that the process of ethicizing begins and these are the condi-

ground. Every effort to solve the riddle by somehow identifying the two has failed. To account for the existence of a finite world of indefinite extensibility side by side with a universe *ex hypothesi* infinite is impossible. Instead of seeking to explain let effort go toward utilizing. Let the *world* be used instrumentally for the purpose of verifying the existence of *universe*." *Ibid.,* p. 134.

tions to be transformed. Actual conditions are, in this important sense, the beginning, middle, and end of ethical striving.

Since any actual situation is, as it were, grist for the ethical
mill, every person is equally in a position to put forth *his*
maximum effort. An individual's natural condition may prevent him from achieving a particular goal, or it may make
such a specific achievement a simple or trivial matter. But the
effort, the striving, and the direction the striving takes, define
ethical activity. It is not defined in terms of any specific goal
to be reached. The total empirical matrix, then, includes the
external conditions and the actual people involved at a particular time in a particular place. And no situation totally precludes the possibility of some ethicizing.

Worth and Empirical Man

Adler constantly reminds us of the distance between the finite and the infinite realms and of the difference between the
ideal and the actual. Of particular interest is his discussion of
worth in relation to man as an empirical being. In lectures
given at Columbia University, Adler analyzed four attempts to
find a basis for human worth. He claimed that the ability to
account for worth in *every* human being is the test of the
soundness of an ethical philosophy. The four systematic attempts with which he dealt are (1) the system that appeals to
human pity and tenderness, (2) the aesthetic view, (3) the
evolutionary view, and (4) the Kantian position.[31]

The appeal to pity, tenderness, and sympathy defines these
qualities as moral qualities, and the moral person as one who
has them. But, Adler argues, many people do not possess this
instinct and "by excluding them from the class of moral beings it strips them of their worth; for it must be remembered
that human beings have worth only insofar as they are
moral."[32] He argues further that the ethics of pity assumes the

[31]The following discussion is taken from material in Adler, *Ethics Based on
the Organic Ideal*, pp. 11-20.
[32]*Ibid.*, p. 18.

need for pity, which in turn presupposes evil in the world. But the escape from evil is easy through suicide or the Schopenhauerian denial of life.

Adler attributes the aesthetic view to both Plato and Aristotle. Morality for Plato consists in a love of transcendent beauty, and for Aristotle it is primarily linked with the pursuit of knowledge. In either case worth is ascribed only to the thinker, the philosopher. The large mass of humanity is ignored.

The morality of evolution is charged with the view that contribution to the world's progress, and to the development of the human race, is the prime moral quality. Thus, again, the majority of men fail to exhibit this quality. Even on a generous view of humanity, none of us are contributing all of the time, or even most of the time. Therefore on this principle most of us never have worth.

Given Adler's considerable debt to Kant, it is interesting to see what he chooses as the single criticism of Kant in this context. Adler cites the fact that Kant attributes moral worth to every human being on the basis of man's rational nature: "This is morality according to Kant. A man is moral if he acts according to his rational nature; if he acts according to a rule of universality and necessity. If he exemplifies these he is a moral being."[33] But if this means acting according to the form of Kant's law, then again most men, most of the time, cannot be claimed to be moral or have worth.

There is enough here by way of example to conclude that Adler must be critical of any ethical position locating or defining the moral in terms of any natural characteristic man might display.[34] We know that societies have run the gamut in this respect. There is no act, quality, or capacity that has not at some time in some culture been taken as moral—all the way

---

[33]*Ibid.,* p. 19.

[34]For a similar view, compare G. E. Moore, *Principia Ethica* (London: Cambridge University Press, 1903), particularly Chapters II and IV; also, E. M. Adams, *Ethical Naturalism and the Modern World-View* (Chapel Hill: The University of North Carolina Press, 1960).

from lying, cheating, stealing, scalping, and eating people, to the more "Christian" virtues of poverty, chastity, justice, faith, hope, and charity. And we must not forget Thrasymachus, Machiavelli, Borgia, and Hitler, as they claim the virtue of strength.

The difficulty of defining morality and justifying worth in terms of some natural characteristic that men may display is the fact that men display these characteristics in varying amounts—and in some cases they do not display them at all. For Adler, it is enough if *one* person could not display the characteristic chosen and prized, for the moral theory to fail as a justification of human worth. Adler demands that the claim for worth apply to all human beings.

For additional reasons as well, Adler objects to ethical theories associating morality and worth with the observable characteristics of men:

there are admittedly formidable difficulties in the way of attributing worth to human nature.

The first and most obvious of these is the existence of repulsive traits in human beings, such as sly cunning, deceit, falsehood, grossness, cruelty: *homo homini lupus!* Secondly, there is the prevalent error of employing ethical terms, like good and bad, to denote the merely attractive and repellent traits. Attractive traits, such as gentleness, sweetness, kindness, a sympathetic disposition, are, in those fortunate enough to possess them, pleasing accidents of nature. We delight in them, but have no reason to ascribe the superlative quality of worth to those who possess them. If the evil that men do revolts us, the so-called good in them does not give us the right to surround their heads with the nimbus of worth. Thirdly and perhaps even more deterrent than the ever-present spectacle of evil and the inadequacy of so-called goodness, is the commonplaceness, the cheapness of men.[35]

Speaking on this same point, Adler later states:

Judging from the point of view of bare fact, many of us could very well be spared. Many are even in the way of what is called "progress." And the suggestion of some extreme disciples of Darwin that the degenerate and defective should be removed, or the opinion of

[35] Adler, *An Ethical Philosophy of Life,* pp. 91-92.

others that pestilence and war should be allowed to take the unpleasant business off our hands, is, from the empirical point of view, not easily to be refuted. I can also enter into, if I do not wholly share, the pessimistic mood with regard to actual human nature expressed by Schopenhauer and others. To the list of repulsive human creatures mentioned by Marcus Aurelius in one of his morning meditations,—the back-biter, the scandal-monger, the informer, etc.—might be added in modern times, the white slaver, the exploiter of child-labor, the fawning politician, and many another revolting type. And even more discouraging in a way, than these examples of deepest human debasement—the copper natures, as Plato calls them, or the leaden natures, as we might call them—is the disillusionment we often experience with regard to the so-called gold natures, the discovery of the large admixture of baser metal which is often combined with their gold.

It is imperative to acquaint oneself, nay, to impregnate one's mind thoroughly with these contrary facts, if the doctrine of worth, the sanest and to my mind the most real of all conceptions, is to be saved from the appearance of an optimistic illusion.[36]

The conclusion Adler repeats in many forms is that one cannot make the case for worth on purely empirical grounds. Worth is an ideal, and an ideal is for Adler, by definition, not achievable. Any description of *what is,* any purely empirical account, will not do justice to an ethical ideal. To suggest that *what is* coincides with what *ought to be,* would not necessarily collapse the distinction between *is* and *ought,* but it would be equivalent to saying that this is the best of all possible worlds. This is a path Adler cannot follow. In fact, he almost moves to the other end of the spectrum as he frames his ideas in terms of an infinite aggregate. At its core, Adler's ethics is an ethics of perfection. Ethically, the *is* and the *ought* can never be the same.[37]

How then can Adler make a case for *human* worth? He has conceived a universe the like of which never was and never will be. And it is in such a universe that a human being is

[36]*Ibid.,* pp. 120-121.

[37]At the *ethical* level, the distinction between *is* and *ought* is a distinction between the actual and the ideal, which can never be the same. But the ethical level must be distinguished from the divine, supersensible level. Speaking of the latter, Adler calls the ideal infinite universe "that which truly exists," that is, ultimate reality. In these terms the *is* and the *ought* are identical.

supposed to have worth. Once more, he blocks himself from any claims to worth on empirical grounds:

> The answer. . .is that I do not *find* worth in others or in myself, I attribute it to them and to myself. And why do I attribute it? In virtue of the reality-producing functions of my own mind. I *create* the ethical manifold.[38]

Unlike the content of the empirical manifolds science synthesizes, the content of the ethical manifold is not found or given in experience, according to Adler. But the *demand* to create that manifold apparently occurs within experience, for Adler goes on to say:

The pressure of the essential rationality within me, seeking to complete itself in the perfect fruition of these functions, i.e., in the positing of a total manifold and its total unification, drives me forward. I need an idea of the whole in order to act rightly, in such a way as to satisfy the dual functions within me. My own nature as a spiritual being urges me to seek this satisfaction. This ideal whole, as I have shown, is a complexus of uniquely differentiated units. In order to advance toward uniqueness, in order to achieve what in a word may be called my own truth, to build myself into the truth, to become essentially real, I must seek to elicit the consciousness of the uniqueness and the interrelation in others. I must help others in order to save myself; I must look upon the other as an ethical unit or moral being in order to become a moral being myself. And wherever I find consciousness of relation, of connectedness, even incipient, I project myself upon that consciousness, with a view to awaking in it the consciousness of universal connectedness. Wherever I can hope to get a response I test my power. Fields and trees do not speak to me, as Socrates said, but human beings do. I should attribute worth to stones and to animals could they respond, were the power of forming ideas, without which the idea of relation or connectedness is impossible, apparent in them. Doubtless stones and trees and animals and the physical world itself, are by the screen behind which lies the infinite universe. But the light of that universe does not break through the screen where it is made up of stones and trees and the lower animals. It breaks through, however, faintly, where there is consciousness of relation: and wherever I discover that consciousness I find my opportunity. . .the question is not whether we get the re-

[38]Adler, *An Ethical Philosophy of Life,* p. 121.

sponse but whether we shall achieve reality or truth ourselves; in theological terms, save our own life, by trying to elicit the response.[39]

The demands of which Adler speaks are rooted in what he calls ethical experiences. Distinguishing his theory from Kant's, he says that it "is not a transcendental derivation of ethics. The ideal of the infinite society is a fulguration *out of* ethical experience, to be ever renewed in it."[40] What kinds of experiences are distinctively ethical experiences? It is to the answer to this question, and its significance, to which we now turn.

Ethical Experience and Ethical Theory

The primary problem peculiar to ethical consciousness is one with which we are already familiar: the problem of feeling compelled to attribute worth to all human beings, including ourselves, despite the fact that we and others are always much less than worthy. Horace L. Friess writes:

The special class of facts which ethics is charged to interpret, as Adler saw it, is an order of facts expressive of the efforts of the whole personality to relate itself to other selves in an active and transforming way with respect for ideal potentialities. It may also be defined as the field of the experience of personal worth, of unique and indefeasible selfhood recoiling from twisted relations with others as from an injury and longing for companionship with the best in every nature. It embraces such distinctive inner experiences as violation, remorse, obligation, respect, love, reverence, and the like.[41]

All of these inner experiences are familiar subject matter for the poet, the dramatist, and the social scientist. The critic will be quick to say that there is nothing distinctively *ethical* about any of these experiences. Adler will not, of course, deny that such experiences are proper material for the artist or sci-

[39]*Ibid.*, pp. 121-122.
[40]*Ibid.*, p. 134n.
[41]*Ethical Theory and the Quest for Truth* (unpublished manuscript, 1943), p. 19.

entist. But he finds a characteristic that he takes as the mark of the ethical. The key word in the Friess quotation above is *effort*. A striving toward the highest and most inclusive is the distinctively ethical striving. Such striving requires that the will, the feelings, and the intellect put forth their maximum effort, their greatest stretch in the moment of action.

Stretch, effort, and *action* are terms central to Adler's discussion, as he defines the characteristics of ethical experience. The ethical process is marked by a reaching out of one's own self to other selves. Adler suggests that we think of an ethical energy underlying this "reaching out":

There is in particular one kind of energy to which the quality of worth may well attach itself. It is unlike the physical forces; it is not a transformed mode of mechanical energy. It is *sui generis*, underivative, unique; it is synonymous with highest freedom; it is power raised to the Nth degree. It is ethical energy. To release it in oneself is to achieve unbounded expansion. Morality, as commonly understood, is a system of rules, chiefly repressive. Ethical energy, on the contrary, is determined by the very opposite tendency; a tendency it is true never more than tentatively effectuated under finite conditions.[42]

This leads Adler to say that

ethics is a science of energetics, which has to do with the potencies of our nature in their most affirmative efferent expression. All our higher faculties are active, and touch for good or ill the lives of those who surround us. Even the secret thoughts which seem only to affect our own individuality, inevitably project their influence upon our associates. . .ethics is a science of right energizing.[43]

Adler also speaks of ethics as the science of relations, meaning the science of formulating the ideal relations among people.[44] On the basis of an ethical principle, one idealizes the actual, sees the ethical possibilities in concrete situations; sees, as it were, the *ought* in the *is*. Still another formulation or

[42]Adler, *An Ethical Philosophy of Life*, pp. 92-93.
[43]*Ibid.*, p. 221.
[44]*Ibid.*, p. 233.

characterization of ethics is as the science of the unity of ends.[45] Unfortunately, Adler never synthesized these three characterizations of ethics in a single, systematic statement. We take it that each of these formulations specifies a somewhat different aspect of, or emphasis in, ethical theory.

The clue to Adler's thinking about ends is found in a passage in which he criticizes Kant's conception of an end *per se:*

the notion of end is incompatible with self-consistency as the paramount principle in ethics. For a self-consistent rational being is a being in harmony with himself, one who if this harmony should in some unaccountable way ever be broken would by his own endeavor seek to return to himself. (Kant declares that the morality of any one man cannot be affected by his fellows, by any influence from the outside; it must be his own act.) But an end presupposes some outside object as a means: means and ends are inseparable correlatives. On the other hand, an entity which merely affirms itself, or if somehow alienated from self endeavors without assistance from beyond its sphere to return to itself, is no true end at all, and cannot be designated as such. It is no end because it employs no means.[46]

There is a sense in which energetics, ideal relations, and ends can all be seen as pointing to the *ends* in the means-ends polarity. Energetics suggests potencies, potentialities not yet realized. The ideal relations also are not actual, but only potential or possible at any given time. And *end* itself explicitly refers to the ideal to be sought.

As regards *means:* energetics leads us to a study of human beings as the locus of potentiality; relations suggest the actual human relations which are the very things to be idealized. The unity of ends, considered from the standpoint of means, presents a problem men must resolve—the problem of creating a harmony of the powers of human beings in their relation to one another.

In exploring the differences in Adler's three formulations of ethics, we must turn to the contexts in which these formu-

[45]Adler, "Columbia University Notes" (unpublished notes, New York, 1906), p. 1.
[46]Adler, *An Ethical Philosophy of Life,* pp. 87-88.

lations appear. It seems that energetics and relations apply to
practical ethics. They are meant to lead us to a consideration
of concrete situations. This is partly true of the conception of
the unity of ends as well, but this expression seems to refer
more to theoretical concerns. It is, in the first place, more
openly a conception of an ideal. The unity of ends refers to
the unity of that having the ideal attribute of worth, that is,
the unity of human beings. It also refers to that unity in
which all human beings serve as means for each and every
other human being.

Thus, according to Adler, one starts with ethical experiences as the basic ethical facts. Ethical experiences are inner
experiences which are a function of the relation of a person
with other persons. Ethical experiences are also characterized
by an *effort* of the whole person (or we might say a total effort
by the person) to fulfill or complete himself in relation to
others. Ethical experience is conceived as both dynamic and
teleological. The task of ethical theory is to articulate and do
justice to this experience. The conception of worth is Adler's
interpretation of the fundamental goal of all the dynamic
striving included under the heading "ethical experience." It is
in these terms that Adler speaks of a distinctively ethical approach:

a genuine philosophy of life can only be reached by the ethical approach to the problems of life. This has never yet been consistently
attempted. The approach has been made from the scientific or the
logical side, or as in the case of Plato from the aesthetic, or as in
modern times from the biological. Yet the ethical approach is full of
promise. A philosophy of physical nature may be feasible without it,
a philosophy of art may be possible without it, but not a philosophy
of life. It has not been tried because ethics has lain in the lap of
theology, which was itself corrupted by the attempt to apply to ethical problems the inadequate principle of causality in the form of creation theories, while again in recent times, by way of reaction against
theology, the solution of ethical questions is sought for in the empirical disciplines where a measure at least of objective certainty has re-
warded the investigators. Even Kant, who asserted the independence
of ethics, actually made it dependent on Newtonian science. The

great task now is, strictly to carry out the idea of the independence of ethics, not indeed as if its principles were unrelated to those of science and art, but in the sense of independently investigating the problems peculiar to ethical consciousness.[47]

And in another place Adler says:

To borrow the first principle of ethics from some other field is a common and apparently ineradicable error. Mechanics, aesthetics, and recently biology, have been laid under contribution for this purpose. A consistent attempt to study ethical phenomena on their own ground, to mark off what is really distinctive in the data of ethical experience, and then to search for some principle which shall serve to give a coherent account of them, has to my knowledge never yet been undertaken. Always ethics has been treated as an annex to some other discipline. Always we behold the attempt to assimilate before the distinctive traits and characteristics have been carefully investigated. Never yet has the independence of this wonderful aspect of human nature been truly acknowledged. Kant indeed freed ethics from its long tutelage to theology; but he left it still in subjection, subject to his own favorite study, physical science.[48]

One can see that Adler's line of thought in the above quotations proceeds in the following order: (1) we require a distinctively ethical approach to ethical matters; (2) this approach involves investigations of the problems peculiar to ethical consciousness; (3) we must identify what is distinctive in the data of ethical experience; and (4) ethical principles will be principles that give coherence to the data of ethical experience. Adler insists

that the first principles of ethics be extracted from the study of *ethical facts* and not from the study of physical or biological facts [and that the] attempt to determine what may be the connection of the principles of ethics with the principles of other sciences [must wait] until these ethical principles themselves shall have been established on their own ground and in their own right.[49]

[47]*Ibid.*, pp. 132-133.
[48]*Ibid.*, pp. 84-85.
[49]Adler, "Columbia University Notes" (unpublished notes, New York, 1903), pp. 11-12.

We may conclude this part of our work by trying to summarize Adler's conception of ethical theory, taking as our guide the four points stated in the above paragraph.

The approach Adler takes to matters he would characterize as "distinctively ethical" can perhaps best be pinpointed by noting the major concepts dominating his thought. Ethical concern is a concern with the *ideal,* with perfection. This ideal is the *ultimate end* or *goal* of all *human conduct.* This perfection must include *all human beings* in *relation* to one another.

Ethical knowledge is like other kinds of knowledge insofar as it depends on the reality-producing functions of the mind. It is unlike all other kinds of knowledge in that both the manifold and the synthesis of the manifold of ethics are ideal rather than actual. From the ethical point of view we deal with potentialities rather than actualities.

The problems peculiar to ethical consciousness are the kinds of problems discussed earlier in connection with the historical dimensions of worth. And we have just seen Horace L. Friess characterize them as problems in "the field of the experience of personal worth, of unique and indefeasible selfhood recoiling from twisted relations with others. . . ."[50]

The distinctive ethical aspect of such experience lies in the activity and the effort which it may stimulate. The direction of this effort-full activity is given by Adler in his formulation of the ideal and the supreme ethical rule. It is the supreme ethical rule which Adler offers as the primary regulative rule for ethical conduct.

[50]*Supra.,* p. 129.

Part II. Education

CHAPTER 4

Education for Human Worth

In one sense Adler's ethics is an ethics of perfection. It is in this sense that Adler speaks of persons as *having* worth. The conception of the ideal is Adler's attempt at characterizing that mode of relation among humans, as regards particularly their spiritual being, in which each person can be said to have worth.

But there is an equally important sense in which Adler's ethics is an ethics of development. Human development is, for Adler, the process of narrowing the gap between any given state of affairs and the ideal. It is in this connection, as we have seen, that Adler speaks of ethics as a science of energetics or a science of right energizing. Human development and human relations involve the play of potencies of persons on one another. Such development occurs willy-nilly. To introduce the notion of an ethical development is, for Adler, to introduce a regulative rule, an ideal, which serves to define right relations and right development. It also serves as a criterion for judging instances of development.

For the individual, perfection means full realization of uniqueness: what Adler calls personality. In connection with perfection, Adler speaks of ethics as the science of the unity of ends. The focus is on the spiritual realm in which each person's uniqueness is fully realized and fully efficacious in evoking comparable effective uniqueness in all other persons.

Previous chapters have been concerned primarily with an exposition and analysis of Adler's ethics insofar as it is an ethics of perfection. From the point of view of perfection, the question of development does not arise. As we turn our attention to the question of development, we set the stage for a serious consideration of education, or better, for the process of educating.

If the ideal defines the end of education, it is the process of ethicizing that comprises the most general statement of means for moving in the direction of the end—or, to put this in more dynamic terms—the process of ethicizing defines ethical action. This process of ethicizing not only has impact on others; it also has impact on oneself or on the agent in question. Ethical action is neither simply other-regarding or self-regarding; it cannot be characterized either as altruistic or egoistic. Using these terms, one would have to say that Adler's ethical action is *both*—and at the same time. Ethical action will always be directed toward the goal of a full realization of uniqueness on the part of all persons involved, and a fuller realization of the ideal which no one is ever able to realize wholly. This change, which is deliberately sought for oneself and for others, is the root meaning of education in Adler's thought.

Education as the Process of Ethicizing

The process of education is essentially the process of ethicizing. Adler himself does not make this identification explicit. It is the purpose of this section to show that such an identification is warranted, if not indeed logically implicit in his statements, and further, to examine the import of the identification.

Education, for Adler, is a normative enterprise; it is an activity directed toward an end. Achievement of the end is a criterion for judging the efficacy of the means. An adequate conception of education would include not only efficacious means but also an adequate end. Adler is not unconcerned with means, but his main interest is with a satisfactory conception of the primary end or aim of education. For him, the supreme aim of education must be the realization of the spiritual ideal. But, as we have seen, Adler claims that the ideal can never be actualized. Thus, realization cannot mean actualization. Instead, realization means first, a growing awareness of the ideal and secondly, a working toward actualization in each and every circumstance of life. The effort toward realization should extend throughout life. The ideal marks a direction and defines a way of life. It is not a description of some particular ideal state of affairs.[1]

To say that the supreme end of education is the realization of an ideal which can never be actualized—and that this realization consists in a process of increasing awareness and striving—is to suggest that education can never be fully accomplished or completed. The process of ethicizing is an unending process which is defined by the supreme ethical rule: *"So act as to release the best in others, and thereby you will release the best that is in yourself. Or, So act as to assist in bringing to light the unique excellence in others, and thereby you will bring to light the unique excellence that is in yourself. Or, more precisely still, So act as to evoke in another the efficient ideal of himself as a member of the infinite organism, and thereby corroborate in yourself the same efficient idea with respect to yourself."*[2]

This rule defining the ethical act calls for that kind of action from the agent which will influence or alter others in such a fashion that their unique excellences will become increasingly manifest. This deliberate act on the part of the agent is directed toward others and its explicit concern is with changing them. Such a conception of ethics and ethical action, with its stress on bringing about change in human beings, warrants the characterization of an educational ethics.[3] For it can now be seen that the primary ethical or ethicizing act, defining the change sought in terms of the chief ethical princi-

[1]Friess, "Felix Adler's Conception of Education," *The Standard,* XX:5 (February, 1934), cf. p. 120.

[2]Adler, *The World Crisis and Its Meaning,* pp. 212-213 (italics in the original).

[3]By the same token, Adler's continuing preoccupation with the ultimate end he sets for education suggests that his philosophy of education might well be called an ethical philosophy of education. But to say "philosophy of ethical education" would be to miss the point. For it is not simply a matter of ethical education, if this is taken to suggest a comparison with physical or mathematical education. Ethics is not to be understood simply as a particular subject matter to be taught alongside of other subject matters (although Adler did propose, and Ethical Culture Schools still offer, such a separate course in ethics at every grade level).

ple or regulative rule, must also constitute the primary educative act. It should be added also that since Adler claims that
action on the basis of the regulative rule is the way to ethicize
oneself as well as others, this "chief ethical principle" constitutes a directive for self-education as well as for educating
others.

We must here distinguish sharply between education and
schooling. It should be clear from the above that "educating"
is a responsibility of all men and of all institutions if they
would act ethically. In Chapter VII we will examine Adler's
views on the school's particular obligations and contributions
in this regard. Here we will consider further the breadth of
his conception of education, and the resultant extent to which
Adler identifies ethics and education. Both are revealed elo-
quently in an early address to the New York Society for Ethical Culture. In this address, Adler strongly suggests that his
educational theory is indeed his ethical theory:

> The Ethical Movement stands for the idea that personal relations,
> between individuals and between group and group, are of supreme
> concern. . . .Through right personal relations, that is where you get
> life; there are the springs of the eternal fountain. . . .The Ethical
> Movement stands. . .for the idea that morality is positive and not es-
> sentially negative. The moral man is not the anaemic man. The
> moral man, as I think of him, is exactly the man who exceeds in
> terms of vitality and of supreme effectiveness. The most vitality be-
> longs to and is manifested by the man who most emphasizes that
> which is peculiar to the human being and distinctive of him. That
> includes science, and art, and morality. It means the spiritual gift
> which is really the human thing in us, namely the power of seeing
> together things that seem discrepant and unrelated, the unique
> power of reaching out with the mind and bringing into harmony
> things that seem repugnant. That is the essence of our distinctively
> human qualities.
>
> In this sense, the Ethical Movement is a movement for the educa-
> tion of mankind. And I mean all mankind. I am not confining myself
> to our immediate surroundings in America and in Europe. I am bold
> enough to think of mankind as embracing the Orient as well as the
> Occident. We must judge our western civilization, on its ethical side,
> not by what it means to us alone, but by what it is worth to the east-
> ern civilizations as well, how it affects them in their attempt at ethical

development. In our Movement we can not take a less inclusive point of view, and whatever our numbers may be, this idea of the scope of the Movement is bound to have its way because of the need for it.[4]

Now if we have shown the considerable extent to which ethics and education are identified for Adler, it remains to show the way in which the ethical-educational theory can be brought to apply to specific situations. The theory considered alone does not reveal this—not only because of its generality and breadth, but also because of Adler's strong contextualism. One cannot know how to pursue the ideal at a particular time and place in history without reference to the events and conditions of the times, the spiritual pains these evoke, *et cetera.* Thus the individual who seeks to ethicize or educate must refer to "the empirical substratum" or, more simply, to the relevant facts of his time.

In the following sections we will consider Adler's characterization of the empirical substratum of his own age. The next section deals with Adler's understanding of the most general and pervasive traits of the early twentieth-century Western world. It constitutes a macroscopic look at the contemporary scene. In the following section the focus is on the microscopic, with an examination of the condition of individuals and the specific relations in which they stand to one another. Following these detailed considerations of the empirical substratum, we are ready to consider the question of the nature of ethical development. Thus the closing section of this chapter deals with what we call ethico-genesis.

The Empirical Macrocosm

The following discussion starts with Adler's comments on World War I and his diagnosis of its causes in terms of nationalism, moves then to the problem of individualism, and finally to the issue of specialization. There are two primary purposes for bringing these issues together in one discussion:

[4]Friess (ed.), *Our Part in This World: Interpretations by Felix Adler,* pp. 57-58.

(1) to present some sense of what Adler found in his world, particularly in the first two decades of this century, and (2) to show that what Adler saw as of central concern is always a matter of the relations among people, the relations among groups, and the relations of groups and individuals.

Sometime early in World War I (before the United States entered the war), Adler wrote:

The feeling that should predominate in America at this time is grief, not wrath. Since the world began there has been no such war. But the things now happening are too vast for spite and ancestral animosities, or even for the indulgence of moral indignation. What is it that has thrown civilization so suddenly out of its reckoning? Why this descent from the levels of culture and broadening brotherhood into the depths of brutality? Why do the peasants leave the harvests ungathered, to be themselves mowed down by a sharp, bloody scythe? Why are the gates of the universities closed? Why do the younger generation of scientists abandon their researches into the secrets of nature, prophetic of a beneficent extension of human knowledge, in order to join in the work of destruction? Why do the finest intelligences, the mental elite, fall in line with the dull, equally to lay down their heads on the great block? Why does the musician set aside his instrument on which he was wont to discourse music that touched and uplifted the soul, in order to mingle his voice with the hoarse cries of squadrons advancing to the charge, or with the despairing wail of the wounded? Why do fathers and husbands leave wives and children to slay other fathers and husbands who also have left clinging dear ones across the fatal border? Why do youths reared in all the gentleness of highbred social intercourse, suddenly take, as if they were beasts of the jungle, to the work of slaughter. The voice of lamentation is heard from Ramah; it is Rachel weeping for her children. It is the mother of humanity weeping for all those dead of many nations.

A great cloud has settled on the world. We are at the center of the darkness.[5]

In such a setting we see Adler's ethical theory as it becomes articulate regarding educational concerns. Adler's diagnosis of the causes of World War I is summed up in the following statement: "The unbounded affirmation of nationalism is the

[5]Adler, *The World Crisis and Its Meaning,* pp. 1-2.

ultimate cause of the struggle which we are witnessing."[6] And he goes on to say:

Nationalism has its source in the kinship we feel with those who use the same language, who observe the same manners and customs, who sing the same songs, who have the heritage of a common literature, a common history—in a word, who belong to the same type of human beings as ourselves. There are many types of humanity. You see a certain pattern worked out on a rug or a wall paper; you can follow the lines and the inter-weaving of the colors, their contrasts and their blendings. So there are certain mental patterns. Every one of the great nations represents a certain mental pattern of its own: certain ways of thinking about things, certain ways of feeling, a certain attitude towards life, a certain tincture of sentiment. The soul, the genius of one nation, is different from that of the others, the manners are different. The English lyric is unlike the German lyric. No great masterpiece of one literature has ever been successfully translated into another. It is especially language that distinguishes; a foreign idiom is a straitjacket—very few, even among educated persons, can express themselves freely in a language other than their own; they may be able to read a foreign language fluently, but when it comes to expressing their inmost thought, they feel more or less constrained. The wellspring of nationalism is the feeling of attraction towards those who speak as we do, and who understand us when we speak, those whose minds bear imprinted upon them the same pattern as our own.[7]

Underlying this description of the causes of World War I is a much more fundamental and pervasive mode of analysis which Adler applies to most, if not all, of the actual situations which he confronted. The analysis turns on Adler's understanding of the relation between the one and the many. His criticisms can be understood as application of his notion that the one and the many are polar categories which cannot properly be used separately.

We must notice first that, at the most general or philosophical level of analysis, *one* and *many* are empty of any specific empirical content. Thus, their use as tools for analysis de-

[6]*Ibid.*, p. 18.
[7]*Ibid.*, pp. 19-20.

pends on their relation to one another, *qua* concepts. When Adler writes:

> We are witnessing a vast struggle of the types of civilization with one another, each claiming superlative and exclusive value for itself, and therefore intolerant of the existence and claims of the others. Each of the great stocks that are at war is fighting for its supremacy in the belief that on its supremacy depends the existence of the mental pattern which it cherishes above all else—above peace, above pecuniary property, above the life of the millions who are sacrificed in the conflict.[8]

he is calling attention to, within the context of a plurality (or manifold) of nations, the perception on the part of each nation that its *oneness* takes priority over the existent plurality. Put more strongly, for the nationalist, the unity defined in terms of his nation is the unity which is, and should be accepted by all, as defining culture and civilization—what is highest and best. The logical error is to try to define the manifold in terms of the one. As we remember the use to which Adler puts the logical principle in the framing of his ethical position, we see that this logical error becomes an ethical error. Thus, this exclusive type of nationalism is morally wrong.

It is precisely this same mode of analysis that Adler brings to bear on what he described as excessive individualism. He found this individualism in the laissez-faire conception of man in his economic dealing and in what he took to be a perverted conception of democratic equality. Here an independent, self-sufficient, individual citizen's personal wishes and interests were considered to be the final court of appeal for matters economic, social, political, educational, and ethical.

Adler also saw this individualism manifest in the changing conception of the family and family relations in which mother, father, and children were all autonomous beings each seeking his or her own individual happiness. As the husband-wife relation was perceived as a mutual servicing of the happiness of

[8]*Ibid.*, p. 22.

the other, unhappiness as felt by one of the partners seemed sufficient ground for divorce. Children, too, from the point of view of the parents, were sources of pleasure or displeasure and were valued accordingly. The children in turn learn this mode of evaluation very quickly and accept or reject their parents (and everyone else) accordingly. Adler saw this same extreme individualism as pervading the schools in terms of fundamental aims, the structure of the curriculum, the methods of instruction, and the basis of evaluation, both of the students, *qua* students, and of the school as an institution.

Again, the individualistic error shows itself in insufficient recognition and regard for others. Empirically it does not take into account the actual dependence and even interdependence that links people to one another. This error leads to a mythical conception of the autonomous man. The individualistic position, usually formulated as ethical egoism, fails as an ethical position, for Adler, partly because it completely misreads the empirical facts of human life so that it pays homage to an utter impossibility. But probably more important, as an argument for Adler, is the fact that egoism is incapable of serving as an adequate basis for the one ethical fact which he said he could not doubt, namely, that each and every human being had worth. Adler met the problem of the self-sufficient, atomic individual in Kant's ethical position. His rejection of Kant's views turns, in large part, on the argument that no isolated thing can be said to have worth. It is not enough simply to enunciate a law which applies equally to all individuals. This would be no genuine synthesis of a manifold. An adequate synthesis requires a conception of the interaction or interdependence of individuals. It is just such a rule of relations that all atomistic conceptions of man and all individualistic ethical theories fail to provide. The fruits of this inadequacy, from both a descriptive and a normative point of view, are seen by Adler in such diverse phenomena as an increasing rate of divorce and the First World War.

There is one other very important phenomenon which Adler discussed and which he thought was not only characteristic of his time, but which presented one of the gravest problems to be resolved by an adequate ethical theory in conjunction with a reconstruction of the educational enterprise. This phenomenon is discussed under the heading of *specialization.* Adler is noting a consequence both of the tremendous increase in knowledge and of the range of activities available to people since the Middle Ages. Since Adler's time, not only has there been a substantial increase in knowledge, particularly in the sciences, and a further rationalizing and fragmentation of function in all walks of life, there has even been a marked increase in the rate at which knowledge is accumulating and in the proliferation of kinds of work. We have, therefore, no difficulty in understanding what Adler perceived in the early decades of this century.

Although the primary causes of this specialization in business, industry, and the academic world, were not to be understood in ethical terms, the ethical consequence of this specialization was of particular concern, for it intimately affects the relations in which people stand to one another—both as individuals and as members of groups. Specialization also has a tremendous impact on the way individuals perceive themselves, their relations with others and the world, and, not least, what is possible and what is appropriate as regards their whole life pattern, including work, play, relations to others, community participation, and all the rest. As we shall see, the fact of specialization plays a very special role in Adler's conception of schooling.

What is important to us at this juncture is to see that the conception of specialization offers Adler another opportunity to apply his one-many analysis. Specialization emphasizes the manifold of particular activities in which people engage. Adler has no argument with specialization *per se.* He recognizes it, even applauds it as a necessary response to the increased diversity of kinds of work and knowledge. Given this diversity of jobs and the increase in available knowledge, specialization is the only possible answer to the need for competency. But the price of competency, of expertise, is very high. High competency in one area tends to mean either no, or very low, competency in other areas. Even this, by itself, might not be too serious. The serious issue arises as one perceives what happens to the relations among people who are, with rare exceptions, expert in their own area of endeavor and mostly inexpert in all other areas. The differences in experience, in the language or jargon that builds up around an area of work, and the rather significant consequent differences in perspective—in the way the world is seen—all intensify the difficulty of communication and lead to a peculiar kind of isolation of the expert from the rest of the public, the lay public, which in one way or the other is served by the expert. Adler does not state it in quite this way, but the situation that we have been describing may be stated as a paradox: interdependence creates the need for the specialist, but specialization itself creates a situation that makes it extremely difficult for these specialists adequately to serve the very need which in a sense produced them.[9]

Everywhere Adler looked he saw people defending either an oppressive kind of unity (of the individual or the group) or an anarchic kind of plurality or a combination of both. Adler confronts this issue at every level and in every facet of his theorizing: in his metaphysics and epistemology; in the various aspects of the ethical and educational theory; and in the detailed discussions of such matters as the use of property, the marriage relationship, the nature of vocation, and the problems of an Ethical Culture "Leader." In terms of the present discussion, nationalism, individualism, and specialism are seen, by Adler, as exhibiting the same kind of difficulty. It is, as we have suggested earlier, the central issue of Adler's thought, that is, the problem of worth—but now set in empirical terms.

---

[9]I know of no better statement of this problem as it exists today than that offered by J. Robert Oppenheimer. Many of his papers deal with this issue in detail. See particularly the collection of essays, *The Open Mind* (New York: Simon and Schuster, Inc., 1955). As specialization proceeds in theoretical physics, Oppenheimer is concerned with the breakdown of communication *among* the physicists!

The Empirical Microcosm

Despite, or, in face of the fact, that Adler centered a great deal of his thinking on the problem of the morality of groups, even to the extent of claiming that a more adequate conception of such a morality was the major problem of his day, it is still possible to assert that the individual human being was the basic focus of both Adler's practical and theoretical concerns. His whole theoretical endeavor may be read as an attempt to establish an adequate sense and conception of the worth of the person. We have seen that Adler is not able to attribute worth to man *qua* empirical man. But empirical man is the substratum, the material which one confronts and with which one must deal. Since it is empirical man who is to be ethicized, it is necessary that we know how Adler characterized this man.[10]

In his writings, Adler does not explicitly draw from any

[10]It is necessary to introduce a terminological note. In speaking of the worth of man, he distinguishes between the supersensible and the sensible realms and between the spiritual and the empirical. The affirmation of human worth gains its full meaning as man is considered at the supersensible level. The notions of complete uniqueness and indispensability are likewise "supersensible" ideas. Even the notion of person is, in the strictest sense, a supersensible notion. Thus when Adler speaks of personality and the realization of personality, it is a supersensible reference that he is making. He is talking about man, *qua* spiritual being—a member of the supersensible realm.

Adler uses the term *personality* as a shorthand for referring to the person as a wholly unique member of the universe. The *term* personality adds nothing to what we already know about such a member. We have avoided the term because, for the modern reader, *personality* has primarily a psychological meaning. We now feel that enough of Adler's meaning has been set forth to prevent the reader from taking Adler's notion of personality as a psychological concept. We thus now avail ourselves of Adler's shorthand. But, to avoid any confusion, we will take the added precaution of hyphenating the word when it is Adler's meaning, thus—person-ality—and use the unhyphenated form to carry the more popular meaning.

We now also introduce a stricter meaning of the term *individual*. Up to this point we have been using the term in a loose sense. Now, as we speak of two manifolds, the sensible and the supersensible, *individual* will refer to the unit of the sensible manifold and *person* to the unit of the supersensible manifold. Thus the individual and individuality are, respectively, the empirical substratum of person and person-ality.

carefully worked-out empirical theory of the nature of man. Nor do we find any separate, systematic treatment of this important question. In principle, he would welcome as full an account as was possible, for applied ethics requires as much detailed and accurate knowledge of the individual as possible.[11] But we must suppose that his focus on ethical theory kept him from entering into this field in any detail, for we find him relying on only the most general kind of picturing of the actual human being.

In some of his writings, Adler seems to be operating with a three-part schema of intellect, feeling, and will. Although he speaks of man's soul or psyche in substantive terms, it is not clear whether this three-way distinction is also meant to be taken substantively. For Adler's purpose it does not seem to matter whether intellect, for example, is a manifestation of some part of the soul-substance or whether it is one of the functions of the soul. The same comment applies equally well to feeling and willing. What is important to Adler is that three major kinds of objective experience are correlated with these three parts or functions. Intellect, feeling, and willing are correlated respectively with scientific, aesthetic, and moral experience.

The operation of these three aspects, taken together, constitutes the operation of what Adler calls the human spirit. We remember that as he chose to speak of the spiritual, rather than the rational ideal, it was the limited meaning of *rational* as referring only to the intellect that he meant to avoid. The spiritual ideal was claimed to be objectively grounded as it was supported by the demands of the whole of man's soul or psyche.

Adler does not put it in precisely these terms, but it is clear that he would say that an exclusive emphasis on any one of these three parts of the soul, or the three kinds of experience that they respectively manifest, would constitute a serious im-

---

[11]Adler, *An Ethical Philosophy of Life,* pp. 257-258. This does not imply that theoretical ethics can ignore empirical considerations.

balance for the individual. An excessive stress on the intellect leads to scientism. An exclusive emphasis on feeling leads to the worship of form that is uninformed by either content or direction. If the will is not checked by intellect and feeling, the consequence is utter slavery to every whim and impulse.

What it is important to emphasize here is the rather sharp break that Adler makes with the tradition in philosophy. Although he allows the three-way division of the soul, he does not support the traditional emphasis on the intellect.

As he accepts the division offered by Kant in his three critiques, he is highly critical insofar as he sees Kant writing an ethics of the intellect, that is, writing his Second Critique primarily in terms set by the First Critique. If we look back at our earlier discussion of worth, we see that, from the point of view of the will, Adler has no problem with the claim that each man has worth. In this limited "ethical sense" Adler cannot doubt the fact of worth. His ethical consciousness recognizes this fact. The search for "rational ground" is really an attempt to satisfy the intellect. If we contrast this with Kant, we see that it is the appeal to man's rationality which is taken as primary in Kant. Kant's categorical imperative is self-evidently binding on all rational beings. But Kant does not, in turn, attempt to offer an additional justification for the sake of the will. Adler says that even the claim that God, Freedom, and Immortality are necessary presuppositions of a moral order is, for Kant, a response to the demands of the intellect and not the will. And further, Kant's categorical imperative is a statement of means that a rational being would use insofar as he was a rational being. Adler's criticism is that, although Kant distinguishes between pure and practical theory, he is always thinking of the intellectual, the rational aspect, as the defining character of his moral being.[12]

As far as the nature of man is concerned, we can say that Adler does not introduce new components. Kant's trinity is

[12]Adler, "A Critique of Kant's Ethics," *Mind,* New Series, XI (October, 1902), 165, 171-184.

accepted. The shift that occurs is away from defining man as primarily rational, in the sense of intellectual. Adler's term *spiritual* is intended to introduce the notion that rationality and its attendant objectivity are attributable not only to the products of the intellect but also to the products of feeling and will. Both the products and the canons for judgment are different for each of these three areas of experience. Difficulties are involved in maintaining their individual integrity and at the same time making clear the case for their unity in the human. Empirically, this unity is neither apparent, nor is it claimed that it is impossible for a kind of schizophrenia to occur. Adler claims that it does in fact occur both in practice, as individuals manifest or stress one area to the exclusion of the others, and in theoretical formulations of the nature of man.

It is clear that the kind of characterization that one offers of the nature of man, even at this abstract level, is likely to have its effect on the way in which the education of man is conceived. But we must put off this matter until we have explored Adler's conception of man a bit further.

In order to live, man must work. Such an observation is hardly a new discovery by Adler. But Adler does take seriously the fact that men must *do* something, must be occupied with something. By and large these "occupations" serve to satisfy the range of empirical human needs.[13] They may also be seen as manifestations of human potentialities. And Adler notes that "unless a moral being gives some evidence that his sense of worth is pushing out values, unless the potentialities show themselves potential, by producing some sort of actuality, the mere moral being as such has little standing in his own eyes."[14] The picture here is of energy which will manifest itself in one way or another. Minimum empirical conditions for this manifestation to be considered satisfactory are that the individual is able to survive and that there be sufficient organization of this energy so that something "shows," that is, is

[13] Adler, *An Ethical Philosophy of Life*, p. 261.
[14] Adler, *Culture and Education*, Lecture III, p. 1.

recognized as actual, by the particular individual. Carl Jung, in a radio interview on his eighty-fourth birthday claimed, as a fundamental fact about human beings, that they can not live meaningless lives. It would seem this is the thought that Adler is trying to convey. The idea is not that man ought to work so as to avoid a meaningless life, but rather that the alternative to some meaningful work is death—and not simply psychological death. It is not a metaphorical death-in-life that is meant, but rather the literal and actual end of life. To say the same thing in another way, man, short of death, lives a purposeful life. Man is a "purposing" being. This kind of claim, of course, leaves entirely open not only what concrete purposes people have but also any claim as to what purposes people ought to have. In short, man is a conative being. We will see that this striving plays a central role in Adler's educational theory. In fact, the whole process of ethicizing leans very heavily on this natural characteristic of man.

In the manifestation of energy, individuals display a range of similarities and differences. As we saw earlier, Adler's ethical conception requires that each person be unique. The empirical substratum of this uniqueness is the actual differences that individuals manifest. It should be understood that individual empirical differences are not, *per se,* to be read as uniqueness. Adler says that "difference in the ethical meaning. . .is the kind of difference which elicits correlated difference in all spiritual associates."[15] On the other hand, no specific empirical difference could be set aside *a priori* as not possibly an instance of ethical differences. Adler insists that ethical difference should not be confounded with "mere idiosyncrasy, or originality, not to say eccentricity."[16] But Adler offers no surefire way, nor is there such a way in which one could know in advance how to interpret and deal with a particular difference.

In any event, since Adler places so much stress on the priz-

---

[15]Felix Adler, *An Ethical Philosophy of Life,* p. 142n.
[16]*Ibid.*

ing of "distinctive difference above uniformity or sameness"[17] and since the only clue to this distinctive difference is the empirical traits that individuals manifest, Adler commits one to a very careful empirical study of individual differences.

His own comments, as far as developing these differences are concerned, are at one with Plato's, that is, there should be very careful observation of children starting in the earliest years. The purpose of this observation and even experimentation is to be able to recognize the peculiar bents and interests and abilities of the child. Adler writes:

> To personalize the individual the first step is to discover the empirical substratum in his nature. There is ever an empirical substratum subject to ethical transformations. The empirical substratum of personality is individuality: Individuality manifests itself in a leading interest of some kind, a predominant bias which indicates the thing which the individual is fit to be and do. To discover the bent or bias is the first step, and the difficulties in the way of taking even this first step are admittedly great. Children and even adolescents often show no marked intellectual preferences whatever. Many adults too appear to be neutral as far as their mental life is concerned. Circumstances ran them perhaps into a certain mould—they might have been run into some other just as well. It is the task of the educator to discover the predominant interest where it exists, and to try to produce such an interest where it does not. What nature has not done in such cases art must attempt.[18]

In the discussion of human character, Adler makes the following three points: "that the character of every person contains contrary elements. . .that certain defined minus traits will be found to go with certain plus traits. . .that the distinction must be drawn, and ever kept in mind, between the bright and dark qualities and the virtues and vices."[19]

The first two points Adler offers as hypotheses he believes could be verified. The second point he calls the "principle of the duality of character traits, or. . .the principle of the polar-

[17]*Ibid.*
[18]*Ibid.*, pp. 295-296.
[19]*Ibid.*, pp. 208-211.

ity of character."[20] What impresses Adler is the "bifurcation of human character."[21] He remarks, however, that bifurcation, and even possible multiplication, of contrary characters applies to each and every person at the natural or empirical level, but not in connection with our moral character. It is worth quoting Adler at length:

Wherever bright qualities stand out we are likely to meet with corresponding dark qualities or dispositions, and conversely. There are, I am persuaded, uniformities of correspondence between the plus and minus traits, and it would be of greatest practical help in judging others and ourselves if these uniformities could be worked out. A kind of chart might then be made, a description of the principal types of human character, with the salient defects and qualities that belong to each. Extensive statistical treatment of a multitude of biographies would lay the foundation for such an undertaking; also sketches of the prominent characteristics of nations, like those furnished by Fouilée, would be utilized. Also the study of the character traits of primitive races as partially carried out by Waitz in his *Anthropology* and the character types of animals, so far as accessible to observation, might be used for comparison. Instructed in this manner, we should, on coming into contact with others, either on their attractive or repellent side, be prepared to expect and to allow for the opposite traits. And we should learn to see ourselves in the same manner; we should see our empirical character as it really is, the dark traits side by side with the bright. The courage to wish to know the truth about one's self is rare, and when the revelation comes or is forced upon us, it often breeds a kind of sick self-disgust and despair. The saint at such times in moral agony declares himself to be the worst of sinners. He has striven to attain a higher than the average moral level, and behold he has slipped into only deeper depths. The minister of religion, the revered teacher, the political and social leader, when abruptly shocked into self-examination by some evidence of grossness or deviousness in themselves, no longer to be glossed over or explained away, are fated to go through the same ordeal. A profound despondency is the consequence. It is not only the badness now exposed, but the previous state of hypocrisy that seems in the retrospect intolerable. Some persons live what is called a double life in the face of the world. But who is quite free from living a double life in his own estimate? Achilles said of himself

[20]*Ibid.*, p. 210.
[21]*Ibid.*

ἄχθος ἀροὔρας ("cumberer of the ground"). Many a man has echoed that cry with a bitterness of soul more poignant than that which Achilles felt when he uttered the words.[22]

The matter of the adequacy of the principle of the polarity of character cannot be our concern. We would be surprised if such a static conception of character traits would satisfy many inquirers today. And it seems inappropriate to speak of these traits as fair and foul, bright and dark, or even plus and minus, if the inquiry was not concerned with moral traits from a moral point of view. Nor does Adler give us a way of marking traits as *contrary*. He speaks of R. L. Stevenson's Jekyll and Hyde as an example and cites the French as having recognized "that everyone has the defects of his qualities."[23] But this could hardly serve as a clear way of marking contrary traits or qualities.

These questions, however, are less important than the general line of approach that Adler takes. An exploration of natural traits of character and the search for whatever laws of the clustering of such traits is surely a worthwhile pursuit. In terms of Adler's primary concern, such knowledge would constitute knowledge of the empirical ground of person-ality. We can put it this way: the study of personality is necessary for an understanding of person-ality.

In connection with the third point the distinction between the empirical and the ethical is most urgently asserted. Adler writes:

The bright qualities are not of themselves virtues. The dark qualities are not of themselves vices. To suppose that they are, to confuse the bright with virtue and the dark with viciousness, is the most prevalent of moral fallacies.

A person is found to be kind, sympathetic, gentle, and on this score is said to be virtuous or good. But gentleness, kindness, a sympathetic disposition, while they lend themselves to the process of being transformed into virtues, are not of themselves moral qualities at all, but gifts of nature, happy endowments for which the possessor

[22]*Ibid.*, pp. 209-210.
[23]*Ibid.*, p. 208.

can claim no merit. And sullenness, irascibility, the hot, fierce crav-
ings and passions with which some men are cursed, are not vices,
though it is obvious how readily they turn into vices as soon as the
will consents to them.

The question becomes urgent: What then is a virtue? The fair
qualities are the basis, the natural substratum of the virtues, the material susceptible of transformation into virtues. In what does the
transformation consist? When does it take place?[24]

One might object to the exclusion of the possibility that the
dark qualities might not be transformed into virtues. Adler
certainly recognizes many instances in which the bright qualities manifest themselves as vices. But Adler goes on in a way
that recalls Spinoza's notion that only love can eliminate hate:

When does it take place? The answer is, when the plus quality has
been raised to the Nth degree, and in consequence the minus qualities are expelled. This result, of course, is never achieved. The concept here presented is a concept of limits. But in the direction defined lies growth and continuous development not of but toward
ethical personality. In public addresses I have often said: Look to
your virtues, and your vices will take care of themselves; I can put
this thought more exactly by saying: Change your so-called virtues
into real virtues: raise your plus qualities to the Nth degree. And the
degree to which you succeed in so doing you can judge of by the extent to which the minus qualities are in the process of disappearing.[25]

There is a hint in the first quotation in this series that
should be explored. Adler suggests that the prominent characteristics of nations, primitive tribes, and animals should be
studied. He could have, in keeping with his general conception of groups and individual differences, extended this list to
include families and the various kinds of social, political, and
occupation groups. In short, all kinds of groupings might
supply relevant information. The point to be stressed is both
very general and also central to Adler's view. Adler holds that
each person must be assumed to be unique, to have, potentially at least, a distinctive excellence. Just so, Adler would

[24]*Ibid.*, pp. 211-212.
[25]*Ibid.*

argue that every grouping of persons, from the nuclear family to the nation state, displays characteristic empirical traits which may be seen as the substratum of its distinctive excellence. If raising these selected plus traits to the Nth degree is one part of the story, the other part is the cross-fertilization of these excellences: from nation to nation, profession to profession, nation to profession and vice versa, and so on for all groups and individuals. We will see how this notion not only affects the general structure of the school program that Adler proposes, but also the actual content that is presented.

Adler selects, for special consideration, several kinds of relations among both individuals and groups. The selection is important particularly in connection with practical ethics and education.

Each individual (or group) is related to others who may be characterized as superior, equal, or inferior in one or another respect. In part we may think of this as a relationship to the past, the present, and the future. This temporal reference is not made to imply that people in the past were necessarily superior, that contemporaries are necessarily equal, or that those to come are our inferiors. The reference here is rather to the distinction between work successfully completed, work in progress, and work yet to be done. Also to be considered is the matter of ability and potentiality. Adler seems to want to include, in each of these categories, both the contributor and the contribution.

Superior, in this combined sense, refers to individuals who have successfully contributed something to mankind; who may be said to have achieved some kind of excellence; those who have demonstrated high potential and ability, in particular those who have done "the valid work of ethicizing human relations."[26]

Equal refers to those individuals who are approximately on the same level as regards gifts, opportunities, and achievement. It is important to note that *equal* does not refer to the *kind* of gift or achievement, but only to the level.

[26]*Ibid.,* p. 244.

Finally, *inferior* is to be understood primarily as referring to those individuals (or groups) who are relatively undeveloped. This class clearly has the highest potential and requires the most attention. It includes the as-yet-unborn, the young, and those who have for some reason not realized their distinctive excellence in any substantial degree.

What Adler is concerned with, in making these distinctions and in pointing out these various relations, is the problem of the locus of authority—among people and for the individual. He is primarily concerned with the attitudes that individuals take toward the dead, the alive, and the as-yet-unborn, the great contributors to mankind's progress, the large mass of people of "average" ability and achievement, and the young, the underprivileged, and the backward. And more particularly: the grandparents, the parents, and children; the master-workmen, the journeymen, and the apprentices; the great contributors to the world of ideas, the major run of teachers, and the students.

In 1934, Horace L. Friess published an article in which, in one long paragraph, he beautifully summarized Adler's idea on this question of authority, including Adler's conception of the "threefold reverence." We can do no better than to quote the entire paragraph:

Adler's view represents a species of the modern faith in freedom insofar as it aims to have the self acquire an autonomous authority. He does not recognize any supereminent authority that can be located at some unitary focus beyond the self—whether in Christ, or in the Torah, or in the Ancestor, or in the State. Hence indoctrination in the wisdom and law of such authorities is not the proper method of education for him. But neither do his views coincide with those of the usual self-expressionist and experimentalist schools, because he conceived the process of acquiring and exercising self-authority to go on under conditions which are not usually emphasized by these schools. For instance, in accord with his respect for specialization, he emphasizes the fact that in every field there are master-workmen and journeymen, and apprentices. And again, with respect to conditions of life in general, he stresses the fact that there is always a threefold orientation to be achieved; toward those who are older than oneself, toward those who are younger, and toward one's contemporaries. Extending the perspective one may say also that a threefold orientation toward past, present and future is involved in the process of education. Now Adler viewed the problem as one of achieving an interrelation of the best in each. The apprentice is not to be regarded as simply the servant of the master, but the latter is also an evoker of power in the apprentice. The educational process is not only a transmission of past assets to the present and future, nor even of preserving the so-called best of the past within the present and the future. Adler often emphasized the constant need of reinterpreting and grasping the past, anew. At the same time he is not satisfied to conceive this reinterpretation and renovation as simply a reshaping of tradition for the sake of the present and the future. For him the educational process was always an attempt to move toward what he regarded as the absolute best, toward personal interdependence on the widest scale, and this involved always a fresh evocation and interrelation of powers from masters, journeymen and apprentices, from old, middle-aged, and young, from past, present, and future factors. Speaking of his conception of interrelation between the three generations, he called it the principle of a "threefold reverence." How far he succeeded in making its implications for educational methods clear I am unable to say. But a very important phase of the idea, it seems to me, is that reverence is differentiated. The attempt of the apprentice to relate himself to the best in the master must be of a different kind from that whereby the master seeks to evoke the best in the apprentice. And the various modes of interrelation required cannot be conceived adequately in terms of such concepts as indoctrination, self-expression, or experimentation alone. Adler once said to me "If I have to pick out a word my word is 'linkage.' "[27]

Relations, or linkages, between master and apprentice, teacher and student, parent and child, are all, in the first instance, actual, empirical, natural relationships. The relevance of Adler's concern appears as we consider all of the ways in which these relationships have been conceived and have existed. In each case some analysis of the proper locus of authority or the appropriate way in which the relation shall be set is either implicit or made explicit. Generally, the relationship has been defined primarily from one side or the other-

[27]"Felix Adler's Conception of Education," *The Standard*, XX:5 (February, 1934), 122-123.

—or, in the case of some transcendent reference, from outside. We can safely say that these relationships have been
framed from one point of view, for example, the master's.
The conception of the apprentice is then derived from the
conception of the master. We agree with Friess that a most
important contribution in Adler's notion of the threefold reverence is that the reverence and authority are differentiated.
This is consonant with Adler's concern with finding the locus
of worth, of authority, of distinctive excellence, in each and
every individual. It is, in addition, an instance of the application of the notion of cross-relations within which each individual stands, that is, his linkages with others.

The distinction between the empirical and the ethical is not
easy to maintain at this point, insofar as it is usually the case
that such relations as that between parent and child have a
normative factor embedded or implicit in them. No actual relation between a parent and a child is normatively neutral. An
empirical account, if it is available at all, is to be sought in
biological terms or perhaps within the framework of a
sociological or anthropological theory. But we know that, as
soon as we move beyond a biochemical account of reproduc-
tion, the concepts that enter into our account are "loaded"
with normative material. Biochemistry apart, even to report
the existence of a parental relation is to introduce cultural
elements, including configurations of status, law, expectations,
and a complex of feeling elements.

All this is simply to suggest that it is difficult to extract the
empirical part of Adler's total report and to distinguish it
from the normative or ethical aspects of his view. As we suggested earlier in this chapter, the selection of relations (and
even the naming of them) is to be understood as a function of
Adler's ethical concerns and the ethical theory that he is presenting.

The modern reader will perhaps find the notion of the dif-
ferentiating of reverence and authority not very exciting.
Have not the social sciences and particularly studies in group
dynamics explored this matter with considerable thorough-

ness? Of course. But precisely such a fact helps to make clear the sense in which normative concerns are at work in such empirical or scientific studies.[28] For the choice to consider a relationship from both sides or to define the relationship from both sides is more than just a matter of scientific thoroughness. It involves a selection of materials that are relevant to the discussion of the relationship. There are many conceptions of the family and, for example, the role of the father, that would make consideration of the point of view of the child simply irrelevant.

But given an orientation such as Adler's, there are certain "facts" to be considered as one first *describes* such relations. One must then go further and consider these facts from an ethical point of view. We can perhaps settle this issue, at least terminologically, by saying that the *fact* of differentiation may be distinguished from the *ethical obligation* which Adler affirms in his doctrine of the threefold reverence.

Ethical Development

Adler distinguishes between what he calls the vertical and the horizontal view of ethical development:

According to the latter, the ethical demands are practically identical in all periods of life, whatever the circumstances in which the individual may be placed. According to the former, each period of life has its distinctively dominant ethical note. In each period some one duty or set of duties rises paramount, some one ethical aspect shines out, some special ethical lesson is to be learned. The ultimate goal, indeed, remains the same: it is the summit of the mountain towards which the successive terraces rise. It is ever in view, it is always the aim. The chief ethical rule also remains unchanged. But the successive applications of it to new relations are not mere illustrations: rather are they revelations of the deeper meaning of the rule and they lead to a more penetrating insight into the nature of the ethical aim itself. . . .The ethical aim is the development of personality. Per-

[28]We choose not to put inverted commas around empirical or scientific, or to italicize them, for we do not mean to imply that, because these normative factors are at work, the studies are any less scientific, or are pseudo-sciences.

sonality is to be distinguished from individuality. The individual, insofar as ethicized, is a personality. Empirical man, with his defects and his qualities, is an individual—one of a kind. Empirical man, insofar as he is transformed in a subjection to the rational ideal, is a personality.[29]

Adler divides human life into five stages: childhood, adolescence, early middle life, later middle life, and old age. For each of these stages, he offers what he takes to be the most important facts about that particular period of life and also what he understands as the major ethical task.

Related to this analysis is Adler's discussion of five major social institutions: the family, the school, the vocations, the state, and religious associations. (The fact that there are *five* stages of life and *five* social institutions does not appear to have any particular significance.). Again Adler offers both a factual statement about each of the institutions and then considers them from the point of view of ethicizing.

These social institutions are seen, *qua* ethicized, as the *"successive phases through which the individual shall advance towards the acquisition of an ethical personality."*[30]

We may now consider Adler's discussion of the five stages of life. The primary fact about the child is its dependence on adults. The adolescent craves for independence but is in fact still dependent in many important respects. In early middle life, the primary focus is the beginning of work. Adler speaks of this stage as the first half of the vocational period. It is also the period of early married life. Late middle life is the second half of both the vocational period and of marriage. Competency in one's own work and the assisting of one's children in moving into an area of work are the items that Adler mentions. Old age is marked by the necessity of letting go the reins, of divesting oneself of the power and authority that one has gained.

This brief survey is the groundwork on which Adler pre-

---

[29] Adler, *The World Crisis and Its Meaning,* pp. 207-211.
[30] Adler, *An Ethical Philosophy of Life,* p. 261 (italics in the original).

sents what we might call his idea of ethico-genesis. The primary concepts at work are dependence, independence, interdependence, and reverence. The primary goal is an individual to whom we can increasingly attribute worth, that is, a person. Person-ality is an achievement, not an empirical complex to be investigated.

Adler's method throughout is to identify the salient facts of development and then to ask the question: how can what is given serve or be used to ethicize the individual in accordance with the supreme ethical rule?

The ethical site of the fact of dependence is reverence: "Reverence toward older persons, especially toward parents and teachers, is the specific virtue of childhood.[31] But older persons are not to be construed as authority figures, *per se*. The primary task of the adult is to help the child profit by his dependence by helping to lay down the basis for future independence. Adler suggests three things that the adult can do. He first puts great stress on the fact that the adult must revere the child, that it is the moral attitude of the adult which has the greatest impact on the child: "And by the moral attitude we are to understand principally the unremitting effort in the direction of the moral ideal and the reverence that finds its expression in such effort."[32] In addition, in keeping with the attribution of worth to the child on the part of the adult, the adult, and particularly the parent, must offer a love that is unbought and unmerited. Finally, Adler claims that, from the side of the child, the demand for fairness, for no undue discrimination, must be met by a fine sense of justice on the part of the adult. Taking half a leaf from Machiavelli, Adler writes: "It is important not only that we be just in our treatment of children, but, as far as possible, that we also seem to be just."[33] It should be clear that Adler's point is not that the adult should be revered and respected because it is his due, but because that reverence is the dynamic two-way

[31] Adler, *The World Crisis and Its Meaning*, p. 216.
[32] *Ibid.*
[33] *Ibid.*, p. 218.

linkage that assists the child in coming to a sense of his own worth within an actual condition of almost absolute dependence:

The salient fact about the child is dependence. The outstanding fact about the adolescent is the craving for independence coupled with the necessity for continued dependence because of inexperience and immaturity. The ethical task is to use this craving as a means of advancing a step toward actual independence.

At about the age of puberty, a critical change occurs. The consciousness of separateness is accentuated. The human atom gets loose, as it were, from the molecule. The individual escapes or seeks to escape from the social context and its constraint.[34]

If this analysis of adolescence is not universally true, it at least applies to most children who come under the influence of modern Western civilization. There appear to be three major ways in which this dependence-independence problem is resolved. There may be a lapse back into a pattern of total dependence. There may be the assertion of complete independence, that is, a severing of all past ties. And there may be restructuring of actual dependencies and an acceptance of them. This acceptance opens up the possibility of the perception of areas of genuine independence.

Adler speaks of three kinds of relations in which the adolescent stands (and this analysis could apply to the later stages as well). He distinguishes between the compulsory relations, the pure choice relations, and the choices which eventually lead to compulsory relations.

Adler's statement about the compulsory relations is worth quoting:

Of the first kind, the most important are the filial or family relations. From the bonds of filial and fraternal duty no one can ever escape. To reconstruct, so far as these are concerned, can only mean to revise, to understand more finely, to voluntarily assume that which hitherto was more or less imposed from without. *The best turn that can take place in the relation of adolescents toward parents is based on this new*

[34]*Ibid.*, p. 219.

voluntariness of attitude. The adolescent is to become consciously the companion of the parent. The child ignorantly idealizes father and mother, ascribing to them every kind of perfection and regarding them as a kind of earthly providence, as beings who have no needs of their own, but exist to satisfy those of others. The point of view of the adolescent is to undergo a change in both particulars. The reverence he feels for them is to attach, not to the unreal perfections with which he clothes them, but to the earnest striving after the nobler things of life which he discerns in them. And instead of regarding them as godlike givers, free from want and limitation, his eyes are to be opened so as to see the actual needs and the limitations, physical, mental, or social, under which they carry on the struggle of life. To assist them, if only by understanding sympathy, should be his highest aim.[35]

As regards the pure choice relations, Adler says only that "friendship is the most important. The adolescent should be helpful to the right conception of the specific office of friendship in the development of personality."[36]

Under choices which lead to compulsory relations he cites the choice of a calling or vocation. The other major choice of this kind is the choice of a marriage mate, but this falls into the next stage.

Now we know that adolescence is an extremely difficult period for most people. As regards the parents, they generally tend to err either on the side of becoming more rigid in the face of the thrusts toward independence, or they move to a hands-off policy as they face their own ignorance and/or inadequacy in dealing with the complexities of the youngster's ambivalence. Adler's reference to an unbought and unmerited love might still apply. But we know that even this can be a two-edged sword in the face of the adolescent who requires, even demands a more objective evaluation of himself. The compresence of adoration and contempt which is often directed toward the parents and, in fact, the whole society, is, we have learned, very likely to be a projection of the adolescent's own ambivalance toward himself. But Adler does

[35]*Ibid.*, pp. 219-220 (italics added).
[36]*Ibid.*, pp. 220-221.

not go this far. In his writings he is more concerned with drawing very broad outlines.

If the empirical side of early middle life is primarily focused on gaining first a foothold and then a competency in the work that one is doing, the ethical aspect of this period is concerned with the effect that this chosen line of work has on the individual. Through this work one's distinctive gifts are most likely to become manifest. It is the cross-relation between the individual and his work, as they mutually affect one another, that Adler wants to stress. Competency or expertise can be bought at the price of personality. Unless there is growth in the direction of uniqueness, the work is not serving its ethico-educational function.

Adler assumes that, when one has reached later middle life, one has achieved some mastery in one's own line of work. The primary ethical focus shifts from the effect that the work has on the agent to the effect that it has on others in different lines of work.

Adler reserves the term *vocation* for work—occupation or profession—insofar as it is ethicized and ethicizing. Thus Adler writes, *"So exercise your calling as to quicken the vocational activity of all related callings"*[37]

Keep well within your boundaries. Do not impertinently intrude into your neighbor's precincts. Be not a vocational jingo. If you are a scientist, for instance, do not assume the right to extend the method of the physical sciences, in imperialistic fashion, over the whole field. But all the same, let the touchstone of success within your own lines be this: that the truth you have apprehended is found acceptable by those who work in different lines; that your life becomes life to them, stimulating them to results differentiated from yours. The dangers that appear at this time are those of dilettantism at one extreme, and crusty, Philistine specialism at the other.[38]

In a footnote at this point Adler adds:

The problem, how to be delivered from the disastrous effects of

[37]*Ibid.*, p. 227 (italics in the original).
[38]*Ibid.*, pp. 227-228.

specialism, how to know something well without forfeiting the outlook on the whole, is in some sense the most urgent problem of our times. Simplification, and the conscious interrelating of the central principles of one's work to the central principles of others' work, seem to point the way out.[39]

This question of specialism will be discussed again in connection with schooling.

Finally, Adler spoke of old age and the edge of death:

The ethics of old age is the ethics of abdication. Abdication implies, besides vacating our place, making the way easier for our successor. It has been said that no one can really transmit the benefits of his experience to another; that every new generation must learn the painful lessons afresh. But we can at least facilitate the process of learning these lessons, especially by improving the methods of education and training that obtain in our calling. And we can in addition school ourselves to take the right spiritual attitude toward our successor, whoever he may be, the attitude of welcome towards one of whom we hope that he will eclipse us. *Morituri te salutamus!*[40]

And we must quote Adler's final words here, for we cannot ourselves capture the feeling tone that they express:

The end is in sight. We have finished our pilgrimage. Have we, then reached our goal? Have we achieved personality? We are as far from having done so as ever. We measure as we have never done before the distance that separates the finite from the infinite. The paradox that we forever seek to attain that which under earthly conditions is unattainable, remains. The unique, distinctive excellence, latent, but unapparent in us, is unapparent still. It is a star that shines above us in the highest heavens and we are like beings sunk far, far down in the depths of an abyss, looking *de profundis* toward that star. But it is our star, our essential self, the rays that descend to us are compelling; we are subject to it and therefore akin to it.

Thus, we have not, indeed, realized our ideal, but we have realized the reality of our ideal. It subsists in the world of true being, and we with it. And this, I take it, is the final outcome of it all, this the conviction that brightens our eyes as we stand on the brink.[41]

[39]*Ibid.,* p. 228n.
[40]*Ibid.,* pp. 228-229.
[41]*Ibid.,* p. 232.

This, then, is Adler's ethico-genetic conception. What we have, in its barest outline, is the process of ethicizing as applied to the individual. We turn now to a presentation of Adler's treatment of the major social institutions and the matter of social reform. We will deal, in order, with the family, the vocations, the state, and the religious institutions.

CHAPTER 5

Social Institutions

Social institutions are in a sense the formal and public side of some of the major kinds of relationships in which man stands. These institutions—the schools, the churches, the political and economic institutions, and the institution of marriage and the family—are often seen as representing interests that are in conflict with the interests of the individual. Adler, with a functional and organic approach to these institutions, seeks a basis for claiming that the individual and the social interests are identical. The basis of Adler's attack on these matters is again his conception of the organic ideal. Speaking of the difference between the terms *social* and *ethical,* Adler writes:

It seems to me unfortunate that this difference is so often overlooked. It is an instance of the slippery use of the moral vocabulary due to the lack of explicit analysis, and sure to breed confusion in practice. People speak eulogistically of the social attitude of mind, of the social spirit, and the like, as if the social point of view were necessarily and of itself a commendable one. As a rule, they intend thereby to oppose the selfishly individualistic point of view—that is to say, they pass from one horn of the dilemma to the opposite. The Individual *v.* Society is the case in court. Shall society be sacrificed to the individual, shall egotism dominate? No. Shall the individual be sacrificed to society, shall the State like a huge monster crush the man, shall the multitude submerge the individual? No, a thousand times no. But how shall the two factors be mediated? That is precisely the ethical problem. To emphasize the word Social as if it were synonymous with Ethical is to obscure the problem, to insist on one element, whereas the problem is to bring about an agreement of the two.[1]

[1]Adler, *The Reconstruction of the Spiritual Ideal,* p. 69n.

Adler surely admits that in empirical terms there are many deep and serious clashes of interest. But again we meet the distinction between the empirical and the ethical. To ethicize these major social institutions is to move in the direction in which there will be an ethical identity of interest between the individual and his society. In fact, person-ality is not achievable except through the medium of the social.

Adler construes the social institutions as the *"successive phases through which the individual shall advance towards the acquisition of an ethical personality."*[2] In another connection Adler writes "that every relation in life should be educative" and "that there are a great many different kinds of educators."[3] And further:

The word "education" is unfortunately often restricted in current use to school or college education. But education, rightly understood, applies to the whole of life. All the different relations—citizenship, friendship, vocational experience—are designed to be educative. If not to finish, they are to fashion our moral natures. And marriage, above all, is to be spiritually educative, designed to bring to bear the constant, penetrating, affirmative influence that womanhood at its best is calculated to exert on man, and manhood at its best to exert on woman.[4]

Marriage and the Family

Alder's views on marriage and the family are of particular importance in understanding his educational philosophy. Not only is the family the first milieu which the child enters, but the kinds of relationships within the family are, as we will see, the most amenable to Adler's organic analysis. The family, and particularly the relation between husband and wife, receives full treatment. Adler believes that the family is the absolute core of society and the monogamous marriage relation a permanent ethical achievement of man. The stability of the monogamous marriage, and the family built on such a mar-

[2] Adler, *An Ethical Philosophy of Life,* p. 261.
[3] Adler, *Marriage and Divorce,* pp. 74-75.
[4] *Ibid.*

riage, Adler understands as necessities for the continued ethical development of man.

These are the major empirical conditions of marriage, as Adler presents them: the physical survival of the species depends on some sort of marriage; some arrangements must hold for the sustenance and support of children, at least in the very early years; and marriage constitutes the most sustained and intimate contact, first between husband and wife and then among all the members of the family.

Adler presents his views on marriage against the background of the medieval and the modern views. The medieval marriage was consummated for the sake of perpetuating the family. The family took priority over the individual. Even the dominance of the male prevailed only insofar as he represented the family as the custodian or trustee of its rights and/or property. To marry meant to take one's place in a line of generation and to preserve that line and its tradition by providing heirs. Personal choice of mate and personal happiness were incidental matters by comparison with the interests of the family.[5]

What Adler marks as the modern conception of marriage is a conception that is dominated by the question of the personal happiness of the individuals concerned. The marriage, and the marriage partner, and even in many cases the children, are all seen as serving the happiness of the individual. Such a marriage stands or falls on the participants mutually serving one another as sources of happiness.[6]

The contrast, for Adler, is between a wholly social conception which pays no heed to the individual and an extreme individualism that finds no place for any significant relation between people except insofar as it is self-serving. In the first case, family interest, family property, or dynastic interest prevailed at the almost total expense of the feelings of the young people. In the modern view, these feelings become the ulti-

[5]*Ibid.*, pp. 9-11.
[6]*Ibid.*, pp. 11-12.

mate authority for entering and sustaining, or terminating, the marriage relation. Adler writes:

> My criticism of the older view of marriage then is, that the conception of supereminent and over-shadowing family interest, as it expressed itself in property and privileges, was too narrow and tyrannical. It sacrificed young love to that ogre, the family.
>
> But, on the other hand, I very earnestly maintain that the great fault with the modern conception of marriage is, that it has gone to the other extreme, losing sight of the social end altogether, and over-emphasizing the individual claim to happiness.[7]

Adler expresses his own position as follows:

> The main source of evil lies in the fact that even the worthiest people suppose that happiness is the chief object of marriage. Let me not seem indifferent to the bliss of happy marriage, because I deny that happiness is the highest aim of marriage. Of course, to confer happiness upon one another is one of the duties and pleasures of true wedlock; and in the discharge of the highest functions of marriage happiness must result. But still happiness is an incident, a concomitant, and you cannot make it the highest end, without coming to the intolerable position that marriage should cease when happiness ceases. The highest end of marriage is to perpetuate, promote and enhance the spiritual life of the world, to keep the flame of mentality burning in the universe, and to confer perpetual benefits one upon the other, especially the highest benefits of moral growth. The supreme aim of marriage is to contribute to the growth of character, of the mind, of the feelings,—of the whole nature.[8]

It is extremely common advice today that one should not enter into a marriage relation with the hope or expectation of changing one's mate. Having made a judicious choice, one should accept the person as he or she is. Such acceptance is understood as recognition of the individuality and integrity of the other party. It is important to note that Adler's view is quite different because Adler's conception is an educator's conception (or a conception of marriage as an ethical-educational institution) whereas the others are not. In these

[7]*Ibid.*, pp. 14-15.
[8]*Ibid.*, pp. 47-48.

terms one can justify including a discussion of marriage and the family within the framework of a discussion of Adler's philosophy of education.

According to Adler, the primary duty of a married person is to influence the marriage partner so as to elicit his or her distinctive excellence. This is a direct application of Adler's "supreme ethical rule." But in saying this we say nothing about the distinctive nature of the marriage relations; for Adler would have one act, at all times and with respect to all people, within and outside of marriage, in accordance with this ethical rule. What Adler does wish to stress is the ethical character of the marriage relation, and he does this in explicit opposition to what he takes to be the nonethical "modern" view.

Adler holds that the organic rule particularly applies to the empirical substratum of the marriage relationship. In no other relationship is there so much opportunity for extended and intimate contact. The actual influence of one mate on the other will in any event be immense. It is really not a question of whether or not there will be influence, but in what form and to what end this influence will be exercised. The difficulty that a modern reader will have with Adler's view is that Adler proposes that this influence should be made a matter of conscious concern on both sides of the relation. The concern here is with the development of character, or person-ality. To be concerned deliberately to help develop someone else's character is to admit, even affirm, that improvement is needed. To be on the receiving end of such an intention is to face the fact that the other party does not perceive you as perfect. Given current views, this seems like an appropriate enough arrangement for the student in the classroom, or the apprentice in relation to the master-craftsman, or between child and parent, but not between husband and wife. We stress this fact not only because it is something which Adler took to be very important but also because the view is so foreign to a contemporary audience. It is also sufficiently foreign to contemporary philosophy of education that, although the family is discussed as an educative agency, the marriage relation is not at all dealt with in these terms.

There is an alternative way of comparing Adler's educative view of the marriage partnership with the more common view. It would be true to say that, as regards empirical traits, Adler not only accepts but positively affirms the appropriateness of accepting what is given. The direction of the influence is not so much to change the empirical traits as to improve their use as instruments for the realization of person-ality. In the same way that Adler argues for a distinction between the social and the ethical, he would argue for the need to avoid the confusion of personality and person-ality.

As we consider, in more detail, the kinds of influence that husband may have on wife and vice versa, we are able to illustrate some additional characteristics of Adler's general approach and particularly his conception of the ideal and the real. These points can be brought out through a presentation of Adler's discussion of love.

Adler's *bête noir,* in this connection, is "romantic" love:

A great deal of the disappointment in marriage may be attributed to false expectation founded upon the romantic idea of love, *the false idealization* of the beloved person. To attribute perfection to the object of love is characteristic of the romantic idea. . . .The idea of romantic love is the excessive magnifying of persons, and it is inspired by the desire of each to enjoy the perfection of the other.[9]

This romantic love embodies two principles that are antithetical to Adler's whole position. As idealization is seen as an extremely powerful force in human affairs, it is most serious if the ideal ignores obvious fact. And further, romantic love, as Adler sees it, is framed at the altar of human happiness. For an ethic of character development, happiness cannot be the highest goal. Also happiness cannot serve as a criterion for a good marriage, or for any ethical relation, if there is to be any "presumption of permanence"[10] in the relation. And Adler goes further as he asks:

[9]*Ibid.,* pp. 18-19.
[10]Adler, *The Reconstruction of the Spiritual Ideal,* p. 118.

Why should we not invest one another with this starry mantle? The answer is: Because it is false; and falsehood, especially in the fundamental relations of life, is sure to exact its penalties and to bring reaction in after years.[11]

When the illusion dies,

either the marriage continues intact while love is dead, supported by the force of custom or by fear of exposure. . .[or] the desire to meet the embodiment of one's ideal somewhere, persists, and the attempt is made to find outside of marriage, in unwholesome and illicit ways, the satisfaction which the marriage relation fails to bring. For these reasons romantic love cannot be true love.[12]

It should be clear that we are introducing this material not simply for its own sake but because of its more general significance. Romantic love is a serious problem for Adler, not simply in connection with marriage but because it is evidence of, as he sees things, a widely held misconception of the nature of the ideal. Compare the following citation with the one directly above:

I have drawn, as I conceive it, the ideal of marriage. I have not described actual conditions, for the ideal is never the actual; it is the operative force that transforms and transfigures; it is that to which we may hope to approximate. But it must also be in line with the actual.[13]

An adequate ideal does something: it is operative; it transforms; it transfigures; it makes genuine contact with actuality. An inadequate or a "false" ideal is no less an idealization, but it contains within itself no program for action. No action is called for in the case of romantic love because the ideal is mistaken for the actuality. And what can one do with an actualized ideal except contemplate it? But there is something deeper here with which we have not yet dealt.

In what sense, then, should an ideal, according to Adler's specifications, "be in line with the actual?" A distinction must

---

[11]Adler, *Marriage and Divorce*, p. 19.
[12]*Ibid.*, pp. 19-20.
[13]*Ibid.*, pp. 89-90.

be drawn between the ideal conception and its role as a regulative rule in any specific situation—as it regulates dealing with a particular empirical substratum. The way Adler deals with the role of the woman and of the relation between the man and the woman in the marriage relation serves as a good illustration of the application of the regulative rule. The early years of the twentieth century witnessed a radical change of the actual role of women in society. Roughly we may characterize this change as a move to increasing economic, political, and intellectual freedom. Adler supported and accepted this change as an opportunity for women to discover their individuality and, hopefully, to move in the direction of personality. These changes had their impact on the way in which the marriage relation was conceived. Adler's response was to accept the changes, but to insist that certain facts had not changed. The false idea of marriage, as Adler saw it, which grew up around the increase in *de facto* equality between men and women in certain areas, was that marriage mates were equal in *all* important respects and that the ideal relation between the sexes was the same kind of companionship that existed between men. Now there are all sorts of objections that one might have to this conception of the relation between the sexes. Our interest is in what Adler found objectionable. He objected on two grounds. He argued that this conception of equality simply ignored fundamental empirical differences between the sexes. No ideal can be adequate if it is framed without due regard to all of the relevant facts. He also objected to the conception of companionship as answering to the demands of the marriage relationship. Recall our earlier discussion of the kinds of choice in connection with the adolescent. Companionship or friendship is classified as a free choice that does not lead to a compulsory relation. "Permanent comradeship cannot be imposed. In the very nature of comradeship is implied the possibility of separation."[14]

The ideal of the companionate marriage stumbles on the empirical fact of the physical differences between the sexes

[14]*Ibid.*, p. 21.

and the fact that the continuance of the species requires some kind of presumption of permanency in the marriage relation. Historically, women have been treated as dust; they have been idealized out of this world; they have been treated as absolute equals. But none of these attitudes has been built on an adequate rendering of the actual similarities *and* differences between men and women.

But we must take this argument one step further. It is probably true that at all times women and men have had similar ranges of ability and potential. And there is ample evidence that they have always differed in the same fundamental way sexually. In these respects, one would have pretty stable facts and stable criteria for judging a conception of marriage insofar as it took account of these facts. But what about the facts that change? That is, what can one ethically say about the actual increase in independence of women and the actual increase in their realization of intellectual potential? Adler's view requires that he start with just these facts as facts. If the facts were that women were considered and considered themselves as underlings, then Adler would have to start there in his ethicizing of the marriage relation. A principle of what we might call "ethical readiness" constitutes the sense in which Adler seeks to keep "in line with the actual."

No empirical state of affairs precludes the possibility of ethicizing. But it follows from this that no empirical state of affairs, in itself, comprises an instance of ethicizing. The realization of intellectual potential may be more conducive to the development of a distinctive person-ality than the belief in companionate marriage or the belief that one is an underling with little ability or potential. But ethical transformation is not defined either in terms of the material with which it starts or any set of specific results to be realized. Our expression, "ethical readiness," denotes the fact that any and all empirical situations are available for ethicizing. It also implies that, unless what is dealt with is the empirical situation *as it is,* ethicizing does not take place. The supreme ethical rule as a regulative rule for educating implies that any instance of successful educating is an accommodation between, on the one hand, what is given in the way of human material and institutional facilities (in marriage, the latter would be the whole environment as it has impact on the relevant beliefs, attitudes, procedures, *et cetera),* and on the other hand, the unrealizable ideal itself. So Adler writes:

The true love of marriage differs from romantic love in this, that the romantic lover sees perfection contrary to the facts, and attributes a present perfection to the other; the real lover is he who sees a certain excellence, a certain charm—without the attraction of that there would be no approach—but beyond that, sees the possibility of greater excellence and perfection which is not yet, but which shall be developed through mutual help.[15]

We turn now to an aspect of Adler's conception of marriage that will be surprising to those who knew Adler only as a progressive in religion and education. Adler holds that the marriage bond is indissoluble and, thus, that divorce is ethically wrong—no matter what the circumstances. This view can be seen as a direct application of the ethical ideal. If one is to attribute worth to individuals, then this implies treating them as if they were indispensable. No one may be set aside. No matter how difficult, no matter how painful, the effort must be made to find the person in the individual and to strive to transform the empirical relation into an ethical cross-relation or linkage. This means that the educative function is ethically mandated in every human relation. It is clear that Adler's view precludes "divorce" in any human relations:

The ethical rule applied to human relations is to treat chance relations as if they were necessary relations, to transform them into necessary relations; to treat a companion whom chance has associated with us as if he were indispensable to us in the attainment of our supreme end.[16]

---

[15]*Ibid.,* pp. 23-24.

[16]Adler, *The Reconstruction of the Spiritual Ideal,* pp. 71-72.

In another place Adler writes:

however accidental the first meeting may have been, on the basis of it, with the help of the moral ideal, we shall erect a permanent union, and transform what was perchance mere accident in its inception, into the region of eternal validity and significance.[17]

Both of these citations appear in the context of discussions about marriage and divorce. The second refers specifically to the marriage relation, but the first is clearly meant to apply to all relations. But is there not some difficulty in making the general claim for no "divorce" and Adler's argument concerning the free choice of companions and friends? Several things are at stake. The question arises as to whether Adler can make a case against divorce in the marriage relation.

If companionship can simply end without being construed as "divorce," why is it that one cannot end a marriage? Why cannot one divorce without "divorcing?" But something more important is involved, namely, how Adler uses empirical fact in his application of the ethical rule. Or to put it as a conundrum: when is a divorce not a divorce?

Adler does not answer this second question directly, but he does draw further distinctions which we must consider. Although he holds that divorce is unethical, physical separation is not. Married persons may live separately; but, short of the death of one, they may not ethically remarry. We recognize this as the position of the Roman Catholic Church. And it is, but only externally. For Adler's justification of his position does not rest on any appeal to some supernatural force conceived as a third party in the marriage. For Adler, marriages are not "made in heaven" by God; they are made on earth between two human beings. Man cannot undo God's work, but can he not undo his own work? Empirically, yes. Ethically, no. Adler argues that, once one has entered into an intimate relation of mind and body with another, it is not possible that the fulfillment of person-ality could be fostered by entering the

[17]Adler, *Marriage and Divorce*, p. 27.

same kind of relation with another. Further, it is inconceivable to him that ethical growth would be fostered in children by allowing a divorcee to remarry. He thinks that separation is a sufficient remedy for the reduction of any pain fostered by a bad marriage. Also the presumption of permanency is required to create that atmosphere of necessity that is needed to force people to their greatest effort "to elicit the best in the other." Finally, and perhaps most important to Adler, as he was attempting to counter the prevailing individualistic conception of marriage, is the empirical fact that the union between an individual man and woman is a social act with social consequences. This means, for Adler, that the marriage between two people is not simply a private affair. It has its public side. It is both served by and serves a larger community. This service carries with it obligations that cannot be set aside. These empirical social relations are there: they cannot be denied. The natural necessity of the biological family and of loving care for children must be recognized. Thus Adler argues that the marriage relation cannot be any less binding than the natural social necessities which it serves.

Has Adler made his case? Surely the natural conditions of marriage and family are different from those of friendship, companionship and colleagueship in work, the student-teacher relationship, sibling relationships, *et cetera*. As far as Adler's meaning is concerned, it seems safe to say that he does want to argue for no "divorce" in any of these relationships; but the idea of divorce, like the idea of reverence, is differentiated.[18] Divorce means different things in different relationships. Its root meaning, however, is framed in connection with the primary idea of Adler's entire ethical program, that is, that each person has worth and as such is indispensable: indispensable *in* every relationship in which he stands; indispensable *to* every other person. What this means in any particular relationship is left unspecified by the general claim. This long discussion about marriage and divorce was entered into be-

---

[18]*Supra.*, p. 158.

cause it is one of the specific areas to which Adler devoted extended attention.

As Adler states his case against divorce, it could be weakened. For if it could be shown that the overall results, as regards the development of person-ality (for the marriage partners and/or the children), were better if one allowed an ethically sanctioned divorce, then divorce would be serving the ideal of worth. A legal divorce that was ethically sanctioned would still probably require that whatever natural sources could be tapped in the relationship would have to be the continued focus for mutual effort of the persons involved. Putting this in very mundane terms: no natural stone should be left free of the process of ethicizing.

Having said this much about marriage, we can deal with the family very briefly, only marking out the most salient points that Adler makes—and these we will restrict to what is most immediately pertinent to the process of education.

From the point of view of the child, the family is the first of the series of social institutions into which he enters as an active member. The family, as a social institution, coincides in this sense with the first stage of ethical development. It is of course true that the child also gains membership by accident of birth in a larger community. In some societal arrangements the family role is minimized. Adler would maximize its influence and importance, particularly in the early years:

As a rule no one can so love a child as its own parents do. The plan of state education for infants to replace home education is advocated by some on the ground that professional kindergartners and teachers are more competent to train the budding human mind than unpedagogical fathers and mothers. The function to be performed by the scientific educator in cooperation with the home is doubtless not to be missed; but taking children away from under the care of their parents, assembling them in what would be equivalent to state orphan asylums, is a procedure which precisely for pedagogical reasons would be preposterous. For the parent supplies that concentrated love for the individual child, that intimate cherishing which the most generous teacher, whose affections are necessarily distributed over many, can never give. And the child needs this selective affection.

The love of the parent is the warm nest for the fledgling spirit of the child. To be at home in this strange world the young being with no claims as yet on the score of usefulness to society or of merit of any kind, must find somewhere a place where it is welcomed without regard to usefulness or merit. And it is the love of the parents that makes the home, and it is his own home that makes the child at home in the world.[19]

The family, in Adler's view, is the first opportunity for the child to become alive to the threefold reverence. Parents and grandparents, siblings and other children of about the same age, and younger children, are the empirical basis on which the ideal of this reverence may be first introduced. Differentiated reverence and cross-reverence are particularly difficult to achieve in the modern individualistic kind of marriage in which there is little actual internal organization. Older type families were more tightly organized, but the reverence was entirely undifferentiated insofar as the father was the supreme object of worship.

Given the individualistic family, the parents must earn the reverence they receive. It must "spring from the service the parent renders in bringing to light the specific individuality of the child with an eye to the transmutation which it is to receive in the later terms in the social series. Not only highest gratitude but genuine reverence are due to the parent who performs this office."[20]

The reverence of the parent for the child will elicit a reverence in response: "The reverential relation is mutual. The child will truly reverence the parent who on his side reverences the child's spiritual possibilities."[21] And Adler continues:

The child does not understand the word Spiritual, but is unconsciously affected by the thing itself....A person who has the vision, who has the gift of divining what is as yet unmanifested, will convey to others the illumination of his vision. The child will realize in his parent the presence of something higher, and will revere it, worship

[19]Adler, *An Ethical Philosophy of Life*, p. 252.
[20]*Ibid.*, p. 253.
[21]*Ibid.*, p. 254.

it. Certain looks, certain expressions of the countenance, certain ges-
tures, though not understood in their meaning at the time, will be
imprinted on memory to be recalled in later life and then understood. But it is essential, in order to evoke reverence in the young, to
have it oneself. He who does not steadfastly revere something, yes,
someone greater than himself, will never elicit reverence in others.[22]

We saw earlier, as we were presenting the general ethical
position, that Adler was more concerned to stress the differences between people than their similarities. In the family, the
empirical ground for a complex combination of both
similarities and differences lay with the brothers and sisters. It
is in these sibling relations that Adler sees the greatest opportunity, not only for developing a respect for difference but
welcoming difference:

In current teaching the emphasis on fraternity is placed on likeness.
It should rather be placed on the unlikeness. These exist, and are
sometimes very marked between brothers, and often cause discord
and separation. The novices in life should therefore be taught be-
times to overcome their repugnance to those who are unlike themselves, and the common relation of the brothers and the parents will
be helpful to this end. Naturally we dislike the unlike. Alienness is
ever productive of disharmony. The fact, however, that the unlike
person in the case of a brother is the child of the same parents draws
us powerfully toward him despite the tendency to recoil.[23]

We see that the family is to receive the imprint of the
spiritual ideal. As ethicized, the family is an organization, an
organic group, whose members may differ in the widest possible way, but who are serving one another in the direction of
bringing forth even more distinctive difference. Differences in
sex, age, ability, interest, and knowledge are all to be found in
each family. And here, for Adler, is the first great opportunity for developing the attitude of respecting, fostering, and
welcoming such differences. In short, the family is where one
may be introduced to the sense of human worth, in onself and
others.

[22]*Ibid.*, pp. 254-255.
[23]*Ibid.*, p. 255.

But the family is more than this. From the point of view of development it is a first stage and it is part of the individual throughout life. One does not leave one's family as one moves into active contact with other social institutions. If the ethical development outlined in an early section is seen along a temporal line, Adler's conception of the range of social institutions might best be pictured as an expanding series of concentric circles—or better than circles, concentric spaces of irregular shapes with no clear boundaries that might mark a separation of one from the other.

Through childhood and adolescence particularly, the family and the school are the primary institutions for ethicizing and educating the individual. We are delaying our discussion of the school until later, but this much must be said. Both the family and the school have, in Adler's view, as a primary purpose, the preparation of the individual to engage in some kind of work after adolescence. About the family Adler writes: "It is the vestibule that leads into all the different professions and vocations."[24] "The school is like the hundred-gated Thebes. It leads out into a hundred vocational avenues."[25] And again:

the family does not prepare the young to enter into a vocation for the purpose of securing happiness. It does not regard the vocation as servile to the empirical ends of the individual, but as a phase through which he is to pass on the road to ethical personality, the fulfillment of the objective aims of the vocation being the means of acquiring the ethical development which the vocation is competent to furnish. Thus we regain, but on a much higher plane, what the family possessed before it began to break down under the influence of modern individualism, namely, an ulterior greater purpose imbedded within itself and yet extending beyond itself.[26]

As to the school:

its aim is far greater than merely to prepare the student for that fu-

[24]*Ibid.*, p. 251.
[25]*Ibid.*, p. 292.
[26]*Ibid.*, p. 251.

ture vocation to which he is best suited. It should no less supply the incentive for creating new vocations, and for changing what are at present still occupations into vocations. The school searches out the individuality of its pupils. It undertakes to differentiate and to personalize individualities. But when it has done its part, it sends the pupils into a world where little account is taken of the finer differences of aptitude, where occupations predominate and vocations are few, and where most things, ethically speaking, are still in the rough. The school cannot indeed transform society by merely raising its indignant voice and asking society to pay heed to the finer things which it has fostered, and which often are subsequently crushed. But it can at least contribute to the vocational evolution of society by reiterating its unsatisfied demands.[27]

To the distinction between occupation and vocation, and what Adler means by the "vocational evolution of mankind" we may now address ourselves.

Vocation

As we turn now to the vocations as a social institution, we must draw the distinction between education *for* the vocations and the vocations as themselves educative. Education for the vocations is a matter for the schools and, as such, will be treated in a separate part of this essay. The vocations as educative are our present concern. This distinction is particularly important in Adler's frame of reference because a primary aim of the schools is to prepare the individual to enter successfully some line of work which he will presumably pursue throughout his adult life. For Adler, schooling should be vocationally oriented, that is, it should be *vocational education.* But this idea must be set off from the notion that an individual's work should itself constitute an educative experience. Adler's conception of vocational education calls for ethicizing the entire order of men's occupations and professions.

Vocation, for Adler, means ethicized occupation or profession. A line of work, *qua* ethicized, is a vocation. Adler is not

[27]*Ibid.,* p. 292.

against specialization. Quite the contrary. He puts great stress on the absolute necessity of an individual becoming competent in his chosen work. Adler's own life history exhibits this conviction, and he is explicit about his own decision to specialize. A typical statement is as follows:

> My field is ethics. I am entirely desirous of sticking to my own last, that is, dealing with such concepts as the data of my subject force upon me. I do not wish to trespass, or to seem to trespass, on the domain of my neighbors.[28]

In order to become competent, one must specialize. This means marking off a distinct area of activity and concern. The vital thing is to have a clear channel for the release of energy, for only in this way can an individual hope to manifest his own distinctive excellence. Adler is saying, in effect, that person-ality appears only as a function of the individual's disciplined interaction with the world—both with other individuals and with things.

It should be noted that this idea of specialization does not, in itself, put any limits on what a person might do. Limitations are imposed, but by the individual's capacity and interest and by what is actually available to do. What is being said is simply that an individual should not extend himself beyond an area in which competence is possible for him. An *a priori* decision in terms of presently established "areas of competency" need not be imposed on an individual. In fact, such imposition is most likely to militate against the possibility of an individual's realizing his most distinct potentialities. The possibility of an individual "carving out" his own area of work should not be ignored, even though, for most people, there will be some compromise or adjustment between individual capacity and interest and the established areas of work.

The difficulty connected with specialization, as Adler sees it, is similar to the difficulty faced in framing an ethical conception of the individual. Special*ism* and individual*ism,* as theoret-

---

[28] Adler, *An Ethical Philosophy of Life,* p. 106.

ical formulations, both suffer from overemphasis on the manifold. They, in a sense, validate the manifold and nake no reference at all to a synthesis. Adler's solution for the problem of specialization follows the same line as his analysis of the individual. His conception of person involves a rejection of individualism and statism. The first puts undue stress on the manifold; the second ignores the manifold in favor of an abstract unity. In the same way, specialism emphasizes the manifold and yields an atomic conception of the range of specialities. Generalism, the notion that one should somehow know everything, ignores the complexity of the manifold of areas of expertise. Such a synthesis, is, for Adler, "synthetic" in the most invidious sense of the term.

A person is an ethicized individual, that is, the individual in interrelation with, or cross-linked to, other individuals. A vocation is ethicized work, that is, an area of expertise cross-linked to all other areas of work. Both person and vocation are achievements; they are not given. More exactly, they are ideals which are never fully achieved. But only in the attempt to achieve them can an individual begin to *realize,* that is, come to an awareness of the ideal.

It is important to note also that vocation comprises one of the social institutions *"through which the individual shall advance towards the acquisition of an ethical personality."*[29] Thus Adler connects ethical development and work.

The question to be asked about any specific line of work is: How can it contribute to the development of person-ality? We must quote Adler at length as he takes a major step in answering this question:

In sketching the ideals of the different vocations, I have to consider in what way each contributes to the formation of an ethical personality. There is an empirical side to each vocation. Every vocation satisfies some one or more of the empirical human needs; but in the very act or process of doing so, it ought, in order to deserve the name of a vocation, to satisfy also a spiritual need, to contribute in a specific way toward the formation of a spiritual personality. Agricul-

[29]*Ibid.,* p. 261.

ture furnishes food. The different trades minister to a great variety
of wants. The scientist extends our knowledge of nature. With this
empirical aspect of the vocations, however, I am not here concerned.
A scientific classification of the vocations is not a task to which I need
address myself. *My task is an ethical classification of the vocations.* As this
has never been undertaken the first attempt is difficult and perforce
provisional.

I outline my topics as follows:

1. The theoretical physical sciences (including mathematics) considered from the point of view of the specific way in which the ethical
personality may be developed by those who pursue them.

2. The practical counterparts of the theoretical sciences, e.g., engineering, and the industrial arts in so far as they depend on and
illustrate and use principles and methods furnished by science. Work
in factories, mines, and also in the fields, is to be regarded as the
executive side of theoretical science.

3. The historical sciences, those which have to do with mentally
reproducing the life of the human race in the past, including history
proper, philosophy, archaeology, etc.

4. The vocation of the artist.

5. The vocation of the lawyer and the judge. The vocation of the
statesman. The vocation of the religious teacher.

The three last mentioned are classed together as educational vocations, that is, as vocations which, in respect to their highest significance, are branches of the *pedagogy of mankind,* having for their object
to educate the human race; the ethical object of the lawyer being to
educate society in the idea of justice; of the statesman to educate society in the idea of the state; of the religious teacher to educate society
in the idea of the spiritual universe.[30]

The distinctions underlying this classificatory scheme are the
distinctions among science, art, and ethics. More fundamental
are the distinctions among intellect, feeling, and will. Adler
says:

Ideally speaking, every man participates in all the principal interests
and activities of the human mind. Every man is something of an artist, something of a practical or executive worker, scientist, religious
being. But in each individual the different interests are colored by
his special pursuit, and the influence he wields in return is modified
in the same fashion.[31]

[30]*Ibid.,* pp. 261-262 (italics in the original).
[31]*Ibid.,* p. 267.

This is no more than to say that every man exhibits intellect, feeling, and will. Adler makes the same point in drawing a comparable distinction between what he calls the "three great tasks that occupy human life: To build our finite world (science and its adjuncts); to create in the finite the semblance of the infinite or spiritual relation (art); and to strive to realize the spiritual relation in human intercourse (ethics and religion)."

We might say that Adler's ethical classification into five parts is best seen as a three-way classification of the theoretical sciences, the practical arts and sciences, and the historical sciences. These three are concerned with the finite empirical world. The distinctions between them are of secondary importance. It is in the mastery of a range of empirical phenomena, either in theory or practice, that one can come to a fuller awareness of the finiteness of the empirical. We recall the kind of knowledge Adler attributes to the physicist: "our knowledge of nature is relative, which means incompletely rational, because of the foreign element in nature unamenable to the operation of the rational, the synthetic function."[32] And so it is

> the scientist, who works most successfully in the field of physical truth who must assist the rest of us in escaping from the spell to which we are all subject. He is the one, he who more than others succeeds in unifying the manifold of juxtaposition and sequence, to whom we look to liberate others as well as himself from the deceptive belief that the reality producing function of the human mind can be satisfied in the temporal and spatial manifold.[33]

We learn, with the help of the practitioners of the various sciences, that we cannot know or actually work with the totality of things. This is the message of Kant's First Critique. But it is possible to present to the senses the semblance of that totality. This, according to Adler, is the task of the artist: "to create in the finite the semblance of the infinite; to realize through effort the reality of the infinite."[34] This is achieved

[32]*Ibid.*, pp. 97-98.
[33]*Ibid.*, p. 266.
[34]*Ibid.*, p. 277.

when each part of the work of art contributes to the total effect, each part affecting every other part, and also when the total effect is one of relative completeness. The following is Adler's summary of this idea. He speaks of this as a theory of the relation of art to ethics:

in a work of art each line, color, sound, word, must be irreplaceable, and on that account convincing. Each member must be indispensable in its place and the connection with the rest inevitable. Substitute for line, color, sound, etc. a life—an ethical being,—conceive the members to be not a few but in number infinite, and you have the spiritual ideal, which is the reality whereof the art work is a semblance. This is the relation of art to ethics—the quality which we call in art "convincing," in ethics we call "worth."[35]

This discussion comprises Adler's main points in connection with the vocations. The purpose of eliminating a considerable amount of interesting detail is that by holding to the broad outline of Adler's idea of vocation, we are able to see how it is an application of his most basic pattern of thought. It should be apparent that Adler's analysis of vocation is intimately linked to and informed by his basic metaphysical position: the distinction between the empirical and the ethical; the polar conception of the functions of the mind; the notion that the mind can be analyzed in terms of three major faculties; Adler's conception of finitude and totality—all these and more are etched into the analysis of man's work as ethicized. It was feared that the introduction of any further detail might obscure the basic pattern. The question of the relationship among the various vocations will be discussed in the section dealing with the state, to which we now may turn.

The State and The Organization of States

In keeping with his basic position, Adler presents an organic theory of the state. The primary purpose of the state is to supply the external conditions required for ethical de-

[35]*Ibid.*, p. 286.

velopment by those who pass through the social institutions: the family, the school, marriage, the vocations, the religious institutions, and the many other subgroups in the society. In this external sense, the state is inclusive of all these subgroups. In the developmental sense, it is continuous with these other groups. It follows, as it were, after the vocations, and precedes an "organization of all mankind" and the "culminating social institution," that is, the religious fellowship.

To speak of a series of institutions as a developmental series might suggest a series ordered according to biological or psychological principles. In part, Adler does conceive the move from family to school to vocation as a progressive broadening of experience, with the earlier terms in the series not lost, or even losing their individual character, but rather taken up and included by the later terms. But the principle of order of these terms can be stated without reference to individual experience insofar as each institution is comprised by a larger manifold of individual members than the institution preceding it in the series. We might simply say that the principle of order is size: that the school included more people than the family, *et cetera*. But it should be clear that this would be true only with respect to the number of members *ideally* included. In fact, the order is not an empirical order at all, but an ethical order.

As an ethical order, all the terms of the series are co-present. Each term is defined as a function of the particular relations in which the members stand to one another. In this sense the differences between the institutions are qualitative. In the ascending order of institutions, the differences are quantitative. But it would hardly be possible to say that one institution is more important than another. This is so, even though in a particular situation an individual might have to decide to give more weight to one rather than another. It is important to note that each institution serves specific purposes in the life economy of a person and that they all share in the supreme purpose of development toward ethical person-ality. And so we must ask: What does Adler mean when he says that the state serves to supply the external conditions required for ethical development?

Adler says that the state has two aspects: "(1) It is the balance wheel of the vocational groups included within it. (2) It is the political expression of the national character, and its ethical purpose is to develop this empirical national character into a spiritual character."[36] The interrelations among the vocational groups, in Adler's ethical conception, would be organic. This organ-ization of the vocations comprises the state. Insofar as the vocational groups constitute the economic interest of society, we may say Adler proposes a political order in which the political unit is an economic group. This idea must be qualified, since the vocational classification, on the basis of which Adler would organize the state, is not grounded in economic terms. As we saw in the last section, it is a classification based on the fundamental tenets of the ethical philosophy. Nonetheless, the vocations do serve as the vehicles of economic arrangements in the society.

In both of its aspects, the state is conceived by Adler as an *enabling*[37] institution. It is in this sense that we understand Adler's meaning of *external*. The state supplies no distinctively new purposes or functions in the society as do the other social institutions. According to Adler, however, it should facilitate and harmonize the purposes embodied in the other institutions. The state, in this conception, has no life of its own, but rather is it understood as setting the conditions in which adequate interaction among societal groups, and particularly the vocational groups, may be actualized. As to the other social institutions in the society, Adler comments: "In concentrating attention upon the vocational groups as the entities to be harmonized with one another, account is taken by implication of the family and of the individual. The suborganisms are embraced within the superior organisms."[38]

Adler's ethical conception of the state is that it serves as a

[36]Adler, *An Ethical Philosophy of Life*, p. 305.
[37]This is the author's term, not Adler's.
[38]Adler, *An Ethical Philosophy of Life*, pp. 305-306.

catalyst. But we are led to ask why Adler focuses on the vocational groups. It would seem that, particularly in connection with the state, Adler wants to avoid undue emphasis on the polar conception of unity. Any conception that implies statism is anathema to him. But he also seeks to avoid what he would call excessive individualism. An ethical theory of the state should neither conceive of the state as an autonomous entity nor as a mere aggregate of atomic individuals. This argument may be set in terms of Adler's basic epistemological thesis regarding the dual reality-producing functions of the mind, since it is clear that Adler has this root principle in mind. Negatively, it serves as a basis for rejecting the individual as the basic political unit. It also serves as ground for rejecting the idea of the state as an independent reality. But it does not serve to account for Adler's choice of the vocational groups as the basic political unit and for defining the state as an organization of the vocational groups.

Adler does not offer a direct answer to our question, but we can attempt an answer on the basis of what he does say. First of all, each of the vocational groups includes a sufficient number of individuals, that in the choice of such groups, Adler's view could not be confused with an individualistic approach. Further, these groups are powerful, numerous, and diverse enough that there is little danger in having them disappear as the state is defined in terms of them. Also, on this view, because the vocational groups are brought into the public domain as political units, conflicts of interests get an open hearing that they do not get when they remain in the private sector.[39] Adler contrasts his view with the actual state of affairs in the United States (and elsewhere), where the political units are aggregates of people defined in geographical terms. The difficulty with this arrangement, according to Adler, is that it does not reflect any genuine ordering of interests within the society. And he adds the following:

[39]In this connection, Adler writes: "Government is usually in the hands of more or less selfish coteries, who operate behind the scenes, who do know what they want and who, like the Piper of Hamelin, are past masters of the art of leading the political children whither they will." *Ibid.*, p. 314n.

Representation by geographical districts is the logical outcome of the individualistic conception of democracy. Where this prevails, the state is supposed to take account only of the common interest, those in respect to which all individuals are alike, such as security of life and property, those interests being ignored in respect to which the groups that constitute society, the farmers, the merchants, the industrial laborers, etc. differ. Hence any convenient number of citizens, pursuing their life purposes side by side within a certain geographical area, may serve as a constituency. The absence of regard for the real diversity, and often the clash of interests, between persons belonging to such constituencies, is due to the atomistic, individualistic notion of democracy just mentioned. But sheer individualism is everywhere on the wane, and is bound to become less and less dominant in the degree that the industrial evolution of society proceeds, and the various groups stand out distinctly as different against one another in their functions and in the conditions subservient to those functions. Society is in fact not an aggregate of human atoms. It is already an imperfect organism, destined to become more and more adequately organized. And the system of representation has got to be remodeled and adjusted to this fact and this ideal.[40]

And so it follows that:

The law-making body on this basis will consist of representatives or delegates of the agricultural, the commercial, the industrial, the scientific group, etc. Women belonging to these groups will exercise the franchise within them. There will also be a distinct group of home-makers; motherhood will be recognized as a vocation.[41]

Whether Adler's choice of vocational groups is realistic or not, his criteria for the choice are now clear. Adler seeks (1) a government that is responsive to the diverse interests in the society, and in this he is following his principle that difference is ethically more important than sameness, since it is the best empirical clue to uniqueness; and (2) a government that represents individuals within the area of their interests, activities, and particularly, the area of their expertise. Adler's proposals regarding the state may be seen as an attempt to solve the

[40]*Ibid.*, pp. 310-311n.
[41]*Ibid.*, pp. 310-311.

problem of specialization. The government is to serve as a public forum for communication among the major areas of specialization.

It is not possible, within the scope of this essay, to consider all the ramifications of Adler's combined economic and social theory. But it is necessary that we deal explicitly with Adler's conception of democracy. Much of the discussion in earlier sections has been germane to this issue; but Adler's proposals, as set forth in this section, comprise both his major criticisms of the actual democracy as he saw it, and also his recommendations for a reconstruction of democracy. For Adler is deeply committed to democracy in the sense that he holds that politically, and otherwise, each individual should count and be counted. In a sense, the rest is all a matter of mechanics. But the mechanics reach down deep—right to the basic question of the meaning of worth. We must go back to our early discussion of worth to see that Adler is prepared to affirm that each person has unalienable rights and that the distinguishing characteristic of the democractic ethos is commitment to the worth of each and every man. But, as we have seen, Adler's entire philosophic effort can be read as an attempt to explore both the meaning and the justification of this claim. It is not unfair to rephrase the purport of this effort as an inquiry into the fundamental principles of democracy. As Adler writes, in Kantian terms:

We begin with the affirmation—Man is an end *per se*. This wonderful affirmation, which the democracies are darkly and confusedly trying to express in political and social arrangements, constitutes the problem of all problems.[42]

Adler has a long "Note" on democracy at the end of his chapter on the state. It does not add anything substantially new to what has already been covered here, but it does serve as a summary, and there is some value in having it in Adler's own words:

[42]*Ibid.*, p. 125.

The idea of democracy is often neatly put—all too neatly, into the following formula: In antiquity the individual existed for the sake of the state, in modern democracy the state exists for the sake of the individual. Both of these statements as they stand are mischievous and misleading and require to be qualified. It is not true that in antiquity the individual existed for the sake of the state in the sense that his separate existence was extinguished. The citizen class in Aristotle's state, the rulers in Plato's state, and even a member of one of the inferior classes, each in his own way fulfilled a distinct function. He was not suppressed in the state, he expressed his function by the action appropriate to his station. The philosophic rulers might do the thinking and governing. They were the head of the body politic—others the hands and feet. The underlying conception was what may be called spuriously organic, borrowed more or less from the animal type of organism.

The second limb of the formula is no less superficial. In no modern nation does the state exist, or at bottom is it supposed to exist, for the benefit of the individuals who at any time compose it. If this were the ruling conception, how could the democratic state require its citizens to give up their lives in its defense? If the state existed for the benefit of the individuals, the state would be the means, and the so-called good of the individual the end. And in that case it would surely be irrational to sacrifice the end for the sake of the means, in other words to put an end to one's life in defense of the state, a mere instrument for the protection and prosperity of one's own life.

To reply that the state exists for the sake not of one individual but of all (observe however that the formula says "the individual," and is ambiguous and slippery at this point), nor even only for the sake of all the individuals now living, but also for the sake of the millions yet unborn—to say this is once more to introduce an ideal entity which it was the very object of the formula as quoted to banish. The formula was intended to give us, in place of "the metaphysical entities" of the Greeks and the Germans, a very palpable thing—the good of the individual. The good of the individual seemed to be a palpable thing, though in truth it is the most impalpable thing in the world. And by defining the state in this wise we were supposed to come onto solid ground. But now, behold, it is the good of unborn millions which is to be the object of our devotion, and who can imagine what this good of unborn millions is likely to be?

The fact is that without ideal entities the conception of the state in any noble shape cannot be construed at all. The organic conception must now take the place of the individualistic. The organic conception indeed as it was worked out in antiquity, or as it lived on in the theories of mediaeval writers, or as it survives in the works of certain

German publicists, who use it to defend the feudalistic structure of society, has rightly fallen into discredit,—not because it is organic, but because it is pseudo-organic, that is, based on the type of the animal organism. The individualistic conception of the state at present current in America and in all modern democracies, is a violent reaction against this false idea of organization. The inestimable germ of truth individualism contains is that no such distinction can be allowed as between head and hands or feet in political life, that all the multitudes of "hands" who work in the factories, for instance, must be respected as personalities having not only hands but also heads and heart. But individualism, though it affirms this idea, belies it in practice, as the actual state of society in America and elsewhere abundantly proves. And it is bound to do so, because personality implies more than material well-being, either for a single individual or for all individuals now living or for all future individuals. Personality implies truly organic relations to other fellow-beings—and this can only be achieved by organizing the society in which men live.

The way taken has been, by reaction from pseudo-organization, to extreme individualism and concomitant materialism. The way out lies in the direction of genuine organization.[43]

And by way of further articulation, in another note, Adler adds:

Democracy is at present regarded as a relation between equals. In fact, we have in America the negro population, the illiterate and backward immigrants. A truer conception of democracy depends on our realizing that within each people as well as between people and people there is the distinction of the more advanced and the less advanced groups. Democracy rightly conceived will be found to consist in the effort spent by the more advanced in each vocational group to uplift the less advanced, the more advanced themselves coming into possession of their spiritual worth in the degree that they realize this their task of leadership and its great responsibilities.[44]

As with Adler's conceptions of vocation, here again we find the pattern of the basic ethical position emerging and serving to order another area of data. *Organized democracy* is the microcosm writ large. Instead of cross-linkage and differentiated

[43]*Ibid.*, pp. 319-321.
[44]*Ibid.*, p. 340n.

reverence among, for example, the members of a family, we here have the cross-linkage and reverence written in terms of societal groups. A more fundamental difference between the state and its subgroups, if we read Adler correctly, is that the state is, from a substantive point of view, a derivative institution, in the sense of its having no interests of its own that are not first in the subgroups. For Adler, the state makes possible the kinds of linkages that permit groups to ethicize one another. This is a facet of the idea, which was suggested earlier, that the state is merely a catalyst, an enabling institution. It might be argued that all the social institutions, from the family up, are, in Adler's view, simply enabling in this same sense: that the only underived interests lay with the individual. To argue thus would be to emphasize the fact that the subgroups—family, school, vocation—are enabling. The point is that they are not only enabling, for without them as substantive, Adler would be defending precisely the extreme individualism that he most strongly rejects. We find no evidence that Adler falls into such a contradiction. To avoid another source of misunderstanding, it should be noted that the question of the need or necessity of either the state or its subgroups is not relevant in this connection. Whether or not one or another or all of these institutions is absolutely required for the existence of either the individual or the person is an independent question. The point is simply that one cannot argue from the fact that both the family and the state are necessary and the further fact that they are both enabling institutions, to a conclusion that either one or both were *merely* enabling or formal arrangements. The point is worth making because it is easy, and not uncommon, to slide from the recognition of the necessity of some formal arrangement to the claim that the form is itself a substantive. The pertinence of this short argument is to clarify the opening remarks of this section to the effect that, in Adler's view, the state, that is, an organized democracy, supplies the external conditions required for ethical development.

As "the balance wheel of the vocational groups included

within it,"[45] the state serves the same purposes with respect to the vocational groups as the family serves with respect to the members of the family. The supreme ethical rule applies to the vocational group, *qua* "member" of a manifold, as it would to any member of a manifold. Each member is seen in terms of its distinctive character and excellence (its worthness). Facility must then be made for each member (in the present case, the vocational group) to act or function in such a way that the worth of the other members is elicited, developed, actualized, made to stand forth.

We recall that the other aspect of the state which Adler marks is that "it is the political expression of the national characters. . . ."[46] Adler is here making the same claim about the distinctive character at the level of national groups as he makes about all subgroups and also about the members of the subgroups.[47] It is not necessary that we pursue the details of Adler's discussion of the matter. For our purposes it is sufficient to indicate that the claim to distinctive character at the national level is of the same kind as we have found throughout. Adler supports the claim by reference to the actual traits of various countries. His ethical analysis does not differ substantially from the analysis of the individual.

The same may be said of Adler's discussion of the relations among nations. This is an extension of what has already been developed. Here the members of the manifold are nations. The spiritual ideal is an organization of all mankind in which each nation, with its distinctive excellence, assists other nations to realize their distinctive excellences.[48]

It should be no surprise to the reader who has traveled this far with Adler to see that Adler's "solution" to the problem of excessive nationalism is not, as many have urged, the elimina-

[45]*Ibid.*, p. 305.

[46]*Ibid.*

[47]See particularly, Adler, *An Ethical Philosophy of Life*, Book IV, Chapter 8, and *The Reconstruction of the Spiritual Ideal*, Chapter V.

[48]Adler's discussion of the society of all mankind includes a critique of the League of Nations which bears reading today in connection with the United Nations. See *The Reconstruction of the Spiritual Ideal*, pp. 171-189.

tion of nation states. In accordance with Adler's categorical imperative, to ethicize is not to obliterate. We perceive the same pattern of solution to the three issues which Adler claimed were the major problems of his day: individualism, specialism, and nationalism. In none of these cases does Adler propose a rejection of the empirical substratum, but rather the use of the substratum in ethical ways toward the supreme ethical end. It is true that considerable change would take place if the process of mutual influence were pursued. But these changes, whatever they might be, are of secondary importance to Adler. His primary concern is that the process be initiated and the effort made in all situations. In many areas of activity he gives no clue as to what would constitute the process. And even in those areas to which he did direct his attention, the statements that he made are made at a fairly general level. But it would be an error to try to read off "solutions" from Adler's work for the present or the future without a fresh and very careful scrutiny of the now changed and changing empirical situation. Such independent empirical analysis would not only be consistent with Adler's view; in terms of his view it would be a necessary precondition for adequate ethicizing.

It should be stressed again, in this context, that Adler does not stress the actual results achieved. He is not overly sanguine about any particular success that might be realized. The primary focus is on the life that is being lived and the effort and energy put forth in the attempt to ethicize. With respect to an organization of mankind he writes:

In presenting the ideal of a perfect civilization as the aim of mankind, I have not in view an ethical millennium. It is the creative energy expended in rising to ever higher levels of achievement, and never the actual accomplishment itself, in which human nature must find its satisfaction.[49]

[49]Adler, *The Reconstruction of the Spiritual Ideal,* p. 191n.

The Religious Fellowship

Adler speaks of the religious fellowship as the "culminating social institution":

The religious society is the last term in the series of social institutions, and its peculiar office is to furnish the principle for the successive transformation of the entire series. It is to be the laboratory in which the ideal of the spiritual universe is created and constantly re-created, the womb in which the spiritual life is conceived.[50]

Religious fellowship, in Adler's terms, is not something that one is "born into." Of the three kinds of relations in which men may stand, which we discussed first in connection with adolescence—compulsory, free, and free leading to compulsory[51]—membership in a religious fellowship is a matter of free choice. We remember that in founding the Ethical Society, Adler publicly set aside his membership-by-birthright in the Hebrew religion. This new kind of religious fellowship of which he conceived would seem to require of each of its members an explicit decision to become a member: a decision which is revocable.

The unifying purpose of this religious fellowship is to make the spiritual ideal explicit: to articulate the ideal. By *articulation* we mean to include both the creation and the revision of the ideal which is the supreme end of human existence.

Now, since much of what Adler has to say is either apart from the concerns of this essay, or has already been discussed under other headings, there is only a little more that needs to be said here. We are primarily concerned here with Adler's conception of the relation between the religious fellowship and the rest of the social institutions.

The sense in which the religious fellowship is the culminating social institution refers us not to the actual size of any

[50]Adler, *An Ethical Philosophy of Life,* p. 341.
[51]*Supra.,* pp. 164-65.

given fellowship, but to the object of devotion of that fellowship, namely, the infinite spiritual universe. The membership of the spiritual universe includes all human beings: the dead, the quick, and the as-yet-unborn. In these terms, even the organization of nations is a subgroup.

Since any given fellowship will be located within a particular state, it is necessary that this relation between the religious fellowship and the state be clear. Adler says:

> The state, it is true, is profoundly interested in the flourishing of ethical idealism, and in the constant rebirth in its midst of spiritual ideals. But it is not competent to determine what the character of these ideals shall be. The moment they cease to be freely produced they lose their life-giving power. The state within limits may enforce actions; it may not even attempt to enforce beliefs.[52]

> The greatest danger of Erastianism, of the supremacy of the state in religious matters, is that the state may become the object of worship.[53]

It is in respect to the internal organization of the fellowship that Adler speaks of the vocations. In keeping with his views (1) that it is in one's work that one is most likely to get insight into the nature of the ideal and (2) that it is in terms of one's own work that one can speak with most authority and also have a live perspective in the world, Adler proposes that the fellowships be divided into vocational groups. In this way the ethical teachers or religious leaders will not lose touch with actual conditions: they will be dependent on the expertise in the groups. Thus, as both teachers and pupils, the leaders are less likely to form into a clergy, to see themselves as members of an ecclesiastical body. In this sense, an ethical religious fellowship is a secular fellowship, defined neither in terms of the state or the church(es).[54]

Of course the primary unit of the religious fellowship is the individual member. The fellowship serves him, like other re-

---

[52]Adler, *An Ethical Philosophy of Life,* p. 342.
[53]*Ibid.,* pp. 342-343.
[54]*Ibid.,* pp. 347-348.

ligious groups, in relation to the major events of human life. It may offer support and assistance in time of trouble or need. And it is the agency for the celebration of the major events of life: birth, initiation into a vocation, initiation into citizenship, marriage, and death. Adler speaks of these as festivals and writes:

In place of Baptism the solemn taking of responsibility for the spiritual development of the child. A festival of vocational initiation, like the ancient assumption of the *toga*. Festivals of citizenship, inspired by the ideal of the national character as one to be spiritually transformed. Festivals of humanity in connection with the commemoration of great events in the history of our race and of great leaders who were inspired in some degree by the ideal task of humanity. Festivals of the seasons, deriving their significance from the spiritual interpretation of the corresponding seasons of human life—youth, middle age, old age. And a solemn though not mournful festival in commemoration of the departed.[55]

Of particular interest to us is Adler's conception of the religious teacher. It not only casts considerable light on Adler himself and the role which he defined for himself; but it also brings together, in a concrete way, much of what we have considered up to this point. In Adler's conception of the religious teacher we see more than the ideal which he set for himself:

A teacher in an ethico-religious society will retain something of the character of his predecessors—priest, prophet, rabbi, pastor. The priest is the mediator of grace; the prophet is the seer of visions; the rabbi is learned in the Divine law, and the pastor is the helper of the individual in securing his individual salvation. But these functions will now be seen in an altered light, and will be radically modified in their exercise. The magical attribute of the priest disappears. The confident prediction of future events, based on the assumption that the moral order is to be completely realized in human society, has ceased to be convincing. The Divine law is no longer identical with the Law revealed in the Scriptures and their commentaries, and the salvation of the individual is to be accomplished by other means.

The religious teacher of the new kind is to resemble his predeces-

[55]*Ibid.*, p. 353.

sors in being a specialist. The word specialist in this connection may, perhaps, awaken misgivings, and these must be removed. He is not a specialist in the sense of having a conscience unlike that of others, or in being the keeper of other men's consciences. Nor shall he impose his philosophy of life or his belief authoritatively, but propose it suggestively. His best results will be gained if he succeeds in so stimulating those whom he influences that they will attain an individualized spiritual outlook of their own, consonant with their own individual nature and need. But specialists of this kind are indispensable. The generality of men have neither the time nor the mental equipment to think out the larger problems of life without assistance, and the attempt on their part to do so leads to crudities and eccentricities of which one meets nowadays with many pathetic examples among those who have severed their connection with the traditional faiths, and have tried in their groping fashion to invent a metaphysic or a creed of their own.[56]

In another place Adler speaks more personally.

To discharge competently my own special function [of being a teacher or leader of an ethico-religious society], I saw that I ought to be acquainted with the best ethical thought of the past. This meant an exhaustive study of the philosophic systems of which the ethical thought of the philosophers is the fruit. I ought further to be familiar with the great religions, in which so much of the ethical insight of mankind is incorporated. I ought to acquaint myself with the moral history of mankind in so far as it is accessible, including that of the primitive races. I ought to gain a survey of the variations of moral opinion that have so staggered belief in the possibility of ethical truth. I ought to master at least the general principles of the physical and biological sciences, since it is impossible that the first principles of ethics should not be related to the governing principles that obtain in other departments of knowledge. I ought in addition to master in their ethical aspect the economic and political problems of the present day, as well as the psychology of individual and social life, in order to be able to apply with some degree of competence the directives of ethics to actual conduct. There are in addition other subjects, such as jurisprudence, poetry and the fine arts, that have ultimate relation to ethics, and that may not safely be neglected. Behold, then, the problem of specialism in one of its most appalling forms. For how can any one individual hope to adequately fill out such a programme? And what I have said is but my own personal illustration of a general problem that more and more besets every reflective person

[56]*Ibid.*, pp. 344-346.

in our time. And it is a problem that has direct bearings upon the question of human personality. The personality is not a detached and isolated thing. It is a center that radiates out in every possible direction, and depends for the release of its energy on the influences received in turn from all directions. On the one hand, to have a footing at all in reality one must be a specialist, and the fields of specialism are becoming more and more restricted. To know one thing well is the indispensable condition of the sense of master, yes, of self-respect. And yet it seems to be becoming increasingly clear that one cannot really master a single speciality without knowing of other specialities whatsoever is related to one's own. Narrowness, and loss of power, seems the one alternative. Dilettantism, the other. But again I ask, who can actually fill out such a programme? The frustration of effort thus appears, in its intellectual guise, as one more manifestation of that general fact of frustration which we meet with wherever we turn.[57]

At this point Adler adds in a footnote: "A new conception of culture is needed, based neither on exclusive specialism, nor on the ambition to know everything after the manner of Goethe in his early days, and such a conception of culture must supply the foundation of an educational philosophy."[58]

It is to that conception of culture and Adler's explicit educational philosophy to which we now turn.

[57]*Ibid.*, pp. 65-67.
[58]*Ibid.*, p. 67n.

CHAPTER 6

Culture and the Schools

As we start this part of our work on schooling, we already know a great deal of what Adler has to say on the matters to be considered. No radically new conceptions should be anticipated (although Adler's idea of culture, which we will introduce for the first time here, does add a new dimension to what has gone before). Our task is primarily one of focusing what we know on educating as a deliberate process institutionalized in the schools. Almost all of what has been said before is relevant to this concern, but the most relevant considerations are as follows: (1) the basic ethical position as stated in Part I, including the ever-pervasive concern with worth; (2) the conception of ethical development and the place of schools in the series of social institutions; (3) the conception of the process of ethicizing which we have claimed is Adler's generic conception of education; (4) the centrality of the ideal of vocation as ethicized work and the importance of work for the manifestation of person-ality; and (5) Adler's analysis of individualism and particularly his discussion of specialization.

We might summarize what we already know by saying that the school, in Adler's framework, is the social institution that stands between the "successive phases through which the individual shall advance towards the acquisition of an ethical personality."[1] The school's primary role in eliciting person-ality is that of preparing the individual to enter a vocation. The connecting link between the general aim of eliciting person-ality and a vocationally oriented schooling is the idea

[1] Adler, *An Ethical Philosophy of Life,* p. 261 (italics in the original).

that the unique and induplicable characteristics of each person become manifest as dynamic energy, appearing only as man is active.

Adler's conception of the school's major problem is defined within the context of his analysis of specialization. He is committed to a program of studies and training that, based on the bent and ability of the individual, will lead to thorough competence in some line of work. The great danger of specialization is the potential isolation of the specialist. Specialization as specialism is both narrow and narrowing. It is excessive individualism in the area of work. Adler needs a conception of schooling that will preserve all the virtues of specialization, and so he must steer a path between specialism on the one hand and generalism on the other.[2] He must also frame his position such that it will be consonant with the general ethical theory. Specifically, both the structure and the content of the schooling must reflect and be regulated by the supreme ethical rule.

Adler announces his solution to this problem in the following way: "The cure for narrow specialization is culture. . . ."[3] But, as we have seen, what Adler requires is a new conception of culture.[4] It is such a reconstruction of the idea of culture which Adler offers as the key to his philosophy of education, or what we must here call a philosophy of schooling.[5]

[2]*Supra.*, Chapter IV, Part II., pp. 137-168.
[3]Adler, *Culture and Education*, Lecture I, p. 5.
[4]*Supra.*, pp.
[5]In May of 1923, Adler was in Oxford where he delivered the Hibbert Lectures which were published under the title *The Reconstruction of the Spiritual Ideal.* During this visit in Oxford, Adler also delivered a series of four lectures that have never been published. These lectures contain the major portion of Adler's explicit discussion of his ethical conception of culture. Adler's files contain typescripts of this material. In the case of Lectures I and II it would appear that we have a full record of what he said. For Lectures III and IV, what is available can be characterized as very full notes. For all practical purposes we can say that we have a full record of the series. The envelopes containing the typescripts carry the marking *Oxford Lectures on Culture.* A title page carries the heading *Culture and Education.* We get a better idea of Adler's intention in a line in the first paragraph of the first lecture in which Adler refers to the series as the "four lectures on Education viewed from the stand-

In the first paragraph of Lecture I of *Culture and Education* Adler writes:

I have no polemical intention, and I am not concerned to show up the evils of our present educational systems; but there is one principal defect in our present-day education to which I cannot help referring. It is just the failure to ask the question: "To what end is all this business of education? What is to be the final outcome of it when we have done with the education of the man or the woman; what sort of being do we expect him or her to become?"[6]

When Adler speaks of "the final outcome," he has in mind the ultimate end of education. This ultimate end is, of course, for Adler, nothing more or less than the perfection already described as the organic ideal. Adler characterizes the actual ends pursued in the schools under the heading of "provisionalism." Narrowing overspecialization is a consequence of this provisionalism. Adler's conception of culture, which is to supply the cure, is an articulation of the organic ideal with the educational enterprise taken as the empirical substratum.[7]

point of culture." The four lectures are titled as follows: I—What is Meant by Culture? Matthew Arnold's Conception. II—Goethe's Conception. III—The Ethical Conception. IV—Changes in Education Required by the Ethical Conception of Culture.

In addition to this series, there is a single lecture in typescript titled "The Meaning of 'Culture.' " From the text it would appear that this was an address to an Ethical Society group, but it carries no dateline. Its focus is on moral culture rather than a program of schooling.

[6] Adler, *Culture and Education,* Lecture I, p. 1.

[7] We may note that this conception of culture has relevance not only to schooling but may be understood as applying to the total social fabric. When Adler, in 1876, named the group that he founded the "Ethical Culture Society," he surely had this larger canvas in mind. Extrapolation to this larger framework offers no difficulty, but it is well that we restrict ourselves here to the question of schooling for two reasons. First, this extended treatment of culture is offered by Adler himself within a narrower context. It is consistent with our attempt to be as clear as possible about Adler's views that we present the discussion of culture in the same context in which Adler offered it. Secondly, as we have argued earlier, we think that Adler's generic ideas are educational ideas. We think it no accident that the notion of culture, appropriated by Adler at the founding of the society which was the focus of his life's work, should receive its full due at his hands in terms of a discussion of the schools. We would argue, in this connection, that the primary focus, as Adler

What does Adler mean by "provisional ends"? Ends that are provisional are ends that are framed in response to present conditions—they are temporary, subject to change, are themselves adaptations to changing conditions. Adler writes:

The actuating motive [of modern education] is partly collectivist and partly individualist, partly to keep going the existing civilization, though this object is partly subconscious, partly and chiefly to fit the young person for a place or niche in the existing civilization, that is, to enable him to do some kind of work which is wanted and for which other people will pay; and partly to give him access to some of the amenities of life. . . .The educator in the elementary schools proposes to equip a mass of pupils with the most needful elements, needful, that is, for getting a material foothold in life; bread and butter and a little pleasure and at present also practice in satisfying intellectual curiousity. The educator in the professional schools proposes to turn out efficient doctors, efficient engineers, efficient chemists, and so forth, and in each of these schools the specialities are becoming more and more subdivided; specialization is becoming narrower and narrower. . .the whole business of education being directed towards either certain minimum ends of life, or certain major ends of life, but omitting any reference to the maximum end.[8]

Adler's goal then is "to produce and present a system of education regulated by its outlook on the supreme ethical end permeated by that end through and through from the beginning to the finish of the educational process."[9]

Thus Adler offers his conception of culture as a cure for narrow specialization. Through an idea of culture informed by his formulation of the ethical ideal, Adler presents an ethical philosophy of education. It is to this conception of ethical culture that we now may turn.

Culture and the Reconstruction of the Educational Enterprise

The similarity between the two sets of lectures that Adler saw it, of the Ethical Culture Movement is best described not as religious, or as concerned with social reform, but simply as educational. We would judge the other aspects as important, but derivative.

[8]Adler, *Culture and Education,* Lecture I, pp. 2-3.
[9]*Ibid.,* Lecture I, p. 4.

gave in Oxford in 1923 is striking and is worth our careful
consideration. In The Hibbert Lectures, Adler argues for a
reconstruction of society based on a reconstruction of the
spiritual ideal. In *Culture and Education,* Adler is concerned
with a reconstruction of organized schooling, which he claims
requires a prior reconstruction of the ideal of culture. In
Chapter 1 of the present work, we offered an analysis of the
general argument and procedure of *The Reconstruction of the
Spiritual Ideal* that may be summarized as follows:

> Adler's general argument can be outlined as follows: (1) we seek to
> reconstruct society; (2) for reconstruction to be relevant to the time,
> we must reformulate our conception of the spiritual or moral ideal;
> (3) the moral ideal is based upon a conception of the spiritual nature
> of man; and (4) the conception of the spiritual nature will be objec-
> tively based if it is responsive to the spiritual problems of the age, or
> to the "spiritual pain. . . ."
> Adler's procedure is set by the above argument. It requires analysis in
> just the reverse order of which the points as stated above. To write the
> history of ideals according to this scheme, he must first identify the
> spiritual pain experienced at a given time, then show how the spiritual
> nature and the spiritual ideal are connected with that pain. The concep-
> tion of the ideal society should follow the characterization of the spiritual
> ideal. To offer a new reconstruction would require a new identification
> of the pain, anguish and frustration that men are experiencing at a given
> time.
> In the actual analysis that Adler offers, only three phases in West-
> ern history are discussed: the Hebrew, the Christian, and Adler's
> own, which we can call the modern phase.[10]

It is possible to state the argument of *Culture and Education*
in parallel fashion without any loss of integrity. It must be
said that Adler does not present this structure explicitly.
Thus: (1) we seek to reconstruct institutionalized education,
that is, the schools; (2) for reconstruction to be relevant to the
schools as they presently exist, we must reformulate our conception of the aims of education; (3) the aims of education are
based upon a conception of culture; and (4) the conception of

[10]*Supra.,* pp. 55-57.

culture will be objectively based if it is responsive to the most pressing problems of the schools.

Adler's procedure is set by the above argument. It requires analysis in just the reverse order from which the points are stated above. He must first identify the most serious problems concerned with schooling, then formulate a conception of culture that will serve to remedy the problems. On the basis of such a conception of culture, he must then reformulate the ultimate aims or ends of education. Only when there is clarity as regards the ends to be sought can proposals for actual institutional reorganization be seriously entertained and evaluated.

We have already seen what Adler takes to be the most pressing problems of the schools. He characterizes them in terms of provisionalism and specialism. Narrowness, isolation, lack of communication and connection among workers and students in their specialities and among areas of study in the curriculum: this is the price being paid for gaining competence in a given line of endeavor. The demand is for some more adequate conception of perfection, of the maximum end to be sought by each person so that one will not be a slave to lesser ends.

Adler turns to the concept of culture as the historical embodiment of men's ideas of perfection. In *Culture and Education* Adler deals in detail with only three concepts of culture: those offered by Matthew Arnold, Goethe, and his own. His procedure is similar to his critique of historical conceptions of the spiritual nature of man. There he dealt with the Hebrew, the Christian, and then his own conception, recognizing value in the first two, but ultimately rejecting them in favor of his own.

Adler characterizes Arnold as an agnostic and Goethe as a pantheist. They offer different versions of perfection to which correspond different types of culture. So we have agnostic, pantheistic, and ethical culture.[11] We must deal with them in turn.

[11] Adler, *Culture and Education*, Lecture I, p. 8.

Adler uses the term "agnostic" to mean "one who does not know, who does not exercise his intellectual faculty on the problem of the ultimate nature of things."[12] Speaking of Arnold, Adler writes:

He has various circumlocutions for God. God is not a person, not a non-natural man, not the kind of Being described by the theologians. God is the unexplored, the inexpressible. Arnold's tentative approach to definition as "a power not ourselves that makes for righteousness," at which one may question—Does the external power make for righteousness? mean travelling towards, seeking to come at, an unachieved perfection? The eternal is righteousness, or super-righteousness. Again it is a "power *not* ourselves?" or are not we rather as in our essential being a part of that power? And though Arnold is capable of religious feeling, his mood indeed varies, is mournful in the poem "Dover Beach," vivid and almost glowing in certain pages of "Literature and Dogma," yet the point that here matters is that he eschews and censures any intellectual definition of it. . . and therefore, holding still manfully and rightly as he does to the idea of perfection, he is forced to seek a finite substitute for it, to single out the world of finite experience such quasi-perfections as have actually been achieved in it, and he makes these the bases of his culture, and educational structure. . . .He wants definiteness, and since perfection is indefinable he feels himself all the more impelled to practice extreme precision with respect to its finite substitutes. He has a taste, as we know, for sharp contrast, for somewhat forced antithesis, for affixing labels, such as Barbarians, Philistines, Populace; for curious mathematical rating of imponderables, as "conduct is three-fourths of life" or as he adds, passing close to the ludicrous "possibly four-fifths"; and searching for the fragments of a perfection, finitely in acute antithesis, Hellenism and Hebraism; Hebraism for conduct, for the rule of action, Hellenism for sweetness and light, a phrase borrowed from Dean Swift; and in Hebraism he includes without distinction both the Hebrew and the Christian turn of will, curiously combining two attitudes in many ways so unlike. . . .Arnold defines culture as knowing the best that has been thought and said in the world. . ."Everyone knows," he says, "what is the meaning of a man's perfection; it is reaching the best which his powers and circumstances allow him to reach."[13]

Adler has some very substantial reservations about Arnold's

[12]*Ibid.,* Lecture I, p. 9.
[13]*Ibid.,* Lecture I, pp. 9-11, 16.

position. He raises the question of restricting the "best" to Hellenism and Hebraism. He asks whether, even given the restriction, anyone could really assimilate, for example, the best of Hellas. Would this not require reading all the material in the original—the philosophers, the poets, the historians? Arnold admits as much. Without the restriction, which Adler thinks is wholly arbitrary, one must admit the excellent products of all the various civilizations. And one cannot ignore the best of the modern world, particularly in the sciences. Arnold's "precept 'If you would have culture, strive to know the best' must cover the best in sciences and invention as well as in art and in literature."[14] Adler's conclusion is that no one could realize Arnold's definition of perfection. Worse than this: even though a few people might gain some fragment of culture, by Arnold's definition, the vast majority of men would be virtually cut off from anything that might even approach being called culture. Education for culture, in these terms, would be restricted to a very few (strictly speaking, no one). Adler writes:

For the greater number of human creatures he [Arnold] has only to offer sympathy, and that seems to show that he has only an academic sympathy for them; for in his scheme of culture it is hard to see how these toiling, over-wrought millions can be included. . . .He seems to be describing a kind of culture suitable only for an elite, nay, not even within their range. . .but the destiny of every human being, if we regard human beings ethically, points towards perfection; and culture must be defined so as to be possible for all.[15]

Adler also attacks what he calls Arnold's conception of borrowing fragments from the Hebraic and Hellenic ways of life:

Perfection either exists as such, namely, as entire, or it does not exist. The idea of perfection is that of wholeness. Introduce the least imperfection and the notion itself is destroyed. . . .But aside from this, neither the Hellenic objectivity and serenity, nor the Hebrew type of morality are fragments in the sense that like mosaic stones

[14]*Ibid.*, Lecture I, p. 12.
[15]*Ibid.*, Lecture I, pp. 13-15.

they can be lifted from the place where they are found, and combined at pleasure in a new pattern. We cannot borrow objectivity from the Greeks, and spirituality of the Hebrew type from the Hebrews. The objectivity and serenity of Homer is part and parcel of a certain general view of life, a certain particularly Greek relation to things; and the Hebrew type of spirituality is in its turn a part of a general view of life, organically articulated into that view. This view is characterized by the conception of a world-sovereign. And we may draw a certain tranquilizing influence from the Hellenism and a certain inspiring and uplifting influence from Hebraism; but we can no more piece together a culture by borrowing the objectivity of the Greeks and the morality of the Hebrews, than one can take an eye from one body and a hand from another and combine them to make a new organism. We must work out, after all our own general attitude towards life, and in that, and out of that, gain a profounder serenity, a more penetrating spirituality. It is the absence of constructive power in Arnold that leads him to think of culture as borrowing.[16]

Before turning to Goethe's conception of culture, we would like to consider Adler's choice of a position which he characterizes as agnostic. We are concerned with the possibility of extending the notion that the arguments in *The Reconstruction of the Spiritual Ideal* and *Culture and Education* parallel one another. We think that there is more at work in the choice of an "agnostic" or of an extremely influential spokesman for "culture," or of a proponent of the "liberal arts." What we recognize is that both Arnold and the Hebrew, as discussed in the Hibbert Lectures, are, by Adler's definition, agnostic, that is, neither use their intellectual faculty on the problem of the ultimate nature of things. Even as we grant all the differences between Matthrew Arnold and the ancient Hebrew, God for both Arnold and the Hebrews is "a power not ourselves that makes for righteousness." Neither are agnostic in the sense of doubting the existence of such a power. But to both the nature of that power is inexpressible.

Of what significance is it (for understanding Adler) that Arnold, on the one hand, in the face of an indefinable perfection, "feels himself all the more impelled to practice extreme

[16]*Ibid.*, Lecture I, pp. 13-14.

precision with respect to its finite substitutes,"[17] and the Hebrews, on the other hand, claim themselves as "chosen" by the holy, wholly unknowable power? Adler does not draw the parallel. It seems to us, however, that the choice that Adler makes suggests a criticism of a generic mode of thought which we can try to articulate.

What we propose is simply a generalization of the pattern of (1) claiming an ideal to be inexpressible (ineffable, undefinable, sacred beyond mentioning, unknowable, *et cetera*) and (2) proceeding to offer concrete instances of the embodiment of that very ideal. Some of the difficulties involved in this pattern are pointed out by Adler in connection with both the Hebrews and Arnold. There is the problem of the critteria for choice of what constitutes a finite embodiment of the inexpressible. Adler takes issue both with "the chosen people" and the choice of Hebraism and Hellenism. Adler, in fact, argues against making any choice at all in the sense of excluding some person, persons, or groups from contact with the ideal. Adler is also concerned with the mistake, as he sees it, of considering anything in the finite, empirical world as an adequate actualization of the ideal. This is a contradiction in terms, given his definition of *ideal* and *perfection*.

But perhaps Adler's most serious objection to this agnostic pattern of thought is that he believes it necessary to attempt to express the inexpressible. That is, although Adler does claim that one can never know whether one's articulation of the ideal is adequate to ultimate reality, it is necessary to undertake the most painstaking effort to formulate as adequate an ideal as one possibly can, with as much clarity and precision as one can legitimately introduce. The alternative is utter vagueness as regards what Adler calls the maximum end or the highest. The logical and practical consequences of this vagueness are either skepticism and inaction or arbitrariness at the levels both of theory and practice.

Thus we would account for what Socrates called the "first wave," as Adler, in his reconstruction of both the spiritual

[17]*Ibid.,* Lecture I, p. 10.

ideal and the ideal of culture, sets aside what he calls agnosticism which is a composite of mysticism and vagueness, on the one side, and relativism, arbitrariness, and the error of the Golden Calf, on the other. We may now turn to the second wave: Adler's characterization and criticism of Goethe's conception of culture.

Adler sees Arnold as an agnostic seeking fragments of an unknowable perfection. By contrast, he sees Goethe, assuming perfection to be knowable, living his life in search of it. Comparing Goethe with Spinoza, Adler writes:

[The] methodical, minute, mystic Spinoza sought to see all things in one—Goethe, likewise pantheist but not mystic, and not methodically-minded travels in the opposite direction, from the one down into the manifold, and his purpose is not to see the manifold in the one, but the one in the manifold. . . .He abhors unrelieved diversity, he shrinks from the merely manifold because of its complexity.[18]

Adler bases most of his analysis of Goethe's conception of culture on the conclusions that Goethe reaches in *Faust* and *Wilhelm Meister*. In *Faust* the problem is the relation between man and the universe. The solution is a picture of a self-unified man.

The end of Faust shows that the solution offered was a land won from the seas, which is the symbol of a new opportunity for mankind free from the old shackling traditions, and on this new land Goethe concludes (this is his last word in Faust). The land is for the free men to stand among free men. . .what Goethe meant by freedom is absence of any external shackles that prevent man from being unified in himself. He is to be self-unified—And how about his relations to the universe? He is to be his actual, his essential self. By unity, through cognition, through feeling, through the purposes of the great rulers of the world, he is to stand on his own feet on new made land. In Europe this is not yet found, it has to be won from the ocean, from the chaos of things, and he is to achieve unity in his own person. But that is to be explained, seeing that the quest was unity with the universe. . .in Wilhelm Meister. Here the language of the problem is somewhat different. The question is how now shall

[18]*Ibid.*, Lecture II, pp. 3-4.

the ideal be realized. The ideal is unity with the universe
. . . .Goethe—that is Wilhelm Meister—becomes a surgeon, and Phillene, the butterfly of the early part of the novel, become a dressmaker. That is the solution. There is the analogue in the new-made land won from the ocean, a community which Wilhelm and Phillene and the principal persons in the novel join, and which emigrates to Pennsylvania, and America is the new made land—no traditions, no shackles, a new start for mankind. And in this new ideal community, this social Utopia, we find the answer to the question what does he mean at the end of Faust by saying that a man should be unified in himself, apparently abandoning the problem of unity with the Universe. What he meant was that every person shall become a specialist in his vocation, absolutely the typical functionary, his function whatever it be, whether distinguished or humble, to be the utmost conceivable in what he does in his particular business in life. And how is this specialism reconciled with the idea of unity? The only reconciliation is to be found in that fact that all these specialisms form parts of a society which itself is conceived as a work of art. Everything is to be arranged artistically—town planning, road planning—and music is to accompany every stroke of the hammer. . . .[And] how is the person who is united in himself connected with himself? The answer is as an archetype. I have seen what seems to me a clue to the abysmal difference between the beginning of Faust and the end of Wilhelm Meister, a clue to the specialism and the relation of the specialist or the man who becomes one with himself. The meaning of that phrase to become one with himself is to become archetypal in the discharge of one's functions. . . . What we have in Arnold is culture confined to the elite class. What we have in Goethe is something else. The working man, the humblest seamstress is cultured insofar as she is the typical cutter of gowns, and the man is the typical healer of bodies.[19]

Goethe finds a place for everyone with a conception of perfection as archetypal efficiency. Goethe stands for specialism as a cultural ideal. Adler speaks of this ideal as "frozen." Each person does his work with superb expertness, but there is no play of life, there are no active relations among these experts. All of Adler's criticisms of specialism come to bear on this conception:

though Goethe himself is set up by his admirers as a universal har-

[19]*Ibid.,* Lecture II, pp. 8-13.

monious personality, and though he undoubtedly aimed at something of the kind, he ended by standing for specialism; and specialism is the blight, the great and ever-increasing evil (the logical consequence is seen in the system of German expertness); and culture is to cure the malady of specialism, to take the individual who has become a fragment, and give him back his integrity. This can only be done by changing the fragment into an organ. . . .Perfection is characterized by mastery. The problem is how to combine efficiency, or mastery in your specialty with inclusiveness, which would seem to be mean mastery in every other specialty; because it is absurd to say: I will be master in my own, and a dilettante in everything else. That is what President Lowell of Harvard said: "I will drink deeply out of my own cup, and sip a little of other men's vintage." The mastery of my speciality must give me something more than a smattering of acquaintance with other men's specialities.[20]

Before turning to Adler's own formulation of the cultural ideal, we want to consider more carefully the nature of this "second wave." In *The Reconstruction of the Spiritual Ideal,* Christianity was the second stage of Adler's historical reconstruction. Since pantheism has always been a heresy in Christianity, it would appear that the claim to a similar pattern in the two Oxford series breaks down. But there are two important facets to Goethe's work, as Adler characterizes it, that suggest a significant similarity of motive for Goethe and the early Christian. In Adler's characterization, the Christian seeks a home in the world and discovers it in relation to God. But God demands a purification of the soul, a separation of the clean from the unclean, the holy from the unholy.

And Adler writes: "To understand Goethe's ideal of culture one must follow the road which he travelled in the course of his endeavor to reconcile himself to life, to make himself at home in the universe."[21] And again:

The deeper object in his [Goethe's] composition is, as he himself tells us, a purification of his own nature, a liberation. The things that trouble him, his sorrows, his love, his distractions, all the turbid elements of his nature, he sought to clear by externalizing the things

[20]*Ibid.*, Lecture III, pp. 2-3.
[21]*Ibid.*, Lecture I (extra notes), p. 1.

that were chaotic in him, and simply rising above himself, as it were, and looking down on the emotional ferment in his own bosom, lifting himself above his own chaotic inner life, and framing all these inner emotions and giving them unity in a work of art, in lyric, in a piece of lyric art.[22]

The Christian, according to Adler, concludes with an ethic that is individualistic and private. The relation between man and God bypasses human society—man's public world. Purification is bought at the price of attention to the dynamic relations among human beings. Is there not an important similarity between this Christian view and the image that Adler draws of Goethe? Like the early Christian, Goethe could not find a way out of chaos in the Europe in which he lived. So he offers a Utopia in America, based on artistic principles, with a committee of overseers to make sure that the archetypal citizens form a harmonious whole. What might constitute a public world in which humans relate to one another is accessible only to the overseers. The citizens, except with respect to their area of expertise, are not agents or loci of responsibility in relation to other citizens. The overseers play the role of God. The principle of specialism offers a basis for an ethic internal to the area of specialization but affords no ground for ethical relations among the specialties or between a specialty and the public at large. Goethe's conception can be seen as the Christian idea writ large. As Adler wrote: "The metaphysical idea latent in the Christian ethic. . .is that of self-conversation, self-affirmation, 'self' meaning an indefeasible, unitary entity."[23] We may say that the Christian view and Goethe's view both stand for what Adler calls excessive individualism. The difference between them lies in what they take to be a unitary entity.

The discussion of Goethe also serves Adler's purposes in another and more direct way. Adler singles out the work that a person does as the single most important medium for the realization of personality. Goethe starts with roughly the same

[22]*Ibid.*, Lecture II, p. 5.
[23]Adler, *The Reconstruction of the Spiritual Ideal,* p. 42.

premise but arrives at an individualistic conception of work in terms of which Adler's conception of vocation (that is, ethicized work) would be impossible. Goethe's "error," then, serves as a good introduction to Adler's own view of culture:

> Perfection is characterized by mastery. The problem is how to combine efficiency, or mastery in your speciality with inclusiveness, which would seem to mean mastery in every other speciality....I am to become more aware of my work by putting forth values. The putting forth is the thing that matters, not so much that which is put forth; the producing, not so much the product. Hence it follows that what I am to get from other specialities outside my own is the movement of life in them, the consciousness of development of the vital process, of the energy of production, above the knowledge of the products.
>
> One might say that the object of culture is to identify oneself, the individual, with humanity in its various branches. And the idea of perfection would signify the goal towards which all this striving of humanity tends. *To be cultivated, then, is to have the sense of the striving of the human race towards perfection,* the striving being realized by acquaintance with novelties, the new efforts in all lines, that have from time to time been put forth. (The relation of perfection to the striving would be something like that of Aristotle's God to the yearning world. To be a cultivated man would be to experience the yearning of the human race in all its divisions and congregations toward the manifold Godhead.)[24]

Perfection is an unactualizable ideal. It can never become manifest except in the striving of men toward it. And "it" is not a single all-embracing one, but a manifold Godhead, a unity in and as diversity. The various perfections exist as perfections in their organic relation to one another. The unity lies in the mode of relation, the diversity lies with the manifold of relata.

Both Arnold and Goethe err on the side of speaking of an actualized perfection. For Adler, this is characteristic of the artist, who has as his business the collection and presentation of a realized perfection of some sort.[25] The mistake is to offer

---

[24]*Ibid.,* Lecture III, pp. 3-4 (italics not in the original).
[25]*Ibid.,* Lecture II, p. 2.

the artistic presentation as if it were the real thing. Arnold, as an agnostic, offers fragments. Goethe, as a pantheist, seeks for full realization of perfection in the actual world and ends with an atomistic conception of the expert. Arnold's cultured man must thoroughly know the best of the Hebrews and the Greeks. Goethe's cultured man epitomizes, is a paradigm case of, a particular line of work. Arnold must exclude most of mankind from the possibility of being cultured, while Goethe's conception includes everyone, but in utter disconnection from one another.[26]

The primary thing that Adler has in common with Arnold and Goethe is the concern with perfection. But Adler has both his own conception of perfection and his own idea of what it means to be a cultured person.

The organic ideal is, of course, the perfection of which Adler speaks. And it is in terms of that ideal that worth has its place. In this sense we may say that Adler offers nothing particularly new as he develops his conception of culture: it is no more than a particular rendering of the ideal. But it is worth considering what aspect of the ideal is here emphasized. Over and above mastery of one's own work, Adler calls for a sense of the striving of others and of knowledge of the effect of the different lines of work on one another.

If the spiritual effort is manifest at all, it is manifest in the active producing and striving of men to achieve their goals. Adler does not assume that this activity is, or has been, consciously inspired by the ideal of worth. But in terms of this striving one can more fully come to realize the ideal. We recall that the ethical imperative requires great effort and that the effort never yields anything more than partial success. The other side of this partial success is failure and deep frustration. With the failure comes the possibility of some clarification of the nature of the ideal. Adler would see the striving of men, with its consequent success and failure, as the movement

[26]Adler is quite prepared to say that Arnold and Goethe bespeak significant facets indicative of both distinctive strengths and serious weaknesses in British and German culture and education.

of men in the direction of perfection—and this whether men know, report, or even deny such a goal.

Part of what is required of the cultured man is that he see the accomplishments of men, not simply or primarily as results, but as issuing from human beings, active agents striving to realize something. The stress is on the process and production, rather than on the product.

There are several important facets to the stress on process rather than product. First, it allows the possibility of every man's being cultured. To define culture in terms of a specific product requires that a man, to be cultured, has to achieve, and has to be able to achieve or master, that product. But there is no product that is accessible to all men. Arnold's conception in terms of products is simply an extreme case of definition, such that most people, even perhaps everyone, falls by the wayside.

But even more important is a point that was raised in connection with Arnold, that is, to specify a product is to actualize what is not actualizable. Perfection, or the ideal, may be sought by men; they may come to fuller *realization* of the ideal, but a fuller *actualization* of the *ideal* cannot occur. Conditions can be improved, energies may find fuller scope, social institutions may be reconstructed to facilitate linkages among people and the release of more and more distinctive differences. But none of this should be confused with the *actualization* of the ideal. In fact, part of the growth of realization of the ideal is the recognition of the always infinite gulf between the actual and the ideal.

From the point of view of training for the vocations, it may seem that the stress on expertise is a stress on product. Mastery is a necessary condition for membership in a vocation, but what vocation a man *can* master is less important than that he masters something. And this mastery is a necessary, but not a sufficient, condition for vocational activity, as Adler's criticism of Goethe should make clear. The mastery, the expertise, is the empirical substratum. The distinction between occupation and vocation is relevant here. Expertise is all that is required to pursue an occupation—to hold a job. Vocation calls for something more. We might say that the stress on process assumes product as a consequent but does not prescribe what product should be forthcoming. This may appear to be the giving up of the possibility of evaluation. But it is clear that Adler does not mean to dismiss results entirely. Tangible results are important as they serve as evidence of effort. Criteria for evaluation of results are as necessary as ever, but criteria for evaluating the direction of the effort supervene.

To see product as part of process is to see it as the result of something and the cause of other things. And the primary context for evaluation is set by (1) the effort, the striving of human beings, and (2) the effect of that striving, including the tangible products of the striving, on the individual and on other individuals. In terms of vocational efforts, it is the striving in a particular line of endeavor and the effect on the strivers plus the effect of that striving and its products on other lines of work or on other vocational groups.

What this comes to is that Adler's conception of culture focuses on the effect on human beings of the work that they do.

Culture as Cultivating

We may say that *culture* refers to a process that is defined, in part, by the kind of dynamic relations among individuals. But Adler must also consider the individual, *per se*. And so he writes:

The term "culture" is a horticultural metaphor. It implies a living thing of some kind to be cultivated. It implies secondly a power of growth from within, that is, cultivation in the modification of intrinsic process. It implies next the possibility of improvement; and implies fourthly improvement in a certain direction, with a view to achieving a certain end.[27]

Adler's notion of intrinsic process is best understood in

[27] Adler, *Culture and Education,* Lecture I, p. 5.

connection with his idea that there is a substantive entity in each individual:

There is in particular one kind of energy to which the quality of worth may well attach itself. It is unlike the physical forces; it is not a transformed mode of mechanical energy. It is *sui generis,* underivative, unique; it is synonymous with highest freedom; it is power raised to the Nth degree. It is ethical energy. To release it in oneself is to achieve unboundled expansion. Morality, as commonly understood, is a system of rules chiefly repressive. Ethical energy, on the contrary, is determined by the very opposite tendency; a tendency, it is true, never more than tentatively effectuated under finite conditions. And because the energy is unique, it points toward a unique, irreducible, hence substantive entity in man, from which it springs. This entity is itself incognizable, yet the effect it produces requires that it be postulated. The category of substance, which is almost disappearing from science, is to be reinstalled in ethics. Ethics cannot dispense with it.[28]

We are here less interested in the difficulties of defending this idea of substance than with what Adler does with it as he proceeds. Adler does not, in fact, offer any extended argument for this postulation, except to say that if one can postulate unobservable entities in physics, one can do it in ethics also. The test in both areas will be in the results obtained from such theoretical formulations.

Adler does not say it in so many words, but it seems fair to surmise that if asked to define *human,* he would answer: not *homo faber,* nor *homo sapiens,* nor rational or symbolic animal, but rather that kind of living thing that had the potentiality for growth through mutual action and reaction with others of its kind—in short, the ethical animal. But Adler's conception of a substantive entity and of intrinsic process must be distinguished from simply defining man as having some particular essence. He scarcely finds an approach to his conception in any period in human history:

epochs in human history in which there was a passion for culture are

[28]Adler, *An Ethical Philosophy of Life,* pp. 92-93.

like rare clearings in a dense forest. They are chiefly the age of Pericles, the Renaissance, and the period which is best distinguished by the name of Goethe.[29]

And what immediately follows in Adler's text marks his view off from most traditional substantive conceptions of man:

So long as the weight of the supernatural rested on men, they would not attempt to cultivate themselves, as the gardener cultivates plants, by discovering a law of growth from within, because they felt themselves dependent for the laws of their being on the commandments of the supernatural powers, and were alarmed by their incapacity ever adequately to fulfill those commandments. The state of man engendered in this was one of timidity, and sometimes of abjectness. The relation of man to the supernatural, which is not to be confounded with the supersensible, is unfavorable to self-confidence; and self-confidence, the belief in the possibilities of self, in an intrinsic not extrinsic law of growth, is indispensable to culture.[30]

The complexity of Adler's application of a horticultural metaphor can be seen if we contrast it with John Dewey's concept of growth and his criticism of notions of education as "unfolding."[31] Dewey is concerned to avoid anything that might be construed as "external dictation." Growth, for Dewey, is the "cumulative movement of action toward a later result."[32] And he says further "that life is development, and that developing, growing, is life. Translated into its educational equivalents, this means (i) that the educational process has no end beyond itself; it is its own end; and that (ii) the educational process is one of continual reorganizing, reconstructing, transforming."[33] And further, "Growth is regarded as having an end, instead of being an end."[34] Dewey's criticism of "education as unfolding" is embodied in the following two paragraphs:

[29]Adler, *Culture and Education,* Lecture I, p. 6.
[30]*Ibid.*
[31]Dewey, *Democracy and Education,* Chapter V, Part 2.
[32]*Ibid.,* p. 49.
[33]*Ibid.,* p. 59.
[34]*Ibid.,* p. 60.

The conception that growth and progress are just approximations to a final unchanging goal is the last infirmity of the mind in its transition from a static to a dynamic understanding of life. It stimulates the style of the latter. It pays the tribute of speaking much of development, process, progress. But all of these operations are conceived to be merely transitional; they lack meaning on their own account. They possess significance only as movements *toward* something away from what is now going on. Since growth is just a movement toward a completed being, the final ideal is immobile. An abstract and indefinite future is in control with all which that connotes in depreciation of present power and opportunity.

Since the goal of perfection, the standard of development, is very far away, it is so beyond us that, strictly speaking, it is unattainable. Consequently, in order to be available for present guidance it must be translated into something which stands for it. Otherwise we should be compelled to regard any and every manifestation of the child as an unfolding from within, and hence sacred. Unless we set up some definite criterion representing the ideal end by which to judge whether a given attitude or act is approximating or moving away, our sole alternative is to withdraw all influences of the environment lest they interfere with proper development. Since that is not practicable, a working substitute is set up. Usually, of course, this is some idea which an adult would like to have a child acquire. Consequently, by "suggestive questioning" or some other pedagogical device, the teacher proceeds to "draw out" from the pupil what is desired. If what is desired is obtained, that is evidence that the child is unfolding properly. But as the pupil generally has no initiative of his own in this direction, the result is a random groping after what is wanted, and the formation of habits of dependence upon the cures furnished by others. Just because such methods simulate a true principle and claim to have its sanction they may do more harm than would outright "telling," where, at least, it remains with the child how much will stick.[35]

Now Adler's goal is perfection, which is, as we have emphasized, unattainable. In fact, we read Dewey's general characterization as quite applicable to Adler's position. We might even surmise that Dewey was familiar with Adler's ideas, since they were at Columbia University at the same time in the Department of Philosophy. Though Adler offered courses on a part-time basis, they met with some regularity at

[35]*Ibid.,* pp. 66-67 (italics in the original).

meetings of a faculty philosophy seminar. The specific views which Dewey criticizes are those of Froebel and Hegel, but perhaps he had Adler in mind in the following passage:

Some of Hegel's followers sought to reconcile the claim of the Whole and of individuality by the conception of society as an organic whole, or organism. That social organization is presupposed in the adequate exercise of individual capacity is not to be doubted. But the social organism, interpreted after the relation of the organs of the body to each other and to the whole body, means that each individual has a certain limited place and function, requiring to be supplemented by the place and functions of the other organs. As one portion of the bodily tissue is differentiated so that it can be the hand and the hand only, another, the eye, and so on, all taken together making the organism, so one individual is supposed to be differentiated for the exercise of the mechanical operations of society, another for those of a statesman, another for those of a scholar, and so on. The notion of 'organism' is thus used to give a philosophic sanction to class distinctions in social organization—a notion which in its educational application again means external dictation instead of growth.[36]

Now it may be thought that just because his characterization of a general position under the heading of "unfolding" comes so close to what Adler holds, it is applicable to Adler's views. We think, in fact, that almost none of the strictures that Dewey offers, either of a view of education as unfolding, or of an organic conception of society, apply to Adler. It is, then, in the interests of clarifying Adler's conceptions that we introduce Dewey's criticisms.

Taking the last Dewey passage first, Adler is quite explicit in his rejection of what he calls a natural conception of organism. Adler rejects both supernaturalist and naturalist conceptions as he writes:

The difference between "supersensible" and "supernatural" is capital. I do not encourage relapse into supernaturalism. The supernatural is the opposite of the supersensible. It is an attempt to represent in natural or sensible guise what is supposed to be beyond the

[36]*Ibid.*, p. 70.

senses; and the naturalistic representation of the supersensible is
then taken not metaphorically but literally.[37]

and on the other hand:

> I use the word Organize in its spiritual sense. The empirical animal
> organism is commonly taken as the type upon which the notion of
> organism is modeled. The animal organism, however, fails to express
> the implicit idea, for the following reasons: The number of members
> is limited; the combination of organs is, so far as we can know, acci-
> dental, and the relation is hierarchical,—there are inferior and
> superior organs. The spiritual conception differs in each of these
> points. The number of members is infinite; the relations are neces-
> sary, and they are equal, that is, of equal worth. To distinguish the
> spiritual pattern from the animal type the term metaorganic may be
> used for the former, in analogy to such terms as metaempirical,
> metaphysical, etc., and the system of ethics expounded. . .may be
> called the metaorganic system of ethics.[38]

It would be hard to find in this what Dewey speaks of as "a
philosophic sanction to class distinctions in social organization." It is also worth noting that Adler emphatically rejects
Hegel's position.[39]

Both Adler and Dewey are concerned with avoiding external dictation. The issue centers around the compatibility of
such avoidance with a conception of perfection. Dewey says
they are incompatible and so must insist that the developmental process must have no end beyond itself; that growth involves having rather than being an end. Adler's major criticism of education is that its ends are provisional, opportunis-
tic. Or as he speaks more sharply: "our educational system,
despite certain advantages, is pointless."[40]

Can the concrete activities involved in an educational program have meaning on their own account if the ultimate criterion of development is a conception of perfection? Must the
basis for distinguishing between good and bad development

---

[37]Adler, *An Ethical Philosophy of Life,* p. 128n.
[38]*Ibid.,* p. 310n.
[39]*Ibid.,* p. 139.
[40]Adler, *Culture and Education,* Lecture I, p. 6.

be *a priori* and hence arbitrary, as Dewey claims it is for all "transcendental" positions?[41] We can put this in other terms and ask: Is any conception of perfection compatible with a stress on process and a refusal to define any product as a manifestation of that perfection?

We can say that it is at least Adler's intention to offer a philosophy of education that does locate significance in the actual educational process and to avoid deriving the meaning of that activity from some external source. In effect, this requires that his conception of perfection be itself an educational conception. And this is precisely what we argued at the beginning of Part Two of this work. Dewey and Adler are perhaps closer in view than would appear on the surface. Dewey's criterion for "good growth" is growth that leads to more growth. Adler's criterion for adequate ethicizing is that influence which gives rise to the further eliciting of differences. Good differences are those differences which elicit more differences. Bad differences lead to a leveling-off, an increase in similarity. Both Dewey and Adler hold what we may call a fission theory of development, that is, that development is good which leads to more and ever more development.

Both of these conceptions need the idea of an intrinsic process in order to avoid the *bête noir* of external control or an extrinsic law of growth. Adler postulates this intrinsic process as a power within the individual. Dewey locates the intrinsic power of growth within human experience. The conditions of growth are immaturity and plasticity. Dewey writes:

We may mean by potentiality a merely dormant or quiescent state—a capacity to become something different under external influences. But, we also mean by capacity an ability, a power; and by potentiality potency, force. Now when we say that immaturity means the possibility of growth, we are not referring to absence of powers which may exist at a later time; we express a force positively present—the *ability* to develop.[42]

---

[41]Dewey, *Democracy and Education*, p. 68.
[42]*Ibid.*, p. 49.

And with respect to plasticity,

> The specific adaptability of an immature creature for growth con-
> stitutes his *plasticity*. This is something quite different from the plas-
> ticity of putty or wax. It is not a capacity to take on change of form
> in accord with external pressure. It lies near the pliable elasticity by
> which some persons take on the color of their surroundings while re-
> taining their own bent. But it is something deeper than this. It is es-
> sentially the ability to learn from experience; the power to retain
> from one experience something which is of avail in coping with the
> difficulties of a later situation. This means power to modify actions
> on the basis of the results of prior experiences, the power to *develop
> dispositions*. Without it, the acquisition of habits is impossible.[43]

In Adler's ethical formulation, we read the following:

> Now frustration after partial achievement has the effect of making
> more explicit the idea of the plan of relations as it ought to be car-
> ried out in human life. And in this sense I would have the reader
> understand the main practical argument of the book—that frustra-
> tion is the condition of our intensified conviction as to the reality of
> the supersensible universe.[44]

In this one quotation from Adler both the ideas of immaturity and plasticity are implied. Ethical growth takes place
through frustration and pain. We have always less than a full
and mature conception of the ideal by which to guide our
conduct in new situations, and the capacity to reformulate the
ideal and our conduct in keeping with the combination of partial success and failure is the capacity to be plastic.

What Dewey refers to as a person's "own bent" is what
Adler attempts to account for in his conception of a law of
growth intrinsic to the individual. We find no counterpart to
this notion in Dewey's writing. In fact, it would seem that
Dewey's emphasis on experience is part of a deliberate effort
to avoid extraexperiential postulations. Adler wants to study
the individual with the greatest care to read what signs one
can of the "bent" of that individual. And this study is not just

[43]*Ibid.*, pp. 52-53 (italics in the original).
[44]Adler, *An Ethical Philosophy of Life*, p. 137.

a matter for the early years at home and in school but is important throughout life. For it is precisely these signs that lead one to a sense of the distinctive individuality of each person. What must not be forgotten here is that Adler cannot rest with a catalog of types of people, even though he admits such classification to be of value. Strictly speaking, each individual has his own distinctive bent, not duplicated by any other individual. And as Walter Kaufmann has put it so well: "Individuality cannot be measured; individuality is never given in a moment; individuality requires time and appears fully only in a whole life. . . .Individuality is apprehended through the history of an individual.[45]

If there is a theoretical problem with "external control," Dewey might have more difficulty with it than Adler. For Dewey would conceive of "bent" as the product of an interaction between the organism and the environment. It would thus be much more a function of that which is external to the organism than would Adler's rendering of "bent." Of course Dewey does claim that both organism and environment contribute to experience and its growth, but no part of this process is theoretically isolable as *the* contribution of the organism. In practice, both Dewey and Adler, and perhaps all inquirers, make their distinctions between what comes from the side of the organism and what from the side of the environment. But the theoretical, perhaps metaphysical, issue need not be side-stepped. Adler's conception of an intrinsic law of growth requires that one discount the effect of the environment as much as possible, in the attempt to identify the particularity of the individual. But the notion of an intrinsic pattern does not collapse in the face of the fact, which Adler admits, that it is impossible to identify fully the total pattern, that is, the full uniqueness of the individual. The formulation does serve to direct attention to the individual in a way that Dewey's notion of the growth of experience does not suggest. The anomaly here is that Adler's "social ethics" suggests a

[45]*Critique of Religion and Philosophy,* p. 81.

closer look at the individual and his activities than does Dewey's formulation, as much as the latter is concerned to avoid a conception of ends external to the developmental process.

Perhaps the most marked difference in formulation between Adler and Dewey appears as Adler reports that the end of education and the end of life itself is an unachievable perfection and Dewey reports that "education is all one with growing; it has no end beyond itself."[46] These certainly seem like incompatible claims. Dewey refuses to dichotomize means and ends, insisting that nothing is intrinsically only a means or only an end. The distinction between means and ends, as Dewey formulates it, turns on the function that something plays in an ongoing process. Adler's ethical ideal is hardly conceived as something that might at one time be an end in view and another time serve as a means to some further end—for the ideal is a formulation of the furthest, the supreme end. Dewey admits no such conception into his doctrine.

If we look more closely, we see that Adler does not offer a determinate end either for the individual, the educational enterprise, or society at large. His intrinsic law of growth serves to locate the primary source of power within the individual. But the issue is not whether an organism is a locus of natural energies. About this there can be little dispute. Adler is claiming that the individual is the locus of underived *ethical* power. Following one's empirical bent is, Adler thinks, the best possible way of releasing that power. But Adler's primary concern, here as elsewhere, is not with material, but with spiritual (or ethical) release, transformation, and reconstruction. In these terms his criticism of the theologies must be understood. The timidity and abjectness of which he speaks is the timidity and abjectness which man has in the face of an external being who is the locus of all moral law. In such a framework man can have no sense of his primary agency as an ethical being. And this same argument is used by Adler in reference to a

[46]Dewey, *Democracy and Education*, p. 62.

thoroughgoing naturalism. For naturalism, in Adler's view, given its characterization of the whole of reality in causal terms, also allows for no satisfactory conception of ethical agency.

Adler rejects much of what Dewey rejects: external control, a determinate characterization of some supervening end, traditional theology and religion. We think that Adler rejects Dewey's total position, but that Dewey does not capture Adler's view of culture and unfolding in his critique. In this sense Dewey does not so much reject Adler's formulation as bypass and miss it. This, of course, does not make Adler's case. It surely does not follow from the fact that Dewey did not criticize a position that the position is established. This long discussion can only serve to set Adler's views off more sharply from Dewey's and from the "idealisms" usually dealt with in the literature and in this way perhaps make Adler's intent somewhat clearer.

Adler writes that "applied to man, culture means these four things: the living beings, the intrinsic law of growth, the capacity for improvement, and betterment in a certain direction."[47] Ethical culture would thus mean: living individuals containing an underived and unique substantive entity, the unique pattern of release of unique energy, the capacity or power for the increased release of this energy, and the release of this energy in the direction of full and unique personality—and we might add—full ethical agency—or, in short, worth.

We have said that it was Adler's intention to locate significance within the educational process; to avoid importing it from some external source. What can be said for Adler's success with such a theoretical program? If the question asks: Does Adler make a case for empirical development having empirical meaning on its own account? then the answer is clearly no. But Adler does not offer what Dewey speaks of as "an abstract and indefinite future. . .in control with all which

[47]Adler, *Culture and Education*, Lecture I, pp. 5-6.

that connotes in depreciation of present power and opportunity."[48] For Adler there is anything but depreciation of present power. And every empirical situation is seen as an opportunity for ethical action. Further, the indefiniteness of the ideal, as Adler formulates it, is not a function of a distant future. Rather the recognition of the complexity of any empirical situation, whether present or future, makes it impossible to specify in any detail what would constitute an instance of ethicizing in a given situation.

We would say that Adler's "educational process" is not simply an "empirical process" at all. It is an ethical process. This means that it is a peculiar amalgam of the spiritual and the empirical. This entire essay has been concerned with an exploration and articulation of this process, and we are not done. But it is clear that this process, which we can now call, variously—ethicizing, educating, and cultivating—cannot be understood either wholly in supersensible or wholly in sensible terms. The case for the intrinsic significance or meaning of activities composing the educational process is made by Adler as the educational process is conceived as an ethical process. So understood, we can, interestingly enough, import Dewey's formulation regarding growth verbatim. We can say that (ethical) growth is the "cumulative movement of [ethical] action toward a later [ethical] result"; "that life is [ethical] development, and that [ethical] developing, growing, is life." And further: "Translated into its educational equivalents, this means (i) that the educational process has no end beyond itself; it is its own [ethical] end; and that (ii) the educational process is one of continual [ethical] reorganizing, reconstructing, transforming." Finally, "[Ethical] growth is regarded as *having* an end, instead of *being* an end."[49]

We may now turn to some of Adler's specific proposals regarding the schools.

[48]Dewey, *Democracy and Education*, p. 66.
[49]Dewey, *Democracy and Education*, Chapter V, Part 2, pp. 49, 59, 60, 66-67 (italics in the original).

The Schools

According to Adler, the reconstruction of institutionalized education must be based on a reformulation of the aims of education. This in turn requires a conception of culture that is responsive to the most pressing problems of the schools. We have seen Adler identify these problems, formulate a conception of culture and a conception of the ultimate aims of education. It is now possible to consider Adler's proposals for a reconstruction of the school as a social institution and particularly his ideas regarding changes in the educational ladder and the curriculum.[50]

Work, vocation, and culture are the key ideas for understanding Adler's proposals concerning the school. Work, as sustained activity, supplies the conditions for a channeled, disciplined release of that kind of energy which is distinctively human, that is, ethical energy. The idea of vocation is no more than the idea of ethicized work, or work through which there is some measure of release of ethical energy. Culture we might characterize as a meta-vocational idea, for it is really the notion of ethicized vocation (we might speak of second-level ethicizing).

Man can work and the work may be seen as having little more than a material effect on others and himself. Whether this material, or strictly empirical, effect is judged to be good

[50]It is well to distinguish here between Adler's proposals and the schools founded by the Ethical Culture Society. Although Adler had much to do with these schools, particularly the schools in Manhattan and Westchester County (The Fieldston School), a discussion of these schools would present us with the problem of separating what in the schools was and what was not a result of Adler's ideas and influence. This would require a detailed study of the Ethical Culture schools, which is quite beyond the compass of the present essay. It would also tend to obscure the theoretical pattern that we are here attempting to present. It may be said that anyone concerned with exploring the matter of Adler's impact on the schools founded by the Ethical Society should direct their attention to the earliest years of the schools' existence, for it did not take long for very different influences to be felt in both the organization, curriculum and purposes of the schools. This is particularly true at the secondary level.

or bad need not detain us except to remark that Adler considers such effect, in itself, as related to either "minimum" or "major" ends of life, but never to the "maximum" end.[51] A minimum end would be the supplying of food and shelter. A major end would be the discovery of some scientific truth, or creating a work of art. Only the ethical end is maximum. Adler does not mean to derogate the need for food or the search for truth. But he does mean to see these as subordinate to the ethical quest.

Work, as vocation, is seen in terms of the distinctively human effects of the work on the worker himself and on his co-workers. Vocation, within the framework of culture, focuses on the effect of a given vocation on those who pursue it and on other vocations. It is in this sense that the idea of culture provides the general context for Adler's vocation-oriented schooling.

Adler divides the program of formal schooling into four main parts: (1) the exploratory stage, (2) the prevocational stage, (3) the vocational stage, and (4) the adult stage. These stages correspond with the educational ladder as it is generally known today in the United States. The exploratory stage extends through what we know as the secondary school. The prevocational stage takes the place of the college, or undergraduate study. The vocational stage comprises graduate work in the university. As to schooling for adults, Adler has not too much to say. He here follows the pattern that he found, which included advanced work for those who had passed through the earlier stages and some additional facilities for adults who had, as it were, stepped off the ladder at some earlier stage. Adler writes:

The caesura in education will. . .fall about the sixteenth year. Before that the task will be to lay the general foundations and to reconnoiter the individuality of the pupil. After that there will be a system of *prevocational schools*. The college, a legacy which has come to us from a type of society unlike our own, will disappear, and the university

[51]*Vide, e.g.,* Adler, *Culture and Education,* Lecture I, p. 3.

will become an organism of vocational schools succeeding the prevocational.[52]

The concrete manifestations of individuality will be some cluster of interests and aptitudes on the basis of which a vocational choice would be made. Adler does not enter into the dispute over interest and effort that has exercised many educational theorists. It would seem that Adler simply assumed that effort and activity would follow interest and ability. The curriculum in all stages was to be framed in line with these interests. It was only where no interest was shown that the teacher and the school have "to try to produce such an interest. . . .What nature has not done in such cases art must attempt."[53]

Adler sees the college of his day as a survival of "an institution designed for the education of gentlemen."[54] It was also being influenced by its clientele's desire for "materialistic success." Overlaying both of these aspects, the notion of research was imported from Germany. To the extent that colleges set the standards for the secondary schools, a similar analysis could be made for that level.

In rejecting a school for gentlemen, Adler is rejecting a general liberal arts curriculum, much as it still exists today with its avowedly nonvocational orientation. Such a program can never yield more than a smattering: it does not engage a person at the level at which he will be an active member of society. It offers a gloss and supports a superficial and external conception of culture. It draws almost exclusively from the intellectual and artistic attainments of men and deliberately excludes concern with work on the farm, and in industry and business, including even the work of the engineer, the business manager, and the financier.

Adler also wants to reject the combination of an education for gentlemen to which is added a "professional sequence"

[52]Adler, *An Ethical Philosophy of Life,* pp. 297-298.
[53]*Ibid.,* p. 296.
[54]*Ibid.,* p. 299.

answering to the concern with making a living. This can only be a halfway house toward an adequate conception of vocation.

As to the German research idea: this really entered into schools in the United States at the level of graduate studies. But in the same way that the college influences the secondary school, the graduate study influences curriculum. Perhaps the prime mode of influence stems from the fact that the graduate schools provide the faculty for the undergraduate school. We know also that one of the prime criteria for judging both college and university faculty is the research in which they engage and the material that they publish. There is no evidence that Adler sought to reject such research; rather do we think that he prized it most highly. His only criticism was that it was engaged in, and took place in, a context of narrow specialization, unleavened by any active cross-relations among the specialists. This is, according to Adler, Goethe's archetypal ideal become actual.

One must assume that something like what Adler offers as an ethical classification of the vocations would be the basis for organizing the university.[55] This "provisional" classification would call for schools: for the theoretical physical sciences (including mathematics); for the practical counterparts of the theoretical sciences, for example, engineering, management, mining, and factory work; the historical sciences; the various fields of art; legal work; the work of the statesman; the work of the religious teacher. We would expect from Adler's more extended discussion that a school for school teachers would also be included. And we must take seriously Adler's remark about the vocation of home-making. There would have to be a school for motherhood.[56]

Since the political state, as Adler envisaged it, would be or-

[55]*Supra.*, pp. 187-88.

[56]"The law-making body [of the state]. . .will consist of representatives or delegates of the agricultrual, the commercial, the industrial, the scientific groups, *et cetera.* Women belonging to these groups will exercise the franchise within them. There will also be a distinct group of home-makers; motherhood will be recognized as a vocation." Adler, *An Ethical Philosophy of Life,* pp. 310-311.

ganized along vocational group lines, one of the major aims of the university would be to supply leaders for these various groups.[57]

It seems fairly clear that Adler did not think of university study for everyone, but it is not clear whether he thought prevocational school should be arranged for all. We suspect that he would seek to arrange prevocational training roughly up through the age of twenty for everyone. This much time would generally be required for sufficient mastery of the work. Where this was not so, there would be even further opportunity to put the more quickly mastered work into its vocational and cultural perspective. Arrangements, under Adler's political theory, whereby the various vocational groups existed as explicit public institutions, would facilitate organized apprentice arrangements when this was most appropriate. For our purposes, the details are less important than the intent. The notion of education for all youth is part of Adler's program. In this he was supporting one of the major trends in American education.

To return to the exploratory stage, it may be noted that, from the point of view taken by Adler, there is no particular basis for the present division of this ten or eleven year period into elementary, junior secondary, and senior secondary schools. On the basis of judging that the distinction between childhood and adolescence is a fundamental one for the schools, one might find a two-way division within this first stage. But the decision to divide this stage into two or three or more parts would not arise in Adler's primary perspective. We know that presently the arrangement is the result of a diversity of factors: social conditions, both in the United States and Europe; the influence of educators such as Pestalozzi and Froebel; a complex of psychological ideas including notions about needs, developmental tasks, psycho-sexual and psycho-social development, and so on; economic considerations; school arrangements inherited from Europe; and, we can as-

---

[57]*An Ethical Philosophy of Life,* p. 301.

sume, a great deal more. In short, we might say that the internal structure of the nursery school through the senior high school is not the reflection of a single perspective but is in large part what Aristotle would call an accident. It is hard to know precisely what details Adler would choose to preserve. We can know that they would have to be consonant, or at least that they could not be incompatible, with the primary aim of identifying those things which an individual liked most and could do best.

Adler speaks of this exploratory stage as laying general foundations. Here he does not object in any significant way to schools as they have generally been conceived, although his school would include a good deal more of the "nonacademic" subjects such as shop work, industrial arts, and the fine arts, in order to give each child a sufficient exposure to discover any latent interest and/or ability in these areas.

In discussing the educational ladder, we have unavoidably made some few comments on curriculum. Adler's major curriculum proposals, however, require a closer look, as they are the heart of his reconstruction of schooling. We may deal with these proposals under three major headings: the vocation-centered pattern; history; and morality. Under these three headings we find the major changes for which Adler argued. But before considering these proposed changes, it is important to point out that Adler did not offer any concrete proposals as regards the detailed teaching of any of the various specialties, with the exception of history and ethics.

The vocational plan presumes that the individual will become fully competent in his work. Here Adler is in complete agreement with the German notion of thoroughness. There is a clear communication of a stern ethic of duty throughout all of Adler's writings (even a set of lectures published under the title *The Religion of Duty*) and it is particularly evident when the subjects treated are marriage and work. Rigorous standards of performance are called for. But Adler assumes that this technical matter can be well taken care of by the technical specialists. He does think, however, that the explicitly vocational arrangement is more conducive to stimulating both student and master to high standards of performance. As we move on, it is important not to forget that this competence is seen as a *sine qua non* for all vocational areas. The discussion that follows aims at something *in addition to,* not as a replacement of, excellence in the work pursued.

The curriculum pattern which Adler proposed is based on the notion that a single strong focus of interest is the best basis for introducing students to material that at first may seem remote and inert to them. The assumption is that there will be some body of material that will naturally and easily come alive for the student. For one student it will be painting, for another physics, for a third woodworking and so on. It is in terms of the particular focus of interest that Adler would introduce other "subjects" to the student.

Ideally this would call for a curriculum arranged somewhat differently for each student, insofar as even the interest in painting exhibited by two students would be somewhat different. The compromise which Adler makes (and which every individual-centered plan must make if one must deal with groups) is to mark out a number of major areas of interest and to call for a set of programs. Each one of the set would be centered around a particular area of interest.

The image of a center is Adler's. The student is led from his center of natural or spontaneous interest and activity to as wide a range of material and activity as possible. This latter material would be organized and presented in its relation to the center of interest. There is an important sense in which the curriculum is the same for all students. Adler would have each student assimilate as much as possible of what is available of the store of knowledge, skills, and appreciations. The basic material for framing the curriculum would not differ from the standard range of subjects. The difference between Adler's pattern and, for example, the standard academic pattern in our secondary schools and our liberal arts colleges lies in the way this material is organized and presented.

For example, the artist, the physicist, and the carpenter, all have to learn to write well and to develop an appreciation of literature. Instead of developing a writing and reading program which assumes that each of these three students is the same and has the same interest and goal; instead of assuming that since they will all become equal citizens in a democracy, that this political equality calls for equal treatment in the form of the same themes to write and the same books to read—Adler seeks to emphasize and exploit the differences among these students.

The student with artistic interests will be led into writing, literature, in fact all the areas—physics, chemistry, mathematics, history, foreign languages—with an eye both to deepening and expanding and testing the interest, and also to making available the wider area of man's knowledge and skills. The practice would call for a set of interest-centered syllabi and an organization of classes based on the predominant interest. The fuller significance of this arrangement is apparent as we note that "interest-centered" is the individual reading of a vocation-centered arrangement.

But we must emphasize that, for Adler, the concern with interest is not simply a concern with the psychology of motivation. It is surely that. But as we relate these proposals to the larger picture that Adler presents, we see that Adler is mapping a program that he believes would release an individual's active energies, help to make manifest his distinctiveness, and encourage the individual to identify himself with a line of work based on as full knowledge as possible of that work and its ramifications and relations to the world at large. In short, Adler's proposals are framed in line with the idea of treating the individual as if he had worth.

If the organization of the curriculum, as so far discussed, is seen as being aimed, first at identifying a channel of work and second at making the individual expert in that work, Adler sees history in the curriculum as supporting these aims and also moving beyond them. There are two major services that the study of history can perform, and Adler thinks they stand at the very center of a cultural education.

First, it is through the study of the history of one's own line of work that one can come to an awareness of, and identify with, the striving, the efforts, the successes, failures and frustrations associated with that work.

Secondly, history may serve to show the interrelations, the play of action and reaction of one line of work on another. This play of one specialty on another is the empirical ground that is most in need of ethicizing. In these terms, specifically, Adler speaks of ethicizing work in the direction of the vocational ideal. Here vocation gains its full meaning. And here the direction of the solution of the problem of narrow specialization is most clearly indicated. An honest rendering of the actual impact of one speciality on other specialties, followed by a critique based on the supreme ethical rule, is to set the basis for understanding what would constitute the proper pursuit of one specialty in relation to other specialties, that is, what would constitute the pursuit of a particular vocation.

Adler devotes a considerable portion of the third and fourth lectures in *Culture and Education* to illustrating this idea of the play of one line of activity on another. In Lecture III the focus is on religion; in Lecture IV on commerce. Adler's general statement is as follows:

Cultural education would be largely a history, not of art or government or commerce or religion, but a history of the efforts that have been put forth along these various lines. But, again, not a history of each isolated from the rest, for the movement is directed, not towards efficiency, but towards perfection; and each of the great branches of human activity is related to the others; and culture as perfection is inclusive of all, and the effort put forth in one may therefore not be destructive of the progressive development of the others. (Something has always been gained when one branch advanced, and always there has been tremendous loss when others have been injured; and that is the actual history of civilization.)

So that cultural education, if it is to be inspired by the ethical concept, must instruct those who receive it in the efforts that have been put forth in the past, not as if those efforts had been inspired by the ideal of worth, not as if those generations of traders and artists and rulers had been yearning towards the manifold Godhead; but cultural education must rather show forth how the aim has been to produce values, and how either science and religion or something else received any increment of value at the expense of loss to the others; and in this way to raise up before the mind the vision of progress controlled by the organic conception. (The fragment must become organ, both the individual fragment and the vocational fragment. . . .)

I get, therefore, as a specialist, a knowledge, optimistic and pessimistic both, as to the course which the efforts followed in all directions. But I am bound especially and more thoroughly to acquaint myself with those movements in my own specialty, and to learn how the values therein have been produced and how the mistaken shortsighted aim has hurt other vocations and ends, and how the special work of my vocation has been harmed by its harming others. . . .

The ethical purpose of cultural education then is to review the past, the history of the production of values, to note the instrumental advantages gained, the harm done by unilateral value-production, to get knowledge of this particularly in regard to my own specialty, to be the leaven in the lump, to transform the world by transforming my own kind of work in it.[58]

Quite apart from this being a new way of presenting history in the schools, it would call for a new approach to the writing of history. Much of what is known would, of course, be utilized, but the question: What effects has commerce, for example, had on science, law, the state, art, religion, education, *et cetera?* would call for new research and a reorganization of written history. Many studies already made fall within the framework of Adler's notion. Tawney's work on the relation between religion and capitalism is a good example. What is new with Adler is the suggestion that this be made the explicit basis for writing and presenting history in the schools.

Adler makes it clear that history would not be just one subject among others. It is the primary way in which the student is to be brought to awareness of the pervasive process of man striving and "putting forth values." It is man, in his work, having an effect on other men in their work and also, reflexively, affecting himself—this is what Adler seeks to have communicated through a study of history. To paraphrase Adler, this is

[58]Adler, *Culture and Education,* Lecture III, pp. 4-7.

history viewed from the standpoint of ethical culture. It stands at the center of his conception of a cultural education. Without it, in his own eyes, his program would be nothing more than a good technical training.

There is, of course, an important sense in which Adler's entire conception of education could be written under the heading of moral education. We have already seen how his reading of the educational ladder and the content of the instruction is made in what he takes to be conformity to his general ethical view. In addition, Adler offers a considerable amount of additional detail. Taken together, they might be seen, along with the structure of the school's program and the curriculum, as constituting a moral environment.

Adler speaks of these things as serving to put the student "in the way of getting the experience of action and reaction."[59] A combination of this attention to the effect of one's own actions on others and oneself and the principle of the threefold reverence, lay behind most of Adler's specific proposals. The following are among the most important: (1) having the brighter student teach the slower student, (2) a system of student government, (3) community service on the part of the students, and (4) provision for out-of-class contact between students interested in a particular area and the appropriate faculty member.[60]

Since these practices are now fairly common in the schools (with the exception perhaps of number three), such a listing is not likely to evoke much interest. But it is important to see what specific reasons Adler offers for stressing these items.

In the case of the brighter student teaching the slower student, Adler stresses the fact that one learns by teaching; that by activity directed outward toward another, one finds oneself being changed. It is also possible, through such activity, as it is directed toward one who is less developed, to gain a sense of one's dependence on the less developed. This is preparation

[59]*Ibid.*, Lecture IV, p. 3.
[60]Adler, *An Ethical Philosophy of Life*, p. 304.

for a fuller recognition of the third (and Adler thinks the most important) kind of reverence.

Adler sees self-government or student government as primarily an opportunity to place the student in a position of genuine responsibility and "to exercize responsibility is to acquire character."[61] And as the student government has the responsibility for discipline in the school, the opportunity arises, under the guidance of faculty, to raise the whole question of the ethics of punishment.

Through community service Adler would introduce the more privileged students to those who have had less opportunities. Specifically, Adler had in mind the Ethical Culture School in Manhattan, whose students were from families of some means. The school itself was situated in a neighborhood that was even at that time somewhat depressed. By coming into relation with those whom one can help, one faces (as with the brighter helping the slower student) the very difficult and delicate business of assisting those in need such that the results will be beneficial to both helped and helper.

Communication between the adult faculty member and students interested in the area of specialty of the faculty member, Adler sees as an important way of introducing the student to problems seen from an adult point of view. He writes, "There is nothing nearly so educative for the young as to be taken into the counsels of their elders."[62] Instead of the reverence for elders, or those who have already achieved something, being based on some *a priori* rule, the young student can here gain a fuller sense of advanced problems and accomplishments.

These examples may serve to indicate Adler's approach to the details of a school program. In addition to this environmental approach, Adler proposes a course in ethics in each of

[61]*Ibid.*
[62]*Ibid.*, p. 303.

the grades, not only in the exploratory stage, but also in the prevocational schools and the university.[63]

[63]This area of Adler's work has been dealt with elsewhere in some detail. See Adolph Klein, "Dr. Felix Adler's Contribution to Experimental Education" (unpublished doctoral dissertation, New York University, New York, 1935). Also David Lawson, "Changing Modes of Thought in Moral Education" (unpublished doctoral dissertation, Teachers College, Columbia University, New York, 1959). Dr. Klein deals in detail with the matter of moral instruction. Dr. Lawson has a chapter devoted to Adler's ideas of moral instruction and then deals with similar material as presented by John Dewey, Harry Stack Sullivan, and Erich Fromm.

Since this is a question of considerable importance, the reader may be interested in the primary sources in Adler's work. The most extended discussion is in *The Moral Instruction of Children* (New York: D. Appleton and Company, 1892). This is a series of lectures that were given in the School of Applied Ethics, at Plymouth, Massachusetts in 1891. These lectures are divided into three sections. The first section deals with the problem of moral instruction under "unsectarian" auspices. The second and third sections present content for a graded sequence of ethics courses in the primary and secondary school, respectively. The discussion in *The World Crisis and Its Meaning* (New York: D. Appleton and Company, 1915), Chapter VIII, from which we have quoted above, is also relevant. We can also list some unpublished papers which would have to be consulted for any detailed treatment of Adler's views in this area: "Notes on the Ethics Course," "Course of Study for the Elementary School," "Ethics Teaching in the High School for New Year," and a very interesting paper titled "Parent and Child." There are, of course, comments on moral instruction scattered throughout Adler's writings. We offer one further citation. Samuel Frederick Bacon's *An Evaluation of the Philosophy and Pedagogy of Ethical Culture: A Dissertation* (Washington, D. C.: The Catholic University of America, 1933) offers a very detailed discussion of moral instruction based on a study of the Ethical Culture Schools and on the writings of most of the Leaders of the Society. It is not a study of Adler's views, as such, Adler being treated as only one among many; but it is well done and worth close study for one interested in the relation between Adler's thought and the thinking of the men whom he chose or helped choose as Leaders of the Movement that he started.

Part III.
Summary and Evaluation

CHAPTER 7

Summary

Ethics

Adler's ethical theory may be viewed from three major perspectives, corresponding to the three chapters in Part I of this work: worth, rational ground, and the ideal. Each serves not only as an aspect of the general ethical position, but each is also a perspective in terms of which Adler's ethical thought may be studied.

Adler's conceptions of knowledge and the ideal reality, which is the preeminent object of knowledge, serve together as the general context in which we are to understand the claim that each human being has worth. The claim itself can be distinguished from the epistemological and ontological position which Adler developed. Adler would still make the claim to worth, whether or not he thought that he had successfully clarified and justified the claim.

Thus the fact of worth is the primary datum of Adler's ethics. In this connection one may say that Adler's position is human-centered. We may add that in terms of the conception of worth Adler attempts to mark off the realm of the sacred or holy.

The historical roots of Adler's ethical conception lie in early Hebrew and Christian formulations. In both of them, however, whatever is sacred in man is derived from God: from what is supernatural, superhuman, supersacred. In rejecting both Judaic and Christian theism, Adler also must reject their bases for the worth of man. But in a sense this rejection is less than total. For Adler is unable to claim that natural or empirical man *per se* can be judged to be sacred. Adler formulates

251

his idea of a supersensible sense in which man has worth and is sacred. We may read *supersensible* as *ideal*. Then it is the *ideal* that is contrasted with the supernatural, the natural, and the actual. The point worth noting is that the worth of man is not derived from some realm, or being, which is defined in terms other than human. The indispensability of man is to be understood as indispensability of each man to all other men—not indispensability to God. The fact of worth is the ideal of worth of human to human: it is the sacredness of humans to all other humans. Worth is a social ideal.

The historical, psychological, and social dimensions of worth, as discussed in Chapter II, mark Adler's conviction that the experience of man, and particularly the deepest psychic pain that men experience, must be granted ontological status. This pain is understood by Adler as a force which presses men to articulate their highest ideals. The pain is a consequence of the loss of any sense of significance. The ideal, what Adler calls the spiritual ideal, is an attempt to assuage that pain. Man demands some sense of worth, even as he sometimes denies the possibility of worth.

The pain suffered by the Hebrews in their oppression, the Christians in a world that offered no leverage for the individual, the modern in the face of the vastness of nature and his own smallness and impotence in that world, in each case is evidence, for Adler, of the common demand that man, in some sense, makes a difference in the world.

Adler is neither a naturalist nor a supernaturalist. Worth is not to be understood either in terms of the natural order of things or by reference to the God of either the Hebrews or the Christians. The affirmation of the worth of each and every human being must be clarified, made relevant to the present, and must be defended in other than traditional terms. This is the task Adler sets for himself.

From an ethical point of view, perhaps the most important aspect of Adler's epistemological thought is his stress on the idea that the human mind is an active agent. We have seen that Adler attributes ontological status to the deepest feelings of man. Likewise, Adler insists that the root activities of the mind can be understood in ontological terms. The dual, ever-active functions of positing a manifold and of positing a unity of the manifold, are read as *reality*-producing functions. No more than psychic pain are they to be understood merely as subjective phenomena, that is, simply as material for study by the psychologist.

Adler argues that empirical or natural phenomena cannot be fully synthesized. This is to say that we cannot achieve full rational grasp of the empirical or sensible world. But Adler recognizes a supersensible realm that is amenable to complete synthesis. With respect to such a realm complete rationality is possible.

The ideal of an infinite manifold which is entirely synthesized is what Adler offers as a characterization of this supersensible realm. Adler argues from the premise that the root functions of the mind are reality-producing to the conclusion that this wholly rationalized manifold is a reality. This rational system supplies ethics with its demand for a "plan of the whole" in terms of which ethical conduct may be justified. Thus, ethical knowledge consists in referring human conduct to, or seeing human conduct in terms of, this completely rational plan.

The completely rational plan is identified by Adler as the ultimate reality or the divine ideal. As science deals with what is, ethics deals with the ideal, that is, with what ought to be. The reality-producing functions of the mind are thus seen as providing us with a fully articulated ethical ideal—an ideal in terms of which all human conduct can be judged.

The objective status of worth is understood by Adler in terms of the ideal plan of the whole. "No detached thing has worth," he writes. "No part of an incomplete system has worth."[1] Although Adler will say that an individual has worth, he also says that the individual does not have worth *qua* individual, but only as he is indispensable to all other indi-

[1] *An Ethical Philosophy of Life,* p. 99n.

viduals. The infinite manifold is interpreted as being composed of all persons—the living, the dead, and the as-yet-unborn. The flawless and necessary connections among the members of this manifold mark the sense in which all the members are indispensable to one another. Adler uses the analogy of a perfect organism to display his meaning. Not only will a change in any given member effect a simultaneous change in all members, but perfection requires the existence of all the members. None are superfluous. None can be spared.

"A duplicate would be superfluous," he states.[2] Therefore, each member of the manifold is unique. And the manifold must be wholly synthesized. Thus "the ethical manifold cannot be spatial or temporal, since juxtaposition and sequence lapse into indefiniteness, abounding without ceasing, but never attaining or promising the attainment of totality. . .the ethical manifold is non-temporal and non-spatial."[3] And just as neither of the two reality-producing functions of the mind can be derived from the other, so the ethical manifold cannot lapse into unity, nor can the unity dissolve into a plurality.

The unity of the manifold is comprised of a rule which relates all the members of the manifold. Adler speaks of the relation as one of reciprocal universal interdependence. In his words, "the unique difference of each shall be such as to render possible the correlated unique differences of all the rest."[4] Adler's categorical imperative is a formulation of this claim in terms of what it requires of human conduct.

Ethical experience and ethical conduct are marked by the attempt to act according to the categorical imperative, or to what is the same thing, the attempt to achieve worth. Such attempts always fail and always entail great effort and pain. This effort and pain, and the inevitable frustration connected with striving for an ideal, is intrinsic to an ethical life. But to

[2]*Ibid.*, p. 115.
[3]*Ibid.*, p. 114.
[4]*Ibid.*, p. 116.

know failure is to see both the goal more clearly and also more vividly to confront the infinite gap between that goal and any actual human achievement.

Education

In ontological terms, ultimate reality is a perfect realm in which each member of the realm can be characterized without qualification as having worth. This ideal and perfect state of affairs is the ever-unachievable end toward which human beings should strive. The process of ethicizing may be seen as Adler's general answer to the way in which one can move in the direction of that end. Education, understood in its most general terms, can be defined as the process of ethicizing. From the ontological point of view, Adler's ethics is a characterization of perfection. From the educational point of view, we are offered a conception of ethical development whose ultimate end is the full realization of worth.

Briefly, the process of ethicizing is the process whereby the unique characteristics of humans are elicited. Ethical action is action by a human being toward the end of facilitating the release of the unique potentialities of other human beings. Ethical action is thus action aimed at assisting in the realization of the worth of others. Adler claims that such action directed toward others will have a reflexive effect on the agent's realization of worth.

No situation precludes the possibility of ethical action. And there is no human being without some unique potentiality to be realized. Ethicizing, or ethical action, is an obligation that can fall to all men at all times and in all situations.

Ethicizing, seen as activity directed toward the realization of the perfection of others, defines both the activity and the end of education.

In general, the empirical substratum is the actuality that one confronts, that is, the world as it is. It is that which may be ethicized. A general characterization of ethicizing or education does not require any account of the way things are, but any specific ethical act calls for as full and as concrete knowledge of the empirical state of things as possible.

At this juncture empirical science becomes eminently relevant in the context of Adler's views. In order to act ethically one needs as adequate a characterization of the empirical reality as one can get, for it is that reality that calls for ethical reconstruction. Adler offered such a characterization. No attempt will be made here to summarize it, but it may be well to review the general categories that Adler employed.

In respect to contemporary society, Adler found that nationalism, individualism, and specialization of function are the predominant realities. On the nature of man, Adler follows the Kantian three-part division of intellect, feeling, and will. The functioning of these three parts gives rise respectively to the three main divisions of objective experience, namely, scientific, aesthetic, and moral experience.

Adler notes that in order to live man must work. He then stresses the fact that this work is the primary means by which man can release his energies and realize his unique potentialities. As to the relations among men, Adler uses the categories superior, equal, and inferior, building upon them his conception of the threefold reverence.

Both the work which a person can do and his place in relation to superiors, equals, and inferiors is discussed in terms of a description of five stages of ethical development: childhood, adolescence, early middle life, later middle life, and old age; and also in terms of five major social institutions: the family, the schools, the vocations, the state, and religious associations. The relations between the stages of individual development and the social institutions were discussed in detail in the last part of Chapter 5 and in Chapter 6.

The school stands between the family and the vocation. It is one of the stages through which an individual passes on his way to achieving an ethical person-ality. Work is the primary means by which person-ality becomes manifest. Thus the school's major role is to prepare the individual in some line of work. Work that is ethicized is vocation. In this sense, for

Adler, schooling worthy of the name is preparation for vocational activity. Most work suffers seriously from the evil of overspecialization. Adler introduces his conception of culture as an antidote to this evil. Culture relates to men's striving. A vocationally centered education would stress not only competence in one's line of work but a full sense of the striving connected with other vocations and the cross-effects of the various activities of men, both past and present.

CHAPTER 8

Evaluation

Throughout this work, as the various facets of Adler's position have been set forth, we have offered both analysis and some evaluation. It is clear, however, that a full evaluation of Adler's views is beyond the scope of the present work. It is appropriate, though, to offer some preliminary judgments on what is of most value in Adler's ethical and educational thought; to attempt an overall appraisal of Adler's position; and to consider what questions may be most fruitful for further study.

The Problem of the Worth of Human Beings

Adler did not invent the problem of the worth of human beings, but he went a long way in helping us see what the problem is. Or, to put this another way, Adler's work helps us recognize the problematic character of the assertion that each human being has worth. The problem of worth would appear to have at least three major dimensions. There is the question of the meaning of the assertion that each human being has worth. There are also the issues connected with the justification, vindication, or verification of the claim. Finally, there is the question of the practical consequences that flow from the claim, that is, what the assertion calls for in the way of action.

Adler starts with the claim that worth is an indubitable ethical fact which is difficult to justify.[1] His conviction in regard to worth is parallel to Kant's firm belief in the truth of Newtonian physics. And as Kant sought to demonstrate the "possi-

[1]*An Ethical Philosophy of Life,* p. 73.

bility" of the Newtonian physics, so Adler sought to offer a conception of a universe in which worth was a fact. In Adler's work it is not possible entirely to separate his conception of the meaning of worth from his conception of the conditions necessary for worth to be a fact. The reason for this difficulty is that a good portion of what Adler means by worth only becomes clear as he elaborates on the conditions required for its objective existence. Earlier in the present work an attempt was made to identify the meaning of worth, apart from any consideration of the claim that worth is an objective fact. But part of that meaning was drawn from discussions by Adler, in which the primary focus was the issue of the objectivity of worth. We think that no violence was done to Adler's intention by this separation of the portion of his writing relevant to the meaning from the sections concerning objectivity. The value of distinguishing these two dimensions of the general problem lies in the fact that one can, to some degree at least, test the argument for objectivity against a relatively independent *conception* of worth.

Quite apart from any judgment about any of the dimensions of Adler's discussion, the general issue of worth is clarified as dimensions of the problem can be identified in his writings. Our judgment is that, even though Adler did not analyze the problem of worth in exactly the *terms* that we have stated them, his presentation lends itself very easily to such an analysis. At least the dimensions of the problem seem to stand forth; and we begin to see some clarification of the difficult problem of human worth.

The Objectivity of Worth

Worth, according to Adler, is not an empirical characteristic of man. In one sense, it is an unachievable ideal—realizable, but never wholly actualizable. In another sense, worth is seen as a possible achievement. For, although work is not wholly actualizable, men can win partial successes in the empirical world.

Adler attempts to establish the existence of a superempirical or supersensible realm in which worth would be a fact, that is, an ideal fact. If there is a realm in which worth is a fact, then worth has objective status in the universe. But we should note that Adler's entire discussion of the objectivity of worth, insofar as it is read as an ontological problem, may be set aside and dealt with in relative independence of the conception of worth and its implications for the reconstruction of the spiritual ideal, the social order, and formal education. And perhaps the concern with ideals, as they are formulated by men and active in men's lives, is of more significance for ethical and educational theory than a concern with the ontological status of the ideals.

How do ideals which are operative in human affairs come into being? How are they sustained? How do they affect the lives of those who hold them? How do they lose their force? How are they defended and how are they attacked? All such questions are open to empirical inquiry. One could investigate along these lines without ever raising the question of the ontological status of ideals in general, or of any particular ideal.

It becomes necessary here to introduce an important complication. The belief or disbelief, or better, the conviction or lack of conviction in the objectivity of a given ideal has generally been an important element affecting the way in which an ideal enters into the lifeblood of an individual or a group. Thus, a study of ideals would have to include consideration of the concern with objectivity. It would also have to consider how different modes of belief in objectivity affect the viability of an ideal.

This is not to set the ontological issue aside. But if one understood how a belief in the objectivity of an ideal operates, one might be in a better position to evaluate attempts to establish the objectivity.

In this connection, Adler's survey of the changes in the conception of the spiritual ideal are provocative and suggestive. One can imagine an extended historical study of the variety of the ideals of man, considered in terms of the conditions which gave rise to them and the causes of their eventual displacement or alteration. But if, as with Adler, the ideals of the past are seen as preliminary to a new norm, we pass by past ideals too quickly to give any serious consideration to their *modus operandi*. This is true as regards the question of objectivity, or the claim to objectivity. For nowhere in Adler's work is the question raised as to the significance of demanding an ontological basis for the Hebrew or Christian ideals, or for Adler's own ideal of worth. It is simply assumed that a human formulation of a human ideal is neither practically nor philosophically satisfactory. For Adler, if worth is not objective, then it is subjective. This is to say that it is no genuine ideal at all. To be subjective is to be "merely human," and a merely human ideal is clearly insufficient. Adler offers this idea without either proof or explanation. It is not only assumed: it is taken to be self-evident. It is pertinent to note the unexamined notion that historically has supported the grounding of ideals in a wide variety of ways—in God, Nature, Natural Law, the historical process, the evolutionary process, our collective unconscious, a timeless realm of Ideals—to the almost universal exclusion of the notion that human beings develop the ideals and live in terms of them. *If* it is necessary to ground one's ideals in the cosmic process, one might report that human beings are part of that process. Thus the ideals produced by human beings might gain their cosmic ground.

But it would appear to us that the issue of objectivity offers little help as regards the evaluation of a given ideal, or the choice among alternative ideals. If we consider objectivity itself as an ideal, the three dimensions indicated with respect to the problem of worth may be introduced. In these terms we may ask: What is the meaning of a claim to objectivity? How does one justify or vindicate the claim? and What practical consequences flow from the claim? Without full and satisfactory answers to these questions, the demand for objectivity has little force.

However, even if these answers were offered and found to be satisfactory, it is still not clear that it would afford us any basis for choosing among alternative ideals, or for improving upon an ideal, or for understanding how the ideal is best translated into practice. If one assumes that reality can ground only one ideal or one set of ideals, then it would follow that having established the objectivity of a given ideal, no other ideals need be considered.

This assumption (we might call it the assumption of ethical monism) has often been made. But without entering into an extended argument, it may be enough to say that such an assumption does less than justice to the diversity of human beings and human culture and generally reflects and/or leads to the universalization of a parochial point of view.[2]

There are, in fact, two aspects to Adler's attempt to ground his ideal of worth in reality. His historical discussion regarding the reconstruction of the spiritual ideal links ideals to the spiritual pain that men experience. Worth is thus an adequate ideal and is adequately grounded to the extent that it is relevant and responsive to the contemporary spiritual pain. Success in reducing or alleviating the pain is a measure of the relevancy of the ideal.

The other aspect of Adler's argument for the objectivity of worth is related to his conception of the dual reality-producing functions of the mind. It is the nature of mind that manifoldness and unity are given. Perception and understanding always find a manifold, unified in some way and to some extent. Objectivity is thus a function of the operation of the mind. Since the ethical manifold must exclude no one, Adler speaks of it as an infinite manifold. And full reality of an infinite manifold requires complete synthesis of the manifold. It is to the members of the manifold that worth is attributed. Therefore, since the functions of the mind are reality-producing, the worth of the members of the manifold is real, or objective; that is, it is grounded in the nature of things.

The connection between spiritual pain and the reality-producing functions of the mind is not entirely clear. Adler affirms that "the feelings and still more the volition possess intrinsic controls of their own. . ."[3] and "on ethical grounds we

---

[2]For example, Adler's conception of man, with its Hebraic, Greek, and Christian roots, is clearly a "Western" idea and ideal. When one considers that this tradition composes only part of the last 2,000 years of human history, the claim that one is offering a universal and definitive conception seems somewhat dogmatic.

[3]*An Ethical Philosophy of Life*, p. 132.

find ourselves compelled to affirm that there is an object which has worth, and that to account for the inviolableness, indispensableness and preciousness of this object we are compelled to give free rein to the reality-producing functions. . . ."[4] It would appear that the pain forces a certain activity of the mind. But it is not clear why the pain leads inevitably to the positing of a nontemporal, nonspatial, infinite realm. It is surely true that such a manifold yields an interesting framework for speaking of the worth of all men. The only help from Adler is that he reports that the ideal of the infinite society is not transcendentally derived, but is a "fulguration *out of* ethical experience, to be ever renewed *in it.*"[5]

The experience of the spiritual pain compels us to do something to alleviate the pain, namely to give free rein to our reality-producing functions. Intellect, feeling, and will each have legitimate reality-producing functions to perform. Adler interpreted the spiritual pain as a consequence of a lack of any sense of significance or power in relation to nature or to other human beings. The reality to be produced was to supply this lack. In such a reality one would have and know both significance and power. And there is an additional element that should not be overlooked. Although Adler claimed that only the ethically sensitive experienced the pain, he thought that such experience was responsive to the situation in which all men found themselves.

Given the pain experienced by some, it is hardly obvious that all men, if they were more sensitive, would also experience the same pain. An analogy suggests itself: A small number of people are suffering from a particular illness. Therefore all men must submit to the cure. Might not one argue that the demand need only be met for those who experience the pain?

But let us allow Adler's claim to the universal character of this human predicament. Wherein lies the ultimacy of the

[4]*Ibid.*, p. 130.
[5]*Ibid.*, p. 134n (italics in the original).

demand that all men must have significance and all must have power? It is not clear that, simply because the pain is felt and the demand is made, that the demand has legitimacy, that is, that it ought to be met. Adler assumes the legitimacy of the claim and so does not offer any arguments that might help us as we raise the question.

There is a further problem. If Adler's concern is the reduction of intense spiritual pain, then he must face the very considerable evidence that a sense of significance and power tends to induce great psychic pain in many people. As Adler would have each man count and have a full sense of his importance, he must ignore the fact that many people and many traditions find salvation in anonymity. We would suggest the possibility that Adler's conception of the will to ethicized power is a somewhat selective reading of the human situation. It is not surprising that it is set in Judeo-Christian terms. One sees, in particular, the influence of Kant's conception of a "good will." What is even more interesting is the similarity to Nietzsche as regards the fundamental motive of making a difference, of counting, of having power.

It may be that the psychic pain of some is a good index to the situation of all, but Adler has not shown us that this is the case. It may be that having a sense of worth would reduce the pain of those who experience it and would prevent the suffering of the rest of mankind, but there are some serious doubts that can be raised in this connection. We knew too little of the causes of men's pain. We know even less about the effect of different ideals on different men, including what it means to men to judge that their ideal is, or is not, "objective." Adler's work surely stimulates us to raise these questions and to suggest that they are important leads for inquiry. Adler's formulations break important ground, but they cannot be said to do much more than this.

The Meaning of Worth and the Supreme Ethical Rule

That which has worth is indispensable, necessary, irreplaceable, unique, induplicable, incomparable, and the worth itself is both indefeasible and inalienable. As we consider the characteristics of worth, it is clear that worth is a relation. That which has worth is indispensable *to* something or someone else; it is necessary *to* or *for* something; it is not replaceable *by* something else; its uniqueness is only meaningful in relation to other things; it is not duplicable *by* something else; it cannot be compared *to* anything else; and the worth cannot be voided *by* something else or surrendered *to* something else.

Adler's ethical position may be characterized as social, formal, organic, and democratic. It is social in that the primary focus and ethical definition of human beings is the relation in which they stand to other human beings. It is formal insofar as no particular qualities are introduced into the defining characteristics of the prime ethical relationship. This is the sense in which we might say that the ethics is primarily structural rather than substantive. An ethics, such as Aristotle's, that concerns itself primarily with specific virtues would be a substantive ethics. Adler's ethics is organic in the obvious sense in which he depends on a pure organic model to supply the structure of relations among human beings. Finally, the ethics is democratic in that each member of the social organism ethically counts as much as every other member. Ethically, there is no hierarchy.

Adler is neither a socio-political nominalist nor a realist. In accordance with his principle of polarity, neither the individual nor the group can be said to have independent existence. There is no manifold without some synthesis of the manifold, nor can there be a synthesis without a manifold to be synthesized.

Thus we can say that the notion of worth requires both the individual and the organic unity of individuals for its meaning, but it does not refer to either of them. Worth is neither a characteristic of individuals nor a characteristic of a group: it simply means a particular relation that individuals stand in as they are members of the organic group.

If our analysis is correct, then it is at least an unusual sense in which Adler speaks of people *having* worth, or even in which he speaks of attributing worth to others. If worth is a relation, then having worth is a specific case of having relations. Having worth is being related to others in a particular way. And we see that for Adler, worth is a universally reciprocal relation, for if X is worth-related to Y, Y must be worth-related to X, and for X to have worth, all human beings must have worth.

We are led to the following conclusion. Adler's supreme ethical rule is logically entailed by his conception of worth. Adler claims that to elicit the best in others (that is, their worth) will result in eliciting the best in oneself (one's own worth). But it is clear that this is no more than to report that worth is a reciprocal relation.

One cannot criticize Adler for the correctness of his logic. Much of the dramatic and ethical force of his categorical imperative is lost, however, when one sees it as a deduction from his conception of worth. One might report a logical *tour de force,* but hardly a deep ethical insight. If we ask what the imperative means for human action, we are met with the logic of the worth-relation. We are guaranteed that *if* we elicit the best in others, then we will surely elicit the best in ourselves. But the guarantee is the guarantee of the laws of logic. No information at all is being offered about the world, about human motivation or actual human relations. The logical success is an empirical failure.

The core of the failure lies not so much in the logical status of the ethical rule, but in the fact that Adler insists that what constitutes the best or the uniqueness of each member of the ethical manifold is unknowable. Thus we never know whether we are in fact eliciting the best in someone else. Under such circumstances it is even idle to try. Adler buys the universality and necessity of his supreme ethical rule at too high a price. When, as empirical creatures, we turn to decision and action, we are left without a guide.

Uniqueness and Difference

Although uniqueness is incognizable according to Adler, we do have knowledge of the actual, empirical differences among humans. As a guide to practical action, Adler's ethical rule calls for fostering the distinctive differences among people. Such differences are taken to be the empirical counterpart of the supersensible unique excellences. The process of ethicizing focuses on the distinctive traits of individuals, on the different stages of growth of individuals, and on the distinctive characteristics of both large and small groups.

Given the formal ethical position and its stress on uniqueness, Adler argues that it is more ethical to foster differences than similarities. As he speaks of a difference being distinctive, we are led to the idea of that trait or capacity (or those traits or capacities) which would serve as a distinguishing mark of a particular human. In short, Adler is suggesting that the defining characteristic(s) of a person is that which should receive prime ethical attention:

The chief [habit to be acquired] is the prizing of distinctive difference above uniformity and sameness. The ethical quality is that quality in which a man is intrinsically unique. The ethical act is the most completely individualized act (I ought perhaps to say personalized, but the completely individualized act *is* that of a unique personality). In brief, the emphasis is here put on that in which a man differs from all others, and not on the common nature which he shares with the rest; or rather, since the common nature is not denied, the stress is put on the intrinsically different mode in which the common nature is expressed in him.[6]

Adler adds in a footnote, "Difference in the ethical meaning is not to be confounded with mere idiosyncrasy, or originality, not to say eccentricity. It is the kind of difference which elicits correlated difference in all spiritual associates."[7]

[6]*An Ethical Philosophy of Life*, p. 142.
[7]*Ibid.*, p. 142n.

One does not have to celebrate uniformity and sameness to raise questions about such a stress on difference. In practice, there would be considerable difficulty distinguishing a genuine case of ethical difference from other kinds of difference. But this would be a fault in the theory only insofar as Adler does not help us very much in making such a distinction.

A much more serious problem arises as one asks why there should be such stress on difference. The only answer that Adler offers seems to derive from the most formal properties of the organic ideal, that is, in order to be indispensable, irreplaceable, *et cetera,* each member of the organized manifold must be unique. Therefore, one is ethically obliged to stress intrinsic differences. But what might be the consequences of such an emphasis? If this is an empirical question, then the way is open for an extended inquiry. As Adler identifies intrinsic differences with those differences which elicit correlated differences in others, either he is offering an empirical generalization, or the identity is in the meaning of the two expressions. If it is an empirical generalization, then we must at least be skeptical, since no evidence is offered to support the claim. If the identity is one of meaning, that is, if the relation between the two expressions is analytic, then we have no way of knowing whether a given difference is an intrinsic difference. We are offered no empirical marks to distinguish, for example, an instance of mere originality from an intrinsic difference.

We think, indeed, that this is precisely the problem connected with attempting to act in accordance with the supreme ethical rule. The formal or structural character of Adler's presentation gives us no substantive leads on the basis of which to decide which differences to support and which to ignore. This problem is internal to Adler's formulation. But there is a further, and we think, more serious difficulty.

We would say that the argument for the stress on uniqueness is itself purely formal. Adler, quite apart from his argument, may have reasons for being pleased with the result of the conclusions that he is led to by the terms of his organic conception. But we remain unconvinced by a formal approach to the identification of what is most important in the way of human action and human relations. The root meaning of worth makes connection with the live, suffering human being. But the vindication of worth, in terms of the organic ideal, introduces formal conditions that one confronts as *a priori* in the invidious sense of the expression.

One might simply ask: Are there no circumstances in which it would be more important to stress similarities rather than differences? If the matter of spiritual pain is at issue, might it not be the case that the stress on difference would lead to as severe a sense of alienation as would an indiscriminate leveling in terms of similarities?

The Process of Ethicizing

Adler's conception of ethicizing is relevant to any and every empirical substratum. No situation or person is either so good or so bad that improvement is not possible. This is surely an important idea. On the one hand, it is a guard against the sin of pride. On the other hand, it calls for effort no matter how hopeless the case may seem.

But there is another aspect to the notion of ethicizing which is dramatic in its departure from what is generally taken to be an appropriate relation between people. Ethicizing calls upon each person to make judgments with respect to the distinctive excellence of others and to deliberately try to foster that excellence. It is not possible here to enter into the complications of this question. But it is worth pointing out what is perhaps the position at the other extreme, that is, judge not, that ye be not judged. We find it hard to envisage any satisfactory human relations based on either of these positions. The difficulties of making adequate judgments are as great as the difficulty of avoiding judgment entirely. Adler's dictum makes sense in the context of excessive self-centeredness. The call for no judgment at all, interestingly enough, might stem either from the same kind of excessive individualism, or from the view that human beings are totally unable to make any adequate judgments about their fellow men. The difficulties here are not of a logical character. But we would offer the suggestion that a viable social unit is not possible on the basis of either of these extreme positions.

Ethicizing is a process that takes place in the empirical world. Adler offers many examples of the kind of reconstruction that he would effect on the basis of his ethical position. Some of our criticisms might suggest that any concrete proposals that Adler might make would, of necessity, be entirely arbitrary. For what empirical suggestions could follow from a purely formal program? But it is not possible to read Adler without a strong sense of intimate connection between his formal system and his understanding of the whole range of individual and social issues. What is the nature of this connection? Put otherwise: How does Adler use his ethical system when he deals with empirical matters?

We would suggest that the formal system is used by its maker as a heuristic. It serves as a guide for observation. It also serves as a schema in terms of which one may locate what it is most important to report in a given situation and what questions it is most pertinent to ask. It is a structure for understanding, a cognitive map, in short, a model. Adler's formal system does not strike the writer as primarily a model to aid understanding. Its main function seems to be a guide for ethical judgment.

Adler's model supplies the terms in which and by which judgments are made. But it does not supply any specific judgments regarding empirical matters. Some of the criticisms offered in earlier sections of this chapter are directed against Adler on the grounds that he did not supply us with the means necessary for applying his formal system. In terms of Adler's own presentation, we think these criticisms are legitimate. Adler wrote as if one could easily move from the formal system to practical judgment. We think that we have shown that this is not the case.

None of Adler's specific proposals and judgments follow in any strict way from his general system. But they are offered in the terms supplied by the system. This is the basis of what appears to be an intimate connection between the system and the judgments. Cogent proposals, quite different from the ones Adler made, could be offered in the terms that Adler supplied. For example, as regards marriage and divorce, there is little difficulty in conceiving of a convincing case being made for divorce in the best interests of all parties concerned. This would not involve leaving the human race or the human community. It would not call for a total elimination of responsibilities. It would involve a change in the order of responsibility, and it would open up the possibility of new marriages for the divorced parties. Adler's theoretical formulations cannot and do not supply us with sufficient information to decide *a priori* that such a second marriage can never be in the ethical interests of the persons concerned.

The conclusions that Adler comes to in this and, we think, other empirical matters, are to a considerable extent a function of understandings, feelings, judgments, and circumstances that lie entirely outside his formal ethics. The formal ethics supplies a structure for them, but it does not determine their content.

The extent to which specific proposals offered by Adler are found to be cogent and relevant is, of course, in part a function of the formal ethics, but to a very considerable degree it is evidence of Adler's extensive knowledge of, and deep insight into, human affairs.

As we recognize the relevance of knowledge, and even wisdom in human affairs, we may qualify our criticisms of Adler's stress on intrinsic difference. We acknowledge that it is sometimes possible for one to recognize fundamental aspects of another's personality and be blind with respect to oneself. We can and we might well seek help from others in identifying our own basic strengths and weaknesses. In effect, we believe that something approximating the notion of essential traits and even intrinsic differences can be given empirical meaning. But as these traits emerge in a complex historical context, any discussion of them would require full attention to the context. Further, apart from what we recognize as the insight of the wise man, any adequate report about intrinsic differences would require a full-scale theory of man. We note here that these qualifications should not be read as a withdrawal of earlier criticisms of Adler's discussion of intrinsic difference and uniqueness. Also, these remarks offer nothing in respect to Adler's argument for the stress on difference, except the suggestion that close attention to the empirical level opens up complexities that Adler's presentation simply ignores.

To report that fruitful use of a model requires considerable knowledge and good judgment is to report the obvious. Equally obvious is the fact that some models are better than others. One measure of the value of a model would be the questions which it suggests. Using Adler's formal system, the following questions are suggested for further inquiry. We use the term *unit* to refer either to an individual human being or an individual group, with no reference to the size of the group.

Given any unit, we may be led to ask:

1. How is this unit similar to and how is it different from all other units? (If the unit is a person, the question can be put in terms of other persons and also of groups. If the unit is a group, the question can be put in terms of other groups and in terms of individuals.)
2. How is this unit related to other units?
3. Do the differences that exist (see No. 1) and the relations that exist (see No. 2) tend to be productive of further increase of differences and relations, and so on?
4. Questions No. 1 and 3 may be asked with regard to similarities.
5. What are the major factors at work making for the similarities and differences? Related to this—what are the potentialities for change?
6. What specific efforts are being made to support, respect,

and increase differences and interconnections? Also what specific efforts are alive to support the similarities? Further, what specific efforts are alive that are acting counter to both of the above?

7. What are the valuations and the judgments at work in regard to the items in No. 6?

8. What role do nonhuman elements play in relation to the items mentioned above? Nonhuman would refer here to inanimate objects, animate nonhuman things, humans considered as things, and human products such as ideas, habits, customs, institutions, laws.

9. What are the attitudes, judgments, and facilities for dealing with, and acccounting for, the past, the present, and the future?

10. What are the material and intellectual and emotional tools available for creating and coping with change?

11. In the life of the unit, are there any invariant developmental phases or cycles or linear changes which are discoverable? In what framework or context are they invariant? Are they necessary for the existence of the unit regardless of context? What is the range of possible variance of such factors for a given unit? What differences appear with respect to these factors for other units of the same kind?

12. Are there any units whose actual existence is a steady bar to the increase of uniqueness and interdependence? What techniques are available for melioration of such a situation?

13. In introducing a new unit into an existent but ongoing situation, what attitudes, judgments, and instrumentalities are most conducive to both paying respect to the new unit, *qua* unique, and assisting that unit to connect into the existent situation for the mutual benefit of all units?

This series of questions calls for empirical inquiry. The questions do emerge from Adler's formal system. As an explicitly normative system, the questions may be read as those which it is most important to ask or which ought to be asked. We think that Adler's position yields fruit in the way of suggesting significant avenues for inquiry.

Schooling

The highest end for man involves the release of his spiritual energy. Adler holds that the best channel for such release is disciplined work. For this reason Adler proposes a work-centered or a vocation-centered curriculum. Adler also suggests that the work that a person does and the vocation for which he prepares should grow out of that person's major interests and abilities. His stress on interest is not the result of any hedonistic tendencies, but flows from the stress on the ethical value of individual differences and a belief that one's spiritual energy will most likely become manifest in the fostering of one's distinctive interests. As Adler sees it, vocational education does not involve submission to the gross materialism of the day. Nor does he intend that the schools should become service stations for big business. Rather does he see a vocation-centered program as consonant with the highest ends of life.

A conception of culture, translated into educational terms, offers an answer to the question: What should a well-educated man know? Adler's rejection of the views of Arnold and Goethe can be read as his rejection of generalism and of specialism, or excessive functionalism, respectively. The tension between these two extremes can today be felt whenever and wherever the question of curriculum is raised. It seems to this writer that most often the "solution" that emerges is to be read as an uneasy compromise between two powers. The specific result thus depends on the relative power of the contending forces.

Apart from any close evaluation of Adler's specific proposals, it is surely to his credit that he offers a systematic program for the organization of the curriculum. It is also true that the program is responsive to the major values of modern

Western society: the value of competence in increasingly specialized areas of work; the value of responsiveness and respect of others, based on some knowledge of what others are doing; the value of a broad knowledge of one's own and other societies and civilizations; the value of, if not equality, then equivalence of opportunity to develop individual abilities and interests; and, finally, an ethical conception of work. In principle, at least, we think that Adler's proposals for the schools do avoid the extremes of a gentlemen's generalism and a society of, so to speak, "idiot savant" experts.

What we see as perhaps the most serious difficulty in connection with Adler's proposal is the development of a satisfactory classification of areas of interest and areas of work. Adler's conception is impossible if it means a separate curriculum for every specialty. Even to think in terms of the number of departments in a major university would introduce complications with which one could not deal. One might make some progress by attempting to develop some general categories of work, based not on the ever-increasing areas of knowledge, but rather on kinds of work done in the adult society. The specialized areas of knowledge would still have to be served, but this would be done within the framework of nonacademic categories.

There is, as far as we know, no evidence that any such proposal would be of interest to educators today. Both the tendencies which Adler deplored have developed considerably since his time. And given the relative stability of a curriculum already established—institutionalized in terms of the training of the teachers, the organization of the schools, and the materials available in books, courses of study, *et cetera* —modification and revision is much more likely than any wholesale reconstruction.

One need not, however, accept even the general structure of Adler's plan for a vocationally oriented program to be pleased with any attempt systematically to respond to the problem of the education of an expert in a democratic society.

Concluding Remarks

We see Felix Adler's major contributions to ethics and philosophy of education as the formulation of two problems: the problem of worth and the problem of stating a philosophy of education explicitly in terms of an ethical philosophy.

There are few things that are less clear than what we mean when we affirm the worth or the dignity of man. It is perhaps because it is a premise, not only of a great deal of political and social thought, but of many ethical theories (which accept it as a premise without even stating it), that it has remained for so long unexamined. We do not think that Adler has succeeded in the task that he set for himself, that is, to offer a rational ground for worth, but we do think that his work bears serious study for anyone who believes, as Adler did, that clarity with respect to such fundamental ideas is of the greatest importance. It seems to us that one could reject Adler's entire argument for the objectivity of worth and still allow for the significance of recognizing that there is a problem in connection with worth. Worth is problematic both as regards meaning and action. Whatever *worth* means, it is clear that human society often pays little heed to human worth. But no one can read Adler without developing a full sense of how unclear we are as to what we mean by worth.

Adler's second contribution lies not in the fact that he saw education as an ethical enterprise. There is virtually full agreement among all thinkers in the field that there is an ethical dimension to the educational enterprise. The contribution lies rather in Adler's attempt to structure the entire enterprise explicitly in ethical terms. The educational process is saturated with ethical import. Any attempt to make that import explicit, to make it available for public scrutiny, rather than hidden under a mask of ethical neutrality, is a task that ought to be faced and undertaken from the widest range of ethical points of view. As Adler makes the attempt in his own terms, other positions might take up the challenge. The result might well be a deeper understanding of the work of the schools.

The Place of Felix Adler in American Thought

There are degrees in idealism. We learn first to play with it academically, as the magnet was once a toy. Then we see, in the heyday of youth and poetry, that it may be true...in gleams and fragments. Then its countenance waxes stern and grand, and we see that it must be true. It now shows itself ethical and practical.
—Ralph Waldo Emerson, "Circles" (1841)

There was very little that could be called technical philosophic discussion in pre-Civil War America. Outside the colleges, among such thinkers as Emerson himself, there was a great deal of nontechnical, often rough-hewn, speculation upon religion and politics, and even upon the economic ordering of society. But there were few works that even began to consider the range of problems that, from Greek times, have been the special concern of philosophers as such. Within the colleges, there was some attention given to these problems as treated in a number of textbooks (all, before 1835, American printings of British academic authors). Even in the colleges, however, philosophy could hardly be said to be pursued for its own sake. Its professors were for the most part clergymen, often presidents of colleges. The climactic senior-year course in philosophy, as taught by these educational missionaries, was almost always a course on the evidences of the Christian religion, taught out of the work of William Paley, whose *Moral Philosophy* was used as early as 1790 and as late as 1858; *Natural Theology* as early as 1822 and as late as 1871; and *Evidences of the Christian Religion* as early as 1820 and as late as 1889.

Gradually, as the nineteenth century moved through its second quarter, the writings of the highly speculative German idealist philosophers became available in America, either in translation or in summary paraphrase. There were even some American teachers who were capable of reading Kant, Fichte, Schelling, Schleiermacher, and Hegel in the original German. Moreover, special versions of the idealisms of the German romantics were diffused through the popular writings of Samuel T. Coleridge and Thomas Carlyle. With the increased availability of these works came the attempt by many thinkers and teachers to incorporate some of the ideas of the new idealism into the then-favorite teaching instrument in philosophy, the "common sense" realism of the Scottish philosophers. Ultimately, in the latter part of the nineteenth and the early years of the twentieth century, idealism replaced Scottish realism as the dominant academic philosophy.

To a considerable extent, then, we may say that the Scottish philosophy was taught less as a philosophy and more as a dogmatic system justifying "old-time religion," while the new idealistic current, both within and without the colleges, came as a breath of intellectual freedom and speculative openness. Furthermore, as Herbert W. Schneider once pointed out, in America it was the chronologically later figure of Hegel who was studied first and the earlier figure of Kant who was studied later; as a consequence, the critical philosophy of Kant was understood by many American readers as a pruning of the speculative excesses of Hegelian thought.

Thus, of the many developments in American philosophy characterizing the classic period (from the Civil War to about 1930), the earliest to mature was a many-varietied idealism that is still a factor, though every year more negligible, in American intellectual life. The merely epistemological variety of idealism that emerged in the tradition of the British empiricists was never totally discarded. Perhaps it was this form of reductive thinking to which Emerson referred when he spoke of idealism as an academic toy. But the primary influences on the American idealists were German.

This is not surprising. In the nineteenth century the German universities were the finest in the world. They were the Mecca of advanced students from all over Europe and from America, too. By far the majority of the philosophers of America who contributed to the predominance of idealism had part of their professional training in Germany. Quite understandably their teaching and writing reflected their training.

Again we should note that for modern times the nineteenth century was preeminently the age of loss of faith in traditional religious beliefs and in the redemptive role of religious institutions. German idealism, particularly in its Hegelian and post-Hegelian versions, provided a rational substitute for religion, a quasi-religious language for talking about the universe that was not actively or explicitly anti-Christian and which could, therefore, be taught in the many denominational colleges of America without upsetting any but the brightest of theologians who alone recognized its "pantheistic" tendencies.

Hegel and his German followers were, however, metaphysicians and in late nineteenth-century America philosophic metaphysics was not of great concern. As Charles S. Peirce wrote in 1871, in his review of Fraser's edition of the works of Bishop Berkeley,

the minds from whom the spirit of the age emanates have now no interest in the only problems that metaphysics ever pretended to solve. The abstract acknowledgment of God, Freedom, and Immortality, apart from those other religious beliefs (which cannot possibly rest on metaphysical grounds) which alone may animate this, is now seen to have no practical consequence whatever.

The lack of concern with metaphysics is certainly shown in the readiness of the American language to adopt the word as a class-name for occult, spiritualist, mesmerist, and other such nonphilosophic theories.

The thought of Felix Adler (1851-1933) might well be taken as paradigmatic of the development that has been sketched. He was born in Germany and brought to the United States as a child, so that his formal education, through Columbia College, was American, though much of his informal education in the home may well have been more German than American. From his own autobiographical works we know of Emerson as an early influence on Felix Adler's mind; the influence may have been more permanent than Adler himself realized. Then, too, part of his advanced education was intended to prepare him to follow his father into the career of a rabbi in the Reform movement; he was, therefore, familiar with the strongly ethical and prophetic interpretation of Judaism that prevailed in this movement. (Adler called his first book *Creed and Deed,* echoing the saying that "Judaism is a religion of deed, not creed.")

During his period of graduate study in Germany, Adler came deeply under the influence of Kant. From this point on he was in thought and life committed to an idealism "stern and grand," one that "shows itself ethical and practical." His technique of presentation and elaboration of philosophic arguments drew much from the postulational method necessitated by the Kantian *critiques.* After all, Kant had come to the conclusion that "God, Freedom, and Immortality" were not demonstrable but had to be postulated as a basis for human morality. Adler, too, used postulation as a basis for morality by postulating an "ethical manifold"—an ideal universe within which each human being, unique and induplicable, is essential to the whole, because the uniqueness of each lies in his fostering the corresponding uniqueness of the other. Such an imaginary or postulated universe would be truly ethical in its mutuality. Self-serving behavior would consist in serving others. The moral directive for human beings in the real world did not assume the existential reality of the postulated manifold, but only our duty, our obligation to act "as if" all were members of such a society.

But "to act 'as if' " is certainly not an absolutist ideal; indeed, it is far more reminiscent of such a form of pragmatism as that of William James in "The Will to Believe," or of the ill-fated Hans Vaihinger, Austrian pragmatist and author of a book entitled *The Philosophy of "As If."* If Adler's philosophic background and, for the most part, his philosophic vocabulary identify him as an offshoot of the idealist tradition, the forward thrust of his ethical philosophy points toward pragmatism, humanism, even naturalism. The key to this growth and maturation of Adler's thought is, I suggest, to be found in the motto from Emerson's "Circles" that I have placed at the head of this essay. For when idealism becomes more than a toy, more than an aesthetic conception, it is seen to be ethical *and* practical, in the sense that it demands, with all its sternness and all its grandeur to back up the demand, that we act in terms of the ideal. And this means to act *as if* we were members of an ideal universe.

Like so many of his contemporaries, then, Felix Adler began in the idealist tradition of his German postgraduate study. Unlike most, it was from Kant rather than from Hegel that his mature philosophy took its start. This led him (even as it led C.S. Peirce who was also a close student of Kant) to a critical impatience with metaphysical questions. From this point on, however, Peirce and Adler took divergent paths. Peirce concerned himself primarily with questions of logic and philosophy of science, only to be driven later in life by the exigencies of his own thought to the creation of his own metaphysics. Adler strove "to take a new turn in ethical philosophy, to insist that ethical theory shall be based primarily upon ethical data, and shall aim directly, and not by way of circumlocution, at the solution of the distinctly ethical problem." He, too, found that concentration on a limited set of problems ultimately carried him beyond his avowed limits into a metaphysical system. The "ethical manifold" he described as neither spatial nor temporal, created by the "reality-producing" functions of the mind.

Adler shaped for himself a unique career as the founder (in 1876) and the leader until his death of a nontheistic religious movement, Ethical Culture, which spread into a limited number of centers on three continents during his lifetime. He was successful in infusing spiritual vitality into the seemingly cold and bloodless postulation of an ethical manifold. He inspired his followers to live a life of ethical concern and not merely to debate ethical principles. The impact of his ethical thought came chiefly through his own participation in the attempt to resolve the ethical issues in the social order of his day and, through the social ameliorative activities of those whom he stimulated to see and to do, in society. He was an educational innovator, too, under whose direct supervision the Ethical Culture Schools developed a program that was genuinely and not merely verbally centered on realizing to the fullest possible extent the human potential of each student. Finally, he was a respected colleague of the professional philosophers, bridging as very few Americans have the chasm between academic philosophy and the life of society. His place in the history of American philosophy is with those like Emerson and John Dewey who had the blessed talent to proclaim high speculative ideas and ideals in a language and spirit accessible to a larger public.

Joseph Blau
Columbia University
December, 1972

Selected Bibliography

PRIMARY SOURCES

1. Published Works of Felix Adler: Books

Adler, Felix. *An Ethical Philosophy of Life: Presented in its Main Outlines.* New York: D. Appleton and Company, 1918.

————. *Creed and Deed: A Series of Discourses.* New York: G. P. Putnam's Sons, 1877.

————. *Incompatibility in Marriage.* New York: D. Appleton and Company, 1930.

————. *Life and Destiny; or, Thoughts from the Ethical Lectures of Felix Adler.* New York: McClure, Philips and Compnay, 1903.

————. *Marriage and Divorce: Three Addresses.* New York: McClure, Philips and Company, 1905.

————. *Our Part of the World: Interpretations by Felix Adler.* Selections made by Horace L. Friess. New York: Kings Crown Press, 1944.

————. *The Essentials of Spirituality.* New York: James Pott and Company, 1905.

————. *The Moral Instruction of Children.* New York: D. Appleton and Company, 1892.

————. *The Punishment of Children.* New York: The Abingdon Press, 1920.

————. *The Reconstruction of the Spiritual Ideal.* The Hibbert Lectures. New York: D. Appleton and Company, 1924.

————. *The Radical Pulpit: Discourses by Felix Adler and Octavius Brooks Frothingham.* New York: D. M. Bennet, 1876.

————. *The Religion of Duty.* Addresses edited by L. W.

Sprague. New York: McClure, Philips and Company, 1905.

————. *The World Crisis and Its Meaning*. New York: D. Appleton and Company, 1915.

2. *Published Works of Felix Adler: Essays and Articles*

Adler, Felix. "A Critique of Kant's Ethics," *Mind*, New Series, XI (October, 1902), 162-195.

————. "Freedom of Ethical Fellowship," *Ethics and Religion: A Collection of Essays*. Edited by The Society of Ethical Propagandists. London: Swan Sonnenschein and Company, Ltd., 1900, pp. 31-53.

————. "The Ethical Bond of Union," *Ethics and Religion: A Collection of Essays*. Edited by The Society of Ethical Propagandists. London: Swan Sonnenschein and Company, Ltd., 1900, pp. 54-73.

————. "The Moral Ideal," *International Journal of Ethics*, XX (July, 1910), 387-394.

————. "The Problem of Teleology," *International Journal of Ethics*, XIV (April, 1904), 265-280.

————. "The Relation of the Moral Ideal to Reality," *International Journal of Ethics*, XXII (October, 1911), 1-18.

3. *Unpublished Works of Felix Adler*[1]

Adler, Felix. "A Critique of the Prevailing Views on the Chief Object of School Education: Notes for Address to Teachers." November 25, 1913.

————. "Additional Remarks on Ethical Experience." [Diary].

————. "Culture and Education." Four lectures delivered in

---

[1] Horace L. Friess of the Department of Philosophy at Columbia University is Literary Executor of Felix Adler's unpublished work. All the work cited here is typewritten. A date is given wherever one is available. The notations in brackets are identifying marks appearing either on the manuscript itself or on the folder in which the manuscript is filed.

Oxford University, England, May, 1923. [602—Oxford Lectures on Culture].

———. "Ethics Based on the Organic Ideal." Student's notes. Probably 1908. [IV, V].

———. "Experience."

———. "Greene's Prolegomena." [209.07-1].

———. "John Stuart Mill."

———. "Notes for a Paper on Mysticism." [78].

———. "Parent and Child." November 26, 1882.

———. "Preliminary Draft of a Course of Lectures on the Relation of the Ethical Ideal to the School."

———. "Symbol and Experience." [18].

———. "Symbolism." [190].

———. "Symbols." [12].

———. "Symbols." [179].

———. "The Ethical School." December 10, 1877.

———. "The Factors that Determine the Ethical Evolution of Mankind." [55].

———. "University Lectures: Lecture XV." April 2, 1903.

———. "University Lectures: Lecture XVII." April 14, 1903.

SECONDARY SOURCES

1. Published Works

BACON, SAMUEL FREDERICK. *An Evaluation of the Philosophy and Pedagogy of Ethical Culture: A Dissertation.* Washington, D. C.: The Catholic University of America, 1933.

BECK, ROBERT H. "Progressive Education and American Progressivism: Felix Adler," *Teachers College Record,* 60 (November, 1958), 77-89.

FITE, WARNER. "Felix Adler's Philosophy of Life," *Journal of Philosophy, Psychology and Scientific Method,* 16 (March, 1919), 141-151.

FRIESS, HORACE L. "Felix Adler's Conception of Education," *The Standard,* XX (February, 1934), 116-123.

———. "The Relation of Religion and Philosophy for Felix

Adler," *The Standard,* XX (November, 1933), 47-51.
———. *The Vision of Felix Adler.* A Pamphlet. New York: New
     York Society for Ethical Culture, 1951.
KANT, IMMANUEL. *Critique of Pure Reason.* Trans. Norman
     Kemp Smith. New York: St. Martin's Press, 1956.
———. *Kant's Critique of Aesthetic Judgment.* Trans. James
     Creed Meredith. Oxford: Oxford University Press,
     1911.
———. *Kant's Critique of Practical Reason and Other Works on the
     Theory of Ethics.* Trans. Thomas Kingsmill Abbott.
     Sixth edition. New York: Longmans, Green and Com-
     pany, 1954.

2. *Unpublished Works*

FRIESS, HORACE L. "Ethical Theory and the Quest for Truth."
     An unpublished manuscript on Felix Adler, 1943.
     (Handwritten.)
KLEIN, ADOLPH. "Dr. Felix Adler's Contribution to Experi-
     mental Education." Unpublished Doctoral dissertation,
     New York University, New York, 1935.
LAWSON, DAVID. "Changing Modes of Thought in Moral Edu-
     cation." Unpublished Doctoral dissertation, Teachers
     College, Columbia University, New York, 1959.
PRATT, GRACE KIPP. "An Analysis and Comparison of the
     Concept of Social-Self-Realization in the Reconstruc-
     tionist and Ethical Culture Philosophies." Unpublished
     Doctoral dissertation, New York University, New
     York, 1959.

SUPPLEMENTARY SOURCES

ADAMS, E. M. *Ethical Naturalism and the Modern World View.*
     Chapel Hill: The University of North Carolina Press,
     1960.
ALEXANDER, FRANZ. *Our Age of Unreason: A Study of the Irra-
     tional Forces in Our Social Life.* Philadelphia: J. B. Lip-
     pincott Company, 1942.

ARENDT, HANNAH. *The Human Condition.* Chicago: University of Chicago Press, 1958.

BERLIN, ISAIAH. *The Hedgehog and the Fox.* New York: The New American Library of World Literature, 1957.

BRIDGES, HORACE J. (ed.). *Aspects of Ethical Religion: Essays in Honor of Felix Adler on the Fiftieth Anniversary of his Founding of the Ethical Movement,* 1876. New York: American Ethical Union, 1926.

BUCHLER, JUSTUS. *Nature and Judgment.* New York: Columbia University Press, 1955.

———. *Toward a General Theory of Human Judgment.* New York: Columbia University Press, 1951.

CARTWRIGHT, DORWIN, and ALVIN ZANDER (eds.). *Group Dynamics: Research and Theory.* Second edition. Elmsford, New York: Row Peterson and Company, 1960.

CASSIRER, ERNST. *An Essay on Man: An Introduction to a Philosophy of Human Culture.* New Haven: Yale University Press, 1944.

———. *Substance and Function.* Trans. W. C. and M. C. Swabey. Chicago: The Open Court Publishing Company, 1923.

———. *The Logic of the Humanities.* Trans. C. S. Howe. New Haven: Yale University Press, 1961.

———. *The Philosophy of Symbolic Forms.* Trans. Ralph Manheim. 3 vols. New Haven: Yale University Press, 1953-57.

COHEN, FELIX S. *Ethical Systems and Legal Ideals: An Essay on the Foundations of Legal Criticism.* New York: Falcon Press, Inc., 1933. Re-issued Ithaca, New York: Cornell University Press, 1959.

CURTI, MERLE. *The Growth of American Thought.* Second edition. New York: Harper and Brothers, 1943.

DEWEY, JOHN. *Democracy and Education.* New York: The Macmillan Company, 1916.

———. *Experience and Education.* New York: The Macmillan Company, 1938.

DUCASSE, CURT J. *Nature, Mind, and Death.* LaSalle, Illinois: The Open Court Publishing Company, 1951.

Ethical Culture Schools. New York: American Ethical Union, 1900.

FROMM, ERICH. *Escape from Freedom.* New York: Rinehart and Company, 1941.

GABRIEL, RALPH HENRY. *The Course of American Democratic Thought: An Intellectual History Since 1815.* New York: The Ronald Press, 1940.

HARE, A. P., E. F. BURGATTA, and R. F. BALES (eds.). *Small Groups: Studies in Social Interaction.* New York: Alfred A. Knopf, 1955.

HUME, DAVID. *An Inquiry Concerning Human Understanding.* LaSalle, Illinois: The Open Court Publishing Company, 1946.

KAUFMANN, WALTER. *Critique of Religion and Philosophy.* New York: Doubleday and Company, 1961.

LEE, DOROTHY. *Freedom and Culture.* Englewood Cliffs, New Jersey: Prentice-Hall., 1959.

LOVEJOY, ARTHUR O. *The Great Chain of Being: A Study of an Idea.* Cambridge: Harvard University Press, 1936.

MAY, ROLLO. *The Meaning of Anxiety.* New York: The Ronald Press, 1950.

————, ERNEST ANGEL, and H. F. ELLENBERGER (eds.). *Existence: A New Dimension in Psychiatry and Psychology.* New York: Basic Books, Inc., 1958.

MONTAGUE, WILLIAM PEPPERELL. *The Ways of Knowing or The Methods of Philosophy.* New York: The Macmillan Company, 1925.

MOORE, G. E. *Principia Ethica.* London: Cambridge University Press, 1903.

NAGEL, ERNEST. *The Structure of Science: Problems in the Logic of Scientific Explanation.* New York: Harcourt, Brace and World, 1961.

NEUMANN, HENRY (ed.). *Spokesman for Ethical Religion.* Boston: The Beacon Press, 1951.

OPPENHEIMER, J. ROBERT. *The Open Mind.* New York: Simon and Schuster, Inc., 1955.

RAUP, R. BRUCE, *et al. The Improvement of Practical Intelligence.* New York: Harper and Brothers, 1950.

RIESMAN, DAVID, NATHAN GLAZER, and REUEL DENNEY. *The Lonely Crowd: A Study of the Changing American Character.* New Haven: Yale University Press, 1950.

SCHNEIDER, HERBERT W. *A History of American Philosophy.* New York: Columbia University Press, 1946.

Seventy-Five Years of the Ethical Movement: 1876-1951. Special Issue of *The Standard,* XXXVII (January-February, 1951). New York: American Ethical Union, 1951.

SPILLER, GUSTAV. *The Ethical Movement in Great Britain: A Documentary History.* London: Farleigh Press, 1937.

STANLEY, WILLIAM O. *Education and Social Integration.* New York: Bureau of Publications, Teachers College, Columbia University, 1953.

STEIN, M. R., A. J. VIDICH, and D. M. WHITE (eds.). *Identity and Anxiety: The Survival of the Person in Mass Society.* Glencoe, Illinois: The Free Press, 1960.

Tenth Annual Exercises: Reports of the 1st and 2nd Conventions of Ethical Societies. Philadelphia: J. B. Lippincott Company, 1888.

The Fieldston School Plan. Special Issue of *School and Home,* XV (May, 1934). New York: Parents and Teachers Association—Ethical Culture Schools, 1934.

The Fiftieth Anniversary of the Ethical Movement: 1876-1926. New York: D. Appleton and Company, 1926.

The Workingman's School. Handbook Number 17. Albany: The University of the State of New York, 1893.

WHYTE, WILLIAM H. *The Organization Man.* New York: Simon and Schuster, 1956.

Index

ABOUT THE AUTHOR

In 1971 Robert Guttchen was just coming to intellectual maturity when he died of a tragic accident at his summer home in Vermont.

Born in New York City in 1926, Guttchen received his B.A. with Great Distinction at Stanford University in 1948. He received his M.A. in Education at Hofstra University in 1956 and his Ph.D. in Philosophy of Education at New York University in 1962.

Returning to Hofstra after army service, Dr. Guttchen became Associate Professor of the Philosophy of Education in 1967 and Chairman of the Department of the Philosophical Foundations of Education in 1968. In 1969 he co-edited with Bertram Bandman *Philosophical Essays on Teaching* and *Philosophical Essays on the Curriculum*. He contributed to various periodicals, his last article "On Demands" appearing in *Journal of Value Inquiry*, Summer, 1973.